AGENDA

Fiftieth Anniversary Issue

TEAR–OFF SUBSCRIPTION FORM

Pay by cheque (payable to 'Agenda'), or
Visa / MasterCard

SUBSCRIPTION RATES ON INSIDE FRONT COVER

1 Subscription (1 year) = 2 double issues
1 double, 2 single issues
or
4 single issues
(The above is variable)

Please print

Name: ....

Address: ....

....

....

.... Postcode ....

Tel: ....

Email: ....

Visa / MasterCard No: ☐☐☐☐ – ☐☐☐☐ – ☐☐☐☐ – ☐☐☐☐

Expiry date: ☐☐ – ☐☐

Please tick box:

New Subscription ☐ Renewed Subscription ☐

(or subscribe online – www.agendapoetry.co.uk)

Send to: AGENDA, The Wheelwrights, Fletching Street, Mayfield,
East Sussex, TN20 6TL
Tel: 01435-873703

AGENDA

CONTENTS

YOUNG ESSAYISTS/REVIEWERS

NOTES FOR BROADSHEET POETS

POEMS

ESSAYS

TRANSLATIONS

REVIEWS

SPECIAL FEATURE

END PIECE

Lost Footsteps

(from a sequence on Camille Claudel, Rodin's Mistress)

Front cover painting: ***Dream, Think, Speak***, oil on canvas, 1981-2 by **Christopher Le Brun**.
Christopher Le Brun, born 1951 in Portsmouth, studied at the Slade and at Chelsea. His many major credits include Contemporary Voices, New York 2005. A former trustee of the Tate and the National Gallery, and a trustee of the Prince's Drawing School, he is on the Council of the Royal Academy, and in 2000 he became its first Professor of Drawing.

Introduction

Agenda at 50

This double issue celebrates ***Agenda's*** own dignified fifty years of life, and also the ageless poetic life full of vitality, music and essentiality that it has fostered.

A special tribute must be given to William Cookson, founder and long-standing editor of ***Agenda*** (1959-Jan 2003) whose strength, resilience, dedication, shy charm, and sensitive creativity, combined with a necessary stubbornness, carved ***Agenda*** into the highly-regarded journal that it has long been recognised as. William's mentor, Ezra Pound, too, was part-founder and ***Agenda*** is likewise indebted to him.

Appreciation also goes to everyone who has contributed to ***Agenda*** over the past 50 years, and to every reader.

Included in the following pages are poets familiar and new, essayists and reviewers whose inspiring voices, while honouring the past, reach out into the present, and into a time yet to come.

As full-time editor since William's untimely death in January 2003, and co-editor with him for five years before that, I have had a special interest in promoting both a more equal balance of women and men poets, and especially in promoting young poets (and young artists on the website www.agendapoetry.co.uk); also young essayists and reviewers. The online Broadsheets where talented young poets and artists have a vibrant showcase are now up to Number 13. These Broadsheets are accompanied by an ongoing series 'Notes for Broadsheet Poets' published both online and in the journal. These have proved helpful to students, poets of any age, and to their teachers. The work of one or two chosen young poets is given prominence in each issue as well, and, sometimes, a young essayist. This focus, I feel, points ***Agenda*** into the future and it is a future optimistic for poetry with a new generation of such talented young voices.

I have, therefore, in shaping this issue (and it is surprising how each issue seems somehow at the last minute to take on its own particular shape, just as does a poem or an essay – a tinkering by Cookson above perhaps?) placed a group of young poets at the very beginning to highlight them. The general anthology of poems seems to have, as its themes, Song or Music, Dance and Bereavement which, when deeply lived as in the chosen poems, is a form of returning, but also of renewal.

Agenda is honoured to have, here, very fine poems by Nobel Prize-winners Seamus Heaney and Derek Walcott, each of whom have had special issues dedicated to them over the past years. Other names will be familiar to ***Agenda*** readers: Peter Dale, associate editor with William Cookson for a number of years, W S Milne, a former close friend of Cookson, as was Roland John. Other names such as David Jones, Ted Hughes, Robert Lowell, Charles Tomlinson will echo in readers of earlier issues of ***Agenda***.

Be inspired in this celebratory issue, then, by the young voices, by the established and lesser-known ones; by everything that ***Agenda*** represents: a timelessness, a refusal to follow ephemeral poetic fads or fashions for their own sake; a dislike of any 'ism's, an embracing of voices from different cultures, a promoting of long poems or sequences, as well as shorter single poems, and, as always, a concern to promote undeservedly neglected poets. The latter concern is fittingly instanced here by the centenary supplement on Bernard Spencer.

Let us light, then, all the candles in our hearts – without counting – and sing to ***Agenda***:

A Happy Fiftieth Birthday.

The painting on the cover by Christopher Le Brun: *Dream, Think, Speak* is especially chosen to represent the freeing of the imagination in the form of Pegasus, at whose hoof-prints spring up the living source of poetry.

As Seamus Heaney said in a recent letter: 'Blessings on the work!'

Patricia McCarthy
Marcus Frederick

Other memorial issues still available:

Vol 39 No 4: Celebratory issue for William Cookson
451 pages, demonstrating ***Agenda***'s achievements up to
the time of Cookson's death in January 2003.
Special offer: £10 (includes post and packaging)
Normal price £18 incl p and p.

Agenda: An Anthology – The First Four Decades 1959-1993
Edited by William Cookson, Foreword by Grey Gowrie
Published by Carcanet Press
Special offer: £10 (includes p and p)

The above two books can be ordered from The Wheelwrights,
Fletching Street, Mayfield, East Sussex TN20 6TL
Tel: 01435 873703

Young poets

Katie Bishop, 17, lives in Warwickshire. She is currently studying A Levels in English Literature, English Language, History and Law at King Edward VI College, and aspires to be a writer. This is her first poem to be published.

Love Bite

Tender to the touch of my inquisitive fingers;
They stroke the satin flesh
And press on the bruising blossom, tentative and cool.

It is your badge.
Your mark, your primitive, earthy instinct
To brand me yours, with a dark sign,
A yellowing wound, tinged purple, speckled scarlet.
My leash – choking me to you.
Warding away others with your crude signature.

The dull ache brings back
Your frustrated mouth, gasping and desperate.
Clutching, mewling on my skin.
And the savage bite angry and impatient
To wake me.

Yet you go, of course. Hurried and vague.
Until not even your scent lingers on my bones.
But on my skin – pain and chains,
So I know you were here.

Zoë Brigley, 28, is the author of a collection of poetry, *The Secret* (2007), and the editor of the essay volume, *Feminism, Literature and Rape Narratives* (2009). She is lecturer in English Literature and Creative Writing at University of Northampton, but has taken leave this year. She is currently living in Pennsylvania, USA.

Passage

In the beginning, she was a passenger
and the first man she knew was a storm
that stopped her voyage dead in unknown waters.
Later, she was the captain issuing feeble orders
and going down bravely with the ship,
crushed under the weight of water and iron.

Her crew could not conceive of it: a tempest so bloody,
and afterwards the fog fell for seven days,
while the sky hung full of false complements.
She walked the harbour walls, where fishermen
in short-sleeved shirts probed with expensive rods
and from the depths, she caught an autumn moan.

Later, watermen would bid for her, but only stirred
a darkness that they could not satisfy. She recalled
offering herself to the delight of danger and how
a hurricane shook her by the throat and lips.
She blamed her rashness; even the golden, trodden leaves
and headlamps of cars grew severe in watching her.

She pictured herself as lightning, or as an empty sky
with neither sun nor moon. Every night in dreams,
the storm put its hands on her and her distress
pealed out of her like thunder. She dressed herself,
and split, and dressed again; she braved the ocean,
and dressed once more while all the crew perished.

And the storm laid her alight in agony,
a red monsoon: too terrible, glorious, royal.
He offered her over land and ocean; he offered
her in wrecks, the destroying angel of a single day.
She recalled well what could excite her,
too well remembered the water-clogged boat.

Now, she sits on the quayside with the basking women;
the Louisa Brettons go by in the protection of cloisters,
those ladies who are never to sail out of harbour.
Now she watches them pass and knows she is at equinox;
balancing the sun and moon, grief and hope,
she awaits the rise of a resplendent morning.

The Adventuress

Sometimes she finds herself spirited away
as she waits in woods for her bridegroom.
All that is left of her is a silver locket,
that hangs on a branch at the heart of winter.

Awaiting her bridegroom in the frosted woods,
she finds herself bound in a breathless crinoline.
Hung in the trunk, her winter heart
is corseted by the snow-laden oak.

The trees are bound like up-ended crinolines,
as they wade through drifts and foggy sleep.
The snow-laden oak struggles in its corset
so twigs and brushwood collapse to snow-beds.

Fighting the drifts and foggy sleep,
in snow thigh-deep, she digs for her bridegroom.
Her lace collar and petticoat collapse to snowflakes
as she reaches his shoulder frozen by blizzards.

Journeying towards him, she is the secret of the woods
as her silks fall away to a silver locket.
Beneath her dress is a ladder of desire,
that she climbs tonight and every night after.

Caroline Clark, 32, was a chosen young Broadsheet Poet in ***Agenda***, Vol 43, Nos 2-3, and has poems in Broadsheets 8 and 9 which appear on ***Agenda***'s website www.agendapoetry.co.uk Her poems have also appeared in *The Interpreter's House, The Frogmore Papers* and are forthcoming in *Smiths Knoll.* She lives in Montreal, Canada, but comes from Sussex.

Saying Yes in Russian

Place the tip of your tongue
against the roof of your mouth
pressing the point just behind your teeth.
Push up, jaw tough, eyes hard.
Make as if to say *no, nyet,*
think of the negative *n* of never, at least, not yet.
In this position and state of mind,
swiftly release the tongue forward and down;
you must surprise it, yourself and the one who asked.
Then transform that heavy knock of a *n*
into the delicate etiquette of *da*.

Two Words

First you taught me *protálina*,
where earth laid bare
through melting snow
becomes a circle of spring.
There the street dog basks on
last year's grass, warming newly.

Later I mouthed to memory
another: *opúshka*. Where
the forest finally finds its end.
I hear a rush of fir trees as
someone pushes through,
entering meadowed light.

Of all those words whose
shaded paths I've walked,
I find these two growing side
by side, sisters in their lilting land,
whispering tales of places
once unknown, unnamed.

See them step from their
swaying pine and birchwood
sea into warm daylight. How
delicately they wear their names:
Protálina and Opúshka,
the story of a struggle at its end.

Touched

I have not touchéd
she says, sliding a piece
of food from hers to ours,
it makes the rounds,
we refuse, childish squeamish –
what things from under fingernails?
Or perhaps her tongue was there.
A family unlike ours would
drink unthinkingly from
the same glass. We preferred
to keep well apart the pieces
of us that others could touch.

And later we sometimes
joke *I have not touchéd*
and scrape our plates.
Who knows she wanted
to give and to never take.
O, how she gave and was sure
to never take.

Gemma Green, 35, studied Classics at university and gained an MA in Creative Writing at the University of East Anglia under the guidance of Andrew Motion. Her poetry has appeared in magazines and anthologies and in 2008 she won 2nd prize in the *Daily Telegraph* Poetry for Performance competition and was shortlisted for the Bridport Prize.

Imperial 58

My father used to have that typewriter
ribbon divided, half-red, half-black
the top two stripes of a German flag.
He bashed the keys with his forefingers
spent ribbon like a machine gunner
hid mistakes behind a camouflage
of kisses, hammered the cross so hard
he made serifs bleed into the paper.
Now he's gone I keep it in the attic
a Ouija board awaiting a glass
hoping one day it'll spell out a letter
using its ribbon to explain the past;
fill up the page with something that's true
an epitaph, a full stop, some clue.

(50° 73′ North, 3°54′ West)

I'm watching your hands
spidering dishes

pink-hot to the cuffs
in sudsy water

you pull out a glass
breaking its soap caul

fisherman holding
his catch to the light.

Watching you makes me
want to make traces

around this kitchen
the breath-milked windows

draw it all out
longitude, latitude

holding this moment
this simple horizon.

Bathroom

half tiled, with matching coral coloured suite
comprising panelled bath with shower attachment,
pedestal wash basin and low flush w.c. Airing
cupboard containing lagged copper cylinder with
immersion heater; radiator

Mum is reclining
gravid and floating
scaffolding her breasts in foam

Two dark coronas
berry red, bobbing
ripe fruit in an upturned keg

We feel nipple-less
unwritten daughters
cutting our dormant molars

Swelling her belly
our brother wriggles
calculating an exit

She shakes like a dog
casting the bubbles
as Venus shed the water

Sending him rocking
butting surfaces
drunk bee in a rosy hive

Standing in bath towels
two latent wrapped girls
piercing canopies

The Bluebell Tutorial

You took a picture of me walking off.
Caught the back of me, climbing.
Preserved in chemicals those last days of May.

Not a great shot by any standard;
the blur of your finger a foggy intrusion,
betraying your location, giving you away.

Look closely, see the bluebell caught in my hair,
accidental crowning from the forest lair.
Wish I'd kept it, pressed as the perfect memorial,
lasting reminder of my bluebell tutorial.

Martin Jackson, 28, lives in Hackney, London. He gained a BA in English with Creative Writing from the University of East Anglia, then an MA from Goldsmiths College. A brief career in advertising was quit so that he could concentrate on writing. His first novel, nearing completion, is funded by the Arts Council.

Geographers' A-Z Map Co., Ltd

Months before that crack of dawn bundling
he showed you his map
                                        traced a finger
from Ha9 down to Ka11,
'My nine square world.'
                                            How he walked to find
out about Shellness, Grove, Martello;
spiderweb walkways strung across
puddles of parks;
                              the random lefts and rights
that became circles and crosses
amongst the six hundred square miles,
scribbles that meant something and nothing
in the inch thick white frame
                                                Blu-Tack torn
as he was shifted from place to place.

All right where he left it.
                                    This terra
intact within its tattered border.

A kite

a tapered diamond in four brown
moles on your back as again you turn

away from my cruelty: silence, my answer to you
phoning home's accented reminders of how soon –

how short your stay is here
where, holding on still,
I find a reason not to pull and reel

you in
to wind up the taut and tugging string
but cut it
and feel the jolt as something

stops, suddenly;
to watch the wind unleashed:
the rise and plunge away and out of reach

as I rock back and try to capture
one last glimpse
an image
finally sure

of what I already know:
I should write, to let you go.

Anna Lewis, 24, is Welsh on her father's side and she lives in Cardiff, having recently completed an MA in Early Celtic Studies at Cardiff University. She has won several awards for her poetry, most recently the inaugural Robin Reeves Prize in 2008. Her poems have appeared in journals including *Modern Poetry in Translation, New Welsh Review* and *Poetry Wales*, and she is the recipient of a 2008 – 2009 New Writer's Bursary from Academi. She was one of the two Chosen Young Broadsheet Poets in the last, Welsh issue of ***Agenda***.

Glass

i

(Warsaw – Dubno)

Ankles clamping your suitcase,
thighs numb under the sag of the bag on your lap,
you keep pace with the sway of your face in the window:
lips and nose franked on the drab southern fields,
forehead and eyes on the birch-snagged sky.

The window divides you:
you are the boy on his bench in the carriage,
sleep flaking and knotting, muslin-thin, in his head;
you are his twin bumping over the cornrows and furrows,
the streams and plank bridges.

On the last limb of track into Dubno,
sun outscores the carriage's lamp.
Among engine sheds and tenement backs
the twin disintegrates,
scrapes into brick and smoked-up boards.

Between carriage and platform, you descend
from your old Warsaw door to the street,
cross the white slabs of the pavement,

but already the front steps have softened
and the paving stones run together,
as though viewed through steam-crowded glass.

ii

(Dubno – Fălticeni)

The lawns are all torn up,
the walls reduced to rockeries,
trees split at the trunk.
Rats have the run of high street, town square, market hall.

The news comes through in tributaries: garbled, polluted.
You can't be sure.
The glass animals that lined your bedroom shelf –
cow, pig, fantastic elephant – either lie in sandy heaps
or stand, but grim with ash and dust.

Their loss hurts stupidly.
In Fălticeni, safely south of the frontier,
you play mud-footed in the fields,
outwit a cow with scythe-sized horns –
but night after makeshift night, you dream of your menagerie,
its transparent parade along your wall.

Your car, weighted with soldiers – boot, running board
and bonnet – was among the last across the border.
Those who left Dubno five, ten minutes too late

wait, still wait, line the south-bound roads,
bellies vacant, faces set. Their veins and bones
make themselves known against the skin.

iii

(Craiova – Paris)

Below the drawn bow of the Carpathians, the Jiu chimes south,
thicker-voiced with every hour toward winter.
The days collapse, shut one into another,
bordered by broad nights.
An almost-blue moon skims the gables, the turrets and steeples,
as snow blanches your footprints through Romanescu Park.

One frost-trimmed afternoon,
you return from school blowing over your fingers,
and your mother shakes a paper at you in the hallway:
Visa! Like viva – like vita – like life.

Steaming west, your palms are grooved red
from the handles of crammed-up cases,
your mother curses late trains and missed connections,
grinds her teeth to the click of the wheels on the railtrack –

and Paris topples in through the windows, rain-shrivelled
and shuttered, pigeons wetly clumping in gutters.
Chestnut vendors hail you in the street;
your suitcase punches your legs.

In the dim afternoon, from the window of your room
in the Hôtel Perreyve, you watch rain drill the pavements,
a flurry of bowed, covered heads;
press an already-looming bruise on your shin
and feel the ache like a bell call: awake! awake!

iv

(Paris – St. Jean de Luz)

Rain hangs above the beach in slats.
The Basque, the Bay of Biscay: so luminous,
your mother assured you in Paris,
as you folded your shirts down into their creases,
and strapped shut the case –

but above your quiet crowd, the clouds are sour as smoke;
a loose tarpaulin sea flaps beyond the harbour wall,
and chairs and tables tilt along the tideline,
legs snapped with weed. At the highest table
two officers sit: one French, one British,
hands stout about near-empty bottles,
their ashtray's debris thickening to clay.

The ships will take no more on board;
behind their elephantine hides,
soldiers slide rosaries between their fingers.
Your sole hope, now, is the tentative road south:
the Pyrenees, the charmed waters of Lourdes,
Toulouse, the rumour of a French free zone.
As you swarm the coast road's dozen empty trucks,
load yourselves up to the pallets, the officers smoke slowly
on their awkward chairs, and lean and lean into the sand.

v

(Grenoble)

The snow-gristled pavements of Grenoble have hardened overnight.
They slough off footprints, mesh wind-spun leaves and papers.

Soldiers, slouching at each corner of the square,
lift down their caps from time to time, to knock away the white

while you rehearse your spoken French, back to the window.
You wince at the bluff of your voice in the snow-lit room:

Je m'appelle; J'habite. With each word hefted
from your lungs, curved in your throat, released,
the fog that daubs the glass behind you thickens.

vi

(Leicester)

It was not that you decided,
once ringed by this island's cliffs and currents,
that you had seen the last of lorry holds,
of sleeper trains and midnight convoys –
you simply didn't leave, and kept not leaving.

After the war was done with, and Europe closed up
like a greatcoat, lapels drawn across its injured parts,
your parents returned to Paris, took rooms off the Rue D'Assas,
shopped once more in the Marché St. Germain.

They thought you might join them, but you didn't go,
and keep not going. To retreat, you conclude,
is complicated: is like stuffing already-budded twigs
back in the bough, like hanging fallen leaves on winter branches.

Professor Thinks-Too-Much, they call you in the staffroom.
On your way to the morning seminar,
you pass the doorless cars of the paternoster
where they lift and lift beside the lobby,

and pause daily to marvel at its riders:
arms snug with books,
feet leaping the threshold without hesitation.

Ailie MacDonald, 20, originates from Perthshire and graduated this summer in Creative Writing at the University of Warwick. She was the chosen Broadsheet poet in the *Poems on Water* issue of ***Agenda*** Vol 42 No 1 when she was 18 and still at school.

Ice Palace

Outside there is an ice palace
the men of the city have carved
in the city square.
Their coatless backs are drawn up high
to lift the ice, and seem to us quite
inexplicably blue
through the shimmer of the gable walls.
If it were not for the pull of their eyes
under such dark and forceful brows
their shapes would float, undisturbed,
like nár-corpses in the water.
It is not hard to think how
the roof must bear upon the heads of those men
with the weight of old arctic ice
almost opaque but for the low sloped pediments
rising into points of translucency.
Greened bronze figures lean in and consider
like tusks their own wavering counterparts,
who seem to own the cleanness of old
undiscovered caves.
The men from the desert and the steppe
stand close and want to press their palms
into the bricks. The light of such a shallow
sideways sun makes walls turn to clear jellied air
and all the young men do is doff their hats
beckoning to one another
apparently forgetful of the snow.

It occurs to me that
they should house some rare specimen in the ice,
pale creatures set, iridescent and unmoving
in each blue architrave. I cannot help but see its rooms
populated with grotesque rubber flesh,
some tiny-eyed colossal squid.
They would have to trawl its frozen hulking mass

ebony beak clacking, up from the south
its bizarre arms stretching on forever
the warm currents reworking layers of blood-flushed red.
Yet now the snow-dirt clings to our mammalian heat,
to the walls of our great buildings
and the horses, ducking in their harness;
appear as triangle of three
swinging their heads in an eerie troika.

Mackerel Fishing

Digging in a shallow pool of light
and water to the belly of the *yole*
were the hands of an old poetess, she that showed me how
to fold a fleece, to hold all these strangling thoughts
together, in open water.

Her archaism was confined to a matter of truths
soon receding into solemn dusk.

Wha kens noo whaur oor auld banes will fa,
on the mountain or the shore –
sic blameless doctrines, sic strang an measured speech,
all forgotten.

Deid black gruesome fish, gasp and grouw
like two brother lungs in tarry air.
The motion's gone, the belly cut and thrown
to the seabirds, and the sea.

Note: yole means 'yawl', a small fishing boat

The Plague Year

Wade at Snowshill

The man was bruised
his cheekbone blue and amber
where he stood in the lamplight
– It took all his character not to
touch the swollen flesh with his right hand.
He is surrounded by ships
the tides cause his thoughts to rise
and swell; though the rivers here
run far to the sea.
They have broad, airless sails
that clot with dirt.
Forgive me Anna –
All his joys are smeared about with dirt:
the feel and smell of old ivory
and eastern lacquer
has passed itself to his fingertips.
The air had rung;
nothing spoke like those turquoise blue walls
stained with their extraordinary achievement,
with quite so high and mighty a conviction.
Standing in the lamplight he recalls
his grandfather's paces round the stone,
a falsetto voice, his glassy eyes.

What blue, heavy pious sleep he slept
each night – box-bound, and at the crook
his own self-wrought saviour
hanging, brazen from the beams.
He entertains suspicions about the sky;
behind the waxy dullness that he shares
with the shape of the low-lying cloud
there is a peculiar brightness,
that the yellow leaves on the ground reflect –
as garden fires of autumn would,
in spit and crack of smoke the gloaming hours.
The tide goes out, it ebbs.
He has recreated a stillness in this place
this mesh of brick and rafter,
a place where he can
look stiff in his Cromwellian armour;
standing on the steps of Snowshill.

It could be said that
bogus spirits plague this house,
that in the rooms that hold his chorus of
mermaid porcelain dolls, his girlish
rows of soldier men – and sheep and cows
– one feels a hand about one's neck
one feels the sodden force of some unbent vision.
Ann, you drape your velvet curtain round –
And outside yet the trees hang docile,
there is still the blossom, and the dove house
there is an orchard, and the long-fringed lambs;
Wade, Wade –
These beams are not the mast
this floor is not the sea:
the warrior men you meet with
have never risen up in all these years.

The distant footsteps pace around the house
and pause at the darkened door.

Cooled Lava at Camas Nan Geall

The borders of the ocean, the Amazon, Orinoco and Mississippi
Raise their stratus lips to the low steppes skirting these seas

There is a tradition of sudden deluge on the shore;
The Bosphorus, Hellespont, and the Grecian Archipelago

The Western limits bowing, a church under lava-heat
Early eruptions flowered and found in a small number of skeletons

Skaptár Jokul, a cone produced at great depths;
A movement in the stones of two undiscovered obelisks

For such an age the folk have held onto their own earthly psalms,
Told in lilting tongues all night to the heave of the sinking ships.

Each evening a greater number of broken oak barrels
Found their easy way to shore, dry broken edges softened in water.

The talk was always swollen, and pressing gently
On its own delicate boundaries

A momentary thunderhead, a familiar feeling
Bending bodies into a convulsion.

The feeling of it would be forever broken by the movement
Of the gannets to the sea

Each fall cannot fail to act as symbol of irreversible historical process
Not essences but constructs, slow and gray accumulation

The great multitudes have reached their bifurcation;
If we were to break apart, and find another history – another stability

It would need to be gentle. Indeed we have owned each other's histories
Long back from when things split and grew on the dunes.

From what are now cliffs we view humankind's phase transitions
With millennia of strata underfoot, until they meet in this crystal state.

Lallans Sonnet

Tak me tae the winnock, an show me the day
Show me the soond o the laverock's sang
Thouch he is tucked awa in his hoose o gress
Tell me tae peetie the beasts in the dreich o the day.
The doos are aa sauf in their doocot
But oor men are gang awa tae the sea
Claucht atween the een o the luft sae gray
An their ain thochts – pray they skelpit on hame!
In laneliness we'll footer and bide
Tae adore the rising sun; whan the haar is gaan
Whan the lang dreep o scaddows gae lowpin
Aa bousie-shapit frae the muckle muntain heicht.
Yet we ken fu weel the cauld wudnae brak again,
An the gowden hulls o the boats wud freeze eftir the onding.

Christopher Nield, 34, lives in London. His work has been published in *New Poetries IV* (Carcanet 2007) and featured in a range of journals including *PN Review, The London Magazine, Ambit, Magma, The Rialto, Poetry Wales* and *Stand Magazine*. As a professional copywriter he works with a range of charities and NGOs including Cancer Research UK, Friends of the Earth, Sightsavers International and Virgin Unite.

Ghost

How could your beauty never change?

Because it is your eyes,
Those sad emphatic eyes that pierce
The graceless Soho yard with a void
Of mist and fire.

Because it is your voice,
So clear and unresigned beneath the summer rain,
A balance in the air
That fills the trembling nerve with light.

Because it is your touch,
The consequential rush within my hand
That leaves me ravenous, woken to the core.

And, though you smile and walk away,
I write this elegy for time
In the frailest substance known.

How could your beauty ever change?

Rafael

Your name demands a God that heals
And not a God that lies.
Your name is wormwood on my tongue.

Your name demands a world that breaks
Like oil on broken men.
Your name is wormwood on my tongue.

Your name demands a soul that speaks
Of Sinai manna-snow.
Your name is wormwood on my tongue –

Though manna swept *The Seven Stars*
When all of London stood in awe;
We shared a pint and said goodbye.
Within a day, the city burned.

Joshua Roche, 20, is a student at Warwick University. He is studying English with Creative Writing. He travels in his free time, and works boring jobs when he has to. He has recently visited Nepal and plans to go to Tibet next year. He surfs regularly on the Cornish Coast.

Passion Girl

An Italian lover waited for me
In a long walled room,
Dressed in the brightest, most oppressive
Red dress of any time, age or city.
It hung between her breasts,
Languishing like a lioness,
And thick chocolate hair
Piled down her neck like a cascade
In a chandeliered room
Where the ruddy terracotta reds
Bubbled with the firelight
And the glowing mischief in her eyes
Illuminated her

Five long fingers.
No words, my chest's beating checked,
No thought needed, no soft retreating now.
A thoroughfare of hot wind
Sagged between the old windows
And the luxury of her stare
Held that long body in godly pose.

Blue

After John Lee Hooker

The clipper swings by the low wave trough
The men pitching, sing the horn slave song.

Blown by the trade winds, in the gullet drifting.
In their ears pitching, back to New Orleans.

*

Trapped in their churches, crammed in the holes.
Fed to the veins of the earth.

The death-sweat, the deep-dark trees
The lull of long relief.

But something is born. There is some mystery,
Some frothing in hush, and rock.

Absolutely of themselves, the Canaan-Caribbean
like a twisted blue caress.

*

Sax pricked with acacia,
Some double bass from jungle toads.

Shoeless, loveless, listing with
Mourn.

*

Give them no way out,
                                        they said
Let them remember the hush
                                        the rock.

The last line of Ghana,
                                the Ivory Beach.
Give them no way out.

For apology excuses,
apology forgets.
Drive them down to the sea,
wallow.

Give them no way out.
Take the sea,
take the sky.

Let their children remember
This was you,
this was I.

Omar Sabbagh, 28, is a Lebanese/British poet. His poetry has appeared and/or is forthcoming in many journals, such as *Poetry Review, PN Review, Stand, The Reader, Poetry Wales,* and *The Warwick Review*. His first collection, titled, *My Only Ever Oedipal Complaint* is forthcoming with Cinnamon Press in September 2010. He graduated with an MA in Creative and Life Writing from Goldsmiths in 2007 and is currently in his third year of a PhD in English Literature at King's College, London, where he is writing on the representation of time in Conrad and Ford.

The Ecclesiast

For Claudia H, once 18

If you are ever scared, as some dead branches of trees
Look in the starkest blue of a night, moon-made, but moon-free
As well – think of me, or rather, better, think of what it is to think
Of me, which is the better me, my story, and how the world too
Is stored, daily, and forever.
                                                    The sun never shines
And if you'd like to know, I'll tell you why: it's my
Most recent discovery.
                                          Meaning is the light that leads
And leads away
                        from pain and
                                                  also how I loved her.

Muses

In the small square plot of grass
beneath my window
stands a tree, bare knuckled and wintered, bald
but for the curse
of speaking birds perched
on its uppermost bough.

Each morning at four, coloured by the raven-dark,
they arrive on some sirocco wind
of a northern sort, scalding and singed with biting cold,
and stand toe to toe, rigid as statues
speaking in my dreaming sleep
of what death needs of me

before I too go winging.
This is a metaphor, they say –
that's how their black oratory
always begins, as if
what you happen to hear in your sleep
were articulate pain, like poetry.

David Shook, 23, attended graduate school at Oxford. His work has appeared or is forthcoming in *Hayden's Ferry Review, Oxford Magazine, PEN International Magazine, Poetry, World Literature Today,* on the Poetry Translation Centre website, and elsewhere. He grew up in Mexico City. A member of American Literary Translators Association and the National Book Critics Circle, he lives in Silver Lake, Los Angeles, where he edits *Molossus*. He will tour the UK with Mexican poet Víctor Terán and the Poetry Translation Centre in 2010.

The two Mexican poets translated here write in Isthmus Zapotec. Zapotec is Oto-Manguen and has over 60 dialects which are not mutually intelligible. The variant in which these two poets write, Isthmus Zapotec, has about 100K speakers, many monolingual, in and around Juchitan, Oaxaca.

Victor Terán was born in Juchitán de Zaragoza in 1958, and his work has been published widely in magazines and anthologies throughout Mexico. He has had several books of poetry published. Terán works as a media education teacher at the secondary level on the Oaxacan Isthmus.

Victor de la Cruz (b. 1948) is a Oaxacan poet from Juchitán, a hub of Isthmus Zapotec art and culture on the Isthmus of Tehuantepec. He compiled a definitive anthology of Zapotec literature, *The Flower of the Word*. He has a doctorate in Mesoamerican Studies, and has several books of poetry to his name. He works as a professor of social anthropology in the state of Oaxaca and edits *Guaracha' Reza (Striped Iguana)*, a magazine of indigenous literature.

Victor Terán

It's over

It's over
and that is all.
On your new path you will find
the same things you always saw
during the days
that you were her shadow:
dogs, vehicles,
people.
Nothing will change,
and the same grackles
that shat on your head
will whiten that of the kid
that took your place.
And behind the house
where you sat talking
she will cement your absence.
Nothing will change,
only your passion will make you think
the earth lost
its reason for being,
its logic
for sheltering life.
And you will gnaw through your sincerity,
your heart will pound
willing to renounce everything,
and you will stretch
your arms and your legs into awkwardness.
Lost in your place
you will see yourself dumbly moving
your eyes and your arms in no particular direction.

Translated from the Isthmus Zapotec *by* **David Shook**

In the hammock

Right now you're in my arms,
both of us reclined in the hammock
that creaks with each swing.
I'm explaining to you that there is nothing impossible,
there is no knot without its end,
that to make our love last
I will be tireless.
Listen, we will build things,
                                        we will demolish others,
we will found a temple where we will light candles
and burn incense to our love.
You look at me suspiciously,
laugh and press yourself to my side.
I caress your face,
I would kiss your shoulders, your chest,
if you were still with me in this hammock.

Translated from the Isthmus Zapotec *by* **David Shook**

Victor de la Cruz

My fall

Since I left my village
I've fallen to the bottom,
the absolute bottom
of a well of sand
where pain is drawn in
buckets, instead of water.
My heart hurts in the mornings
when I look around
Why do I find myself in these lands?
—I say inside of me—
and I go to sleep
in a bed whose owner
I can't remember.

Translated from the Isthmus Zapotec *by* **David Shook**

The word I forgot

One word,
just one word,
I had just one word
in the palm of my hand,
in my intelligence,
in my heart.
Just one word
to tell you in the night,
when we wake in the blooming flower of the morning,
with the chorus of the birds
above the trees of Lahuoyaga.
Just one word,
one word I've already forgotten.

Translated from the Isthmus Zapotec *by* **David Shook**

Agnieszka Studzinska, 24, was born in Poland. She came to England in the early 80s. She studied Cultural Studies at Norwich School of Art & Design and has an MA in Creative Writing from the University of East Anglia. She has previously worked as a freelance researcher in broadcasting and now teaches and lives in London with her husband and daughter. *Snow Calling* is her debut collection which will be published by Salt next year.

Haunting

i

Through the slats of a February daybreak
when the world no longer sleeps the same
hearing her own spent
in the frost of blackened windows,
an account of one story broken again in its telling
opens –
it begins with winter buying time
for those in hiding,
the snow covering their wisteria steps.

ii

Like shooting stars – you run across the vaults of sundown
a pencil drawn map crumpled in a pocket,
skirting between trees that hold the colour of earth's black –

they veil you in their destroyed elegance
snow capped and angled like sundials –

they are the recordings
of this event and all other happenings
they are the absolute –
in their amputation
they remind you of all those people children,
black keys on a piano –
they saw everything.

iii

Tired breath hits the ground
marking loss in wet dust
in your running
you swallow the invisible hours of grief –
a brother behind you
his quietness like a moonbeam
on your back –
gold coins in your mother's handkerchief
pressed against your breastbone
like stars pressing against abstraction,
they are your Gods –

iv

You imagine that you are living someone else's life
it is easier that way
to accept your fate
geography of light
like a broken sky
over this room, over the farmhouse
hidden
somewhere in Grodno.

Night after night you drink a little, play chess
work out exactly how you got here
and sting yourself with forgetfulness
mime the playing of piano
your brother listening to this blind music
with his eyes shut
arms open as if to beg forgiveness
for being him
as if to embrace his silhouette and let it disappear –

Night after night you make promises
to recreate the sound of daylight,
sometimes you venture outside
imagining the night as morning
inhale the smoke of the fields –
beyond
a nightmare: watching flesh of fields
smell of animal.

v

It's not clear how many years were closed
how many moments wooded
winters cached in purple-dark
how many matchsticks disguised floors
how many butterflies turned into letters
how many hours softened in their inkling
how many meals eaten in a maroon silence
how many afterthoughts became a future
how many voices turned into birds
how many wishes redefined the self
how many snowdrops turned white
how much of nothing became the matter
how much waiting   how
for we are where we are not.

vi

After the war the ravens were the black pearls of the field
glistening with unease like a century changing –

You lived in the impossible
                                        like the burning of snow
– saw the impossible being done
                        nothing from then – frightened

I am the space where I am.

After the war you left for Lodz
                                      in the nettled air of this city
the buildings became free of the streets
streets reinvented themselves in rubble
                                        rubble became new earth
became your haunting –
                              disguised you in its concertina of concrete
the grey orchards of linen –

desire and necessity thickening
                                     a new kind of air –
This city became your mother
who no one ever knew
                            her body in the semblance of things
in the moss of snow.

vii

You wore suits
You listened to your wife
You were lucky
You gave little away
You had two daughters
You sucked the ghost of air.
I am my own hiding place.

Notes on Haunting

Je suis I'espace ou je suis
I am the space that I am – Noel Arnaud

Car nous sommes o nous somme pas
We are where we are not – Pierre-Jean Jove

No one sees me changing – But who sees me? I am my own hiding place – Joe Bousquet

Rory Waterman, 28, was born in Belfast in September 1981, grew up in Lincolnshire, and currently lives in Bristol. He is a graduate of Leicester and Durham, and has returned to the former to write a PhD thesis on the poetry of Charles Causley, R.S. Thomas and Philip Larkin. His poems have been taken by *Stand, PN Review, Staple* and various other publications.

A Wedding Photograph

for both of my parents

At my sun/rain/wind-flushed wedding last November
neither of them knew they both had cancer.
Divorce, a custody war, some twenty-four years;

my happiness had thrust them back together,
had made them seem a pair –
not sickness, or despair.

No endless yestertalk or choking tears,
none of that stuff. But quietly, alone,
we all remember:

I think, now, how I should have hooked your arms
for our photo between those gust-trembled puddles,
the patterns breaking, scattering, regathered.

Where Were You When…

…those girders gave? There were signs we cared:
reams of sympathy, uncertainty;
relentless shots of figures treading air;
wreaths and crosses; services; silences.

We knew it meant that thousands more would die.
Of course. Some said they'd once been in that Square
between them both, and watched illusive sky
overbalance concrete, over there.

In Lincoln, in respect, a few things shut.
Daily, the Minster's tower cut the ground
with shifting shadow, like a huge sundial
no-one could read, and pushed the baskers round.

In The Avenue of Limes

A dribbling afternoon
in Gloucestershire. Through
the National Arboretum,
between broad name-tagged trees,
we squelched in half-blue gloom.

Not like your New England:
postcard reds and ochres
reflected in chill lakes,
drowning the shivered stems
of whitened spires. No: a glum
and quiet way to age,
pallid in a damp-thick
whinny of breezing rain.
Guessing a quick route back

towards the car, we cut
across the regal, bristling
'Avenue of Limes'
where autumn was falling
in ceaseless dribbles of twos
and fours from a quiver
of frail mottled canopy
to clotting mottled ground
where I lost myself in you

dashing to clutch at flurries
of washed-out hearts. Dashing
to clutch at flurries of washed-
out hearts. Dashing to clutch
at flurries of washed-out hearts.

Shrine for a Young Soldier, Castle Drogo

Easy to pick out, Gioconda-faced:
here he crouches in Oxford sepia-blue;
here in the Eton Boys' XI;
here in a family portrait, in casuals;

here in straitening khaki, moustached like a man,
clutching a bayonet proudly: Major Drewe.
'With the Angels in Heaven'.

The day the letter arrived from the Front
the butler stood silent behind the door,
the maids waited, eyes blank, and prayed for their masters
in their cluttered living room, newspapers spread with the War.

The golden child rancid in mud
and horror brought home like a catkill left
on a worn-through scullery floor.

Loveday Why, 25, graduated from Warwick University in 2006, where she founded and edited the poetry magazine, *The Poetaster,* and received the 2006 Derek Walcott Poetry Prize. She subsequently left a Masters in Romantic Literature at Cambridge University in order to travel through Australia and New Zealand. Her work has been published in magazines and journals and she was shortlisted for the 2008 Bridport Poetry Prize. She is also a past editor of *Avocado*, The Heaventree Press's poetry magazine. An essay on **a joint haiku project** with her artist mother comprises **Broadsheet 13** online, including many colourful haiku-prints. www.agendapoetry.co.uk.

Pieces

There were the red sands of Moeraki,
the deep rust,
the cutouts of ourselves
burnt into Eastern sky.

There was you, woven into grasses,
arm's blue scrolling,
filling a bucket with the ground,
and pressing trees into it.

You'd thrown the bush turkey at my door,
shadow, like rummaged rubbish,
pushed into my thigh with feathers.

You'd chased the sun to make me morning,
and then you'd bundled the pig into a sack,
like a mystery play, on the Palmerston highway.

At Tallows Beach, you had rushed me up the cliff,
tired of fruitless wetting,
to watch history heave beneath us.

And now the church floods,

and, just when we're on the cusp,
we hear a noise and
look back and see that it is us,
lurching forwards to grasp this ring
this thing called ossifying.

And already within the waters of me
our joined love slopping, stamping its feet.

The Hut

Light stripes the shadows, dust swirls through the door
to mix with pine needles on the hut floor.
Under the corrugated awning, blocks,
our doorstep, and in the yard of scuffed rocks,
because last night it didn't rain, the stain
of piglets' blood like gerbera petals remains,
beautifully pink in the morning pine shine–
gift from your garden in another time.
The table – manuka flowers, shells, driftwood,
make a painting. To have you here is good,
to take your two sets of hands and adapt,
knee-deep in shovels, dry, the usual scrapped.
On craggy coast, by salt marsh river mouth,
we three stand out, East of the island's South.

Spotlighting

In the back of your dusty Range Rover,
having grown accustomed to butchery,
to take the gun was like learning cookery
backwards. The start is when life is over.
It took twenty four years to discover
this part, the cold bloody treachery,
now so familiar that my own jury
leaves in disgust, shame. I must recover.
I shot a rabbit five times, there, it's said.
Gun, like the dogs, a new acquaintance versed
in death, touched, quickly assimilated.
How the boys spat, drank bourbon, gently cursed;
I was passed a weapon and used it right,
looked through the sights, quivered in the spotlight.

Adam Wyeth was born in 1978 and lives in West Cork. He was a recent prize-winner of the Fish International Poetry Competition, 2009. He was a runner-up in the Arvon International Poetry Competition, 2006. His poems have been anthologized in The Fish Anthology, *Something Beginning with P*, the Arvon 25th Anniversary anthology and a forthcoming Dedalus Press anthology. His work has appeared in numerous literary journals, including *Poetry London, Magma, The Stinging Fly, The Shop* and *Southword.* He was a chosen Broadsheet poet in ***Agenda*** and selected for the Poetry Ireland Introductions Series, 2007. He teaches Creative Writing and is on the Poetry Ireland Writers in Schools scheme. His first collection, *Silent Music,* is being published by Salmon in 2011.

Cinema Complex

The weekend dad didn't come
mum announced we were going out,

she flung her jacket on and we sped off
to the cinema complex; I had never been

just with her. Sitting in the back row
like two young lovers.

We watched *Back To The Future...*
and *I* was Michael J Fox –

going back in time to save his parents.
He had to make sure they danced

to the slow number at the school prom
together, otherwise they would never

fall in love and he would never be born.
But he was getting to know his mum all over.

She was innocent, radiant before she'd
met his father. Fox could have had her

in the scene at the drive-in if he wanted.
He could have warned her, while brushing

his lips against her unexplored ear,
to turn her back on the future...

Deoch an Doris

Those winter nights
I became familiar
to their ways –
all touch-and-go
without a soul
save mine –
prodding a peat fire.
Then, winding down
they'd all trundle in –
fisherman out of the deep
like warriors from battle
sinking pint after pint
of dark ruby stout.
By two-o-clock
they were still drinking
whole-heartedly,
speaking in tongues,
my hands were tied
for who was I –
a tongue-tied blow-in
to show them the door,
to call *deoch an doris* –
one for the road –
as if I were one of them?
Little did they know
my fathers too
fought for this land –
they assumed
by my muted tones
I was pure Sassenach
and after eight hundred years
to keep a sock in it.
Little did they know.
When the fire got low
I stood by the door
and watched them go.

Rough Music

The whole village came out to clamour
and clash – a constant crescendo of pots
and pans outside his house –
like somebody crashing down the stairs.

Ransacking cupboards, empting cutlery
drawers – in a calamity of noise.
One neighbour took his wooden spoon
and whipped up a storm in a beer mug,

while women played merry hell –
smashing saucepan lids like symbols –
and dragging their claws down washboards.
Droves of men hauled necklaces of tin cans –

along the road and marched to the beat
of buckets being battered out of shape
with crowbars. Innovative, like some kind
of travelling circus playing the antithesis

of a Romeolovestruckyouth – serenading
on his lute below a balcony window.
Upstairs the culprit was lying curled up
in bed, like he'd been kicked in the guts –

seeing stars like the ones his wife saw
the night he punched her in the jaw.

Ode to the Globe

Wandering to the bottom of the garden
to cut off the artichokes, you return
with other worlds in your hands.
If they're not picked soon a finely haired
flower sprouts out the top: Resplendent
as fox gloves, you say. A steady steaming
for forty minutes and we're away –
plucking off each soft frond, spading them
in melted garlic-butter – then scraping the flesh
off the saturated leaf with our front teeth.
The leaves getting thinner, allowing our minds
to drift, till there's no flesh left on the inner tips.
We discover the best of both worlds, like Buddhists
journeying towards the centre of the mind,
peeling back layers to reach new realms.
And though we sit in calm repose,
letting clouds of thought come and go
at our ease, it's this we've been waiting for –
the heart of the artichoke, the heavenly piece.
We pull off the yellow tufts of hairs
to reveal the round concaved gem,
and merge into the mind of the universe.

Young Essayists/Reviewers

Caroline Clark is one of the chosen young poets in this issue.

Of All the Places

I was asked to think about what modernism means to me (and Ezra Pound was mentioned in view of his connection to the founding of *Agenda*). So I'll give it a go. I think one of my inner censors has the face of a modernist. The 'compound ghost' of a modernist whose image has filtered through to me. Stern, exacting, demanding newness and at the same time literariness, keeping in line with the myth tradition, yet breaking away from tradition, bringing new life, honouring old life. The perfect censor – contradictory enough to ensure near paralysis sets in. I am not a rebel and I do try to do what's expected of me. It's just that the personal gets in the way, and if it can't be exorcised, I'm not sure where to put it. These Notes are personal; they have to be.

Modernism lies back there somewhere, behind us. 'What lies ahead?' was a question I asked in my first attempt at writing *Notes for Broadsheet Poets*. This time I write these *Notes* not so much *for* young poets but I am, rather, thinking of the source, of where what I have to say is coming *from*. The question of how to speak, how to make an utterance is part of the heritage of the moderns. How to make a start?

Home is where I start from[1]. Home is Lewes, East Sussex, an area that was once host to several of the great moderns. Yes, there were once the moderns. They loom there large on the horizon with their famous profiles. They tilled this land for us. They set the tone, the mood, the palette. I could say the moderns are a place I come from, for when looked at from a distance they become a place, with a tone and colour all of their own. Like the South Downs in the evening, just as a violet light settles into the folds of the hills across the valley (I have a feeling Virginia Woolf noted this phenomenon somewhere). Violet was their colour: a far-off warning light, a fading light. That of shadows, an approaching storm, bruises, memories. The colour of a closing era, worn-out language, still elegant, no longer fresh. In that violet light of a nearing cultural apocalypse, it seems that endings loomed over them; but one would never come:

> Where is there an end of it, the soundless wailing,
> ...

---

[1] To raid and slightly alter Eliot's words: 'Home is where one starts' from 'East Coker'. And the 'compound ghost' in the first paragraph is from 'Little Gidding'.

There is no end, but addition: the trailing
Consequence of further days and hours,
...

In the uncertain hour before the morning
  Near the ending of interminable night
  At the recurrent end of the unending[2]
...

Pound says the poet must be 'on the watch for new emotions, new vibrations'[3] – I would say a sense of the interminable was certainly well signposted by the moderns, whether it be that of physical suffering and spiritual torment or the interminability of lives smothered by convention. In many of its guises the interminable seems to be a descendant of ennui (that late 19th century enemy of the artist), less decadent though, dragging repetitive activity out of its sufferers or forcing them to postpone the present and simply wait – for what? The end (and we know what wonderful absurdities waiting can lead to). Today our lives are no less touched by the interminable: the constant electric drone or drills, tv that is surely without end, hyperlinks that take us further and further away; interminable is the ever-looming postponement of the present that we let eat out our hearts (or livers) again and again. Here's where these thoughts spiral from: I wanted to use the word 'interminable' in a poem but realised I couldn't – it contains too much of a complaint, too much mock agony. (Unless the word is used with humour as in Heaney's poem 'Keeping Going' to describe that pretend bagpipe drone.) The cry of 'when will it all end' is ageless, but to complain of an ending never coming – to sink into the interminable mode – would feel a little worn in a poem these days. We've had enough of endings for now. Today we might find the interminable transformed thus:

Life stretches across all kinds of voids
  without breaking
and even broken keeps up a soft whisper[4]

Instead of sitting it out with the interminable, we find the moment of the poem – like life here – carrying on, not wailing or droning, but with a whisper. Those 'voids' are perhaps full of ennui and the interminable, but they don't create desert wastelands in the present, they don't even make a crack in the pavement: life carries on over them. There's something powerfully gentle here; no echo of

---

[2] First two quotes from 'The Dry Salvages', the third is from 'Little Gidding'.

[3] From 'The Art of Poetry', in *Ezra Pound, Selected Prose 1909-1965*, ed. William Cookson.

[4] From *beautiful, unfinished*, M.T.C. Cronin, Salt, 2003. All further quotes from Cronin are from this book.

that age-long complaint. Our challenge is to deal with the carrying-on of life (the stuff that comes before the end), not to rush to get things over with, push on through to find a miraculous ending. Poets know about the interminable; it is, as I have said, one of their great enemies. Ignorance is interminable (I am talking, in particular, of my own), the young poet's experience of wanting to write is interminable (for as long as the actual writing is deferred). Ideally we would all be able to declare without despair: 'I have begun an endless poem.'[5] Interminable is the indecision, the constant avoidance of risk and it is the release from this that is always miraculous. Poetry and failure are a popular pair often seen together in essays and notes on poetry. But the miraculous is there too, as the third, invisible, element. The miraculous is when something seemingly comes from nothing, when we realise there is more at work here than we are aware of (although, as Pound warns us in his *ABC of Reading*, to believe that something actually can come from nothing, in particular – reading nothing, is either lazy or naïve). Beginnings are miraculous.

Let's start from the heart as Pound says we must:

> I would bathe myself in strangeness:
> These comforts heaped upon me, smother me!
> I burn, I scald so for the new,
> New friends, new faces,
> Places!
> Oh to be out of this,
> This that is all I wanted
> – save the new.[6]
> ...

I'd like to push off from a few key words in this wonderful cry. The strangeness that Pound so longs to plunge into is sought after more than ever by poets today: some seek alienation from all they know and own, including what is most their own – language, others seek out the uncanny, the other, to return newly to what is their own. I certainly am fascinated by that return to one's own which can only be gained by passing through the other, Eliot's:

> In order to possess what you do not possess
> You must go by the way of dispossession.
> In order to arrive at what you are not
> You must go through the way in which you are not.

---

[5] Pound writing to James Joyce, 1917, quoted in *A Guide to the Cantos of Ezra Pound*, ed. William Cookson.

[6] 'The Plunge' in *Personae: the Shorter Poems of Ezra Pound*, ed. Lea Baechler and A. Walton Litz.

–which as the 20th century progressed came to be expressed as Celan's 'step beyond' (which I touched on in my previous *Notes*). But then from the contemporary Australian poet M.T.C. Cronin we read:

> Going out there
>   you usually bring something back
> What of the possibility of it all being here

What a change from the questing impulse of language and poetry! Let's open up the possibilities of the already-present, look inside, as Cronin says:

> Inside something small
>   exists everything

And what of 'the new'? Are poets still here, as Pound says, 'to new-mint the speech'? Well, I won't speak in terms of their 'role', but the new is what they do: dogs bark, birds augur and poets new. But these days we don't roar for the new as Pound does. The new 'new' is the slow grow; it is present in those almost imperceptible shifts, to be found in a 'devastating millimetre' like the one Jen Hadfield's limpet[7] nearly doesn't make.

And what is it that 'smothers' us these days? I have felt smothered at times by the right answers. Those answers, directed at us from A-Levels (I found GCSEs to be mercifully tolerant of independent thought) onwards that gradually seep in to take the place of the original text. Secondary literature or as William Cookson says in relation to Pound's cantos:

> ...the growth of a vast critical industry devoted to explaining and interpreting...[8]

That compound censor of which I spoke at the start is partly a product of not enough reading in source, created before we get a chance to read the original on our own. And it gets much worse at university. More and more often do we find ready formed opinions about those names on our reading lists before we have a chance to take them on in the original. As Cookson advises us in his 'Warning': read the thing first before reading what it's about, quoting Eliot: 'to study even the best commentary on a work of literary art is likely to be a waste of time unless we have first read and been excited by the text commented upon even without understanding it'.[9] How lucky the moderns were in that they didn't have to read themselves as set texts. I certainly felt that

---

[7] In *Nigh-No-Place*, Bloodaxe, 2008.

[8] *A Guide to the Cantos of Ezra Pound*, introduction, xv.

[9] ibid, 'How to Approach *The Cantos:* A Warning', xx.

I had to re-educate myself towards independent thought after completing my formal education. To learn to return to the source: 'go to the TEXTS, the originals.'[10]

Somewhere along the way I got a sense that when reading poetry, this is not yours and you are looking this way by chance, think yourself lucky. A little of that is good (you are lucky), but if we want to encourage more poetry readers less would be better. It is not good to feel so estranged from one's own – that is, achievements in language that seem to be things of the past, frozen there like exhibition pieces. How to break the ice between new readers and Poetry? Let them know it's a thing still done, living. (Perhaps journals could suggest to their readers that they might send a past copy on to local A-level students...). Let them hear the words from Eliot's ghost:

> For last year's words belong to last year's language
> And next year's words await another voice.

And finally what of the 'new places' that Pound invokes? New places mean new selves. Some may say the relationship between self and place seems to be growing more and more fragmented, but perhaps, with rather less sense of doom, we could say it's becoming more multitudinous. I am aware of having not just one place as a reference point, not just one language to understand the world in; I revel in the differences. My Italian grandmother lived in my hometown but came from another place. My first foreign phrase was: *noncapsico, sono inglese* (*I don't understand, I'm English*. I thought *non capisco* was one long word and imagined it to be like some strange sea creature). When visiting Italy, I would release the *noncapisco* whenever spoken to and then add the *sono inglese* as my declaration of otherness. I felt – not quite a fool – but awkward at not being able to understand, but was aware this could be remedied. Later, learning Russian and living in Russia did not teach me that 'we're all the same in the end.' There is such a thing as difference. New places create new senses of centres – that's more than one centre. Are there any truly mono-lingual poets out there? Poetry nurtures the multitudinous; it says (to reassign more of Cronin's words):

> But how silly to be only one

Pound didn't want his use of foreign words in *The Cantos* to alienate the reader, but to give them a sense of the multitudinous world they come from:

[10] From Pound's *The ABC of Reading*. Needless to say, the capitals are not my own.

> Skip anything you don't understand and go on till you pick it up again. All tosh about foreign languages making it difficult... I can't conceal the fact that the Greek language existed.

and:

> ...citations from Homer or Sophokles or Confucius are brief, and serve to remind the ready reader that we were not born yesterday.[11]

Indeed we were not born yesterday and we were not born in an insular culture. But I did read Pound's *ABC of Reading* just two days ago and was delighted to find there:

> The sum of human wisdom is not contained in any one language, and no single language is CAPABLE of expressing all forms and degrees of human comprehension.

and:

> One has to...divide, as it were, those who want to see the world from those who merely want to know WHAT PART OF IT THEY LIVE IN.[12]

but fear not:

> ...I am not insisting even now on your learning a multitude of strange languages, I will even tell you, in due course, what you can do if you can read only English.

Elsewhere he states:

> The essential thing in a poet is that he builds us his world.

– a formulation that is wonderfully helpful for poets and readers alike, prompting us to ask when we read a poet's work: what kind of a place is this? Newness cannot help but bloom when we find poets writing through new experiences of place, foreign languages, other centres.

In his overview of contemporary Australian poetry featured in *Agenda's Australian Issue* (Vol.41, Nos.1-2, 2005), David McCooey talks of the 'worldliness' of Australian poetry:

---

[11] 'An Anthology of Statements by Ezra Pound on *The Cantos' in A Guide to the Cantos of Ezra Pound*, xxiii and xxvi.

[12] All Pound's capitals.

> the contemporary Australian poet is attracted to the 'recombinant poetic' that can be found through any number of antecedents not determined by nationality.

This certainly opens up a supposedly closed category in poetry: we can look to Australian poets for a very new take on place, ownership (of language, land) and self. When McCooey lists the themes that are key to Australian poetry (self, place and the uncanny), I read along ticking them off for contemporary poetry from these isles too. It's the difference that counts though. I shall attempt, just once, the Poundian manner: READ English language poetry that comes from DIFFERENT PLACES.

The world knows the woes of globalisation, but there's also a way to go global in a good way. There is more to us than the place we are from. Of course, the fear that this kind of feeling will lead to losses in terms of language is not unfounded. I sense however that this is a time to try out the many and the multitudinous, not necessarily combining differences but acknowledging them, saying: I am from here and here, and here too now. Maybe even saying, without an end in sight: I want to know more, more of this and this and this. Dis-locatedness has long been a lamented fact of life. But perhaps if we call it multi-locatedness (like the 'fragmented' that could become 'multitudinous'), the relationship between self and place is given more room; a wider plain of interaction becomes possible, is allowed.

N. Bryant Kirkland, 24, read Classics, *magna cum laude*, at Davidson College, North Carolina, where he wrote his honours thesis on the Roman poet, Calpurnius Siculus. He spent a year in Germany on a Fulbright Fellowship and currently lives in London. He is a postgraduate in Greek and Latin literature at University College London.

The Fires by Night: Louise Glűck

Louise Glück's newest book of poems, *Averno*, tells its readers, in effect, to go to hell. Coming from Glück, though, we shouldn't treat this as an insult but rather as an invitation. The underworld is where Glück is going, and we're meant to come along. In a previous collection, *The Wild Iris*, she scoured her garden for clues to meaning. There she wrote

> You ought to know
> I'm never weeding, on my knees, pulling
> clumps of clover from the flower beds: in fact
> I'm looking for courage, for some evidence
> my life will change.

With the same taut focus of that previous search, Glück now moves subterranean. If we met her in the garden, we are now asked to pack for a trip that can occur only after the fall.

But Glück's journey to hell does not reiterate the hell of Dante, the travelogue of tortures and oddities that culminates, at the end of the *Paradiso*, in a vision of harmony and truth. Indeed, the title of the current collection marks an altogether different point of departure. She describes on a preface page the significance of Lake Averno: 'A small crater lake, ten miles west of Naples, Italy; regarded by the ancient Romans as the entrance to the underworld.' Glück's pagan sensibilities mean that her starting point and her ending point will differ from Dante's ascent to paradise. For Glück, such final visions are untenable. In the absence of ultimate dogma, her invitation is perhaps better described as one to Hades, somewhere we haven't been very much in the past two millennia. To go is to admit our desire to see a place we both do and do not know. To go is to admit the polysemic possibilities furnished by a place where life and death ambiguously coexist.

We often misuse the word *myth* nowadays to mean something commonly believed but in fact false. Glück knows what a myth is, and her book depends on its proper definition as a story commonly known in which an element of truth inheres, even if the manner of telling is fanciful. *Averno*, then, engages in an extended poetic exploration of several recurring mythical and archetypal themes. The poet explores, with moments of splintering incision, the myths of Persephone and Demeter, the difficulty of reconciling the dying body to an earth that itself seems at once death-bound (headed for winter) yet renewable (headed for summer), and the strange regions between life and death that, like the titular lake, the soul fitfully inhabits in a world often devoid of comfort or assurance. 'Weren't we necessary to the earth?' Glück asks upon the realization that winter has returned, and that the garden, a work of human hands, has become ice.

The word Averno is from the ancient Greek for 'birdless.' At the membrane between life and death there is no flight, no winging away. But many parallel deaths precede the final death, and it is in these defeats of self, from which there might be the chance for escape, where Glück locates losses that prefigure the inescapable one. When the narrator's sister tells her that falling in love is like being struck by lightning, the narrator can't help but see the other possibilities of electric shock:

> I reminded her that she was repeating exactly
> Our mother's formula, which she and I
>
> Had discussed in childhood, because we both felt
> That what we were looking at in the adults
>
> Were the effects not of lightning
> But of the electric chair.

This riff of memory shoots downward, without end-stopped phrases, like its own electric bolt on the page. The effects of distance, between mothers and daughters, between earth and sun, between lover and lover, are everywhere present in the collection. The space between the daughters and their mother regarding electricity in love in the above passage finds its ancient antecedents, as here evidenced in 'Persephone the Wanderer':

> When death confronts her, she has never seen
> The meadow without the daisies.
> Suddenly she is no longer
> Singing her maidenly songs
> About her mother's beauty and fecundity. Where
> The rift is, the break is.

Persephone, in the field of flowers, gives herself over to her lover and loses her mother and her life. Glück fortifies this connection between love and disappearance, maturity and darkness, through her consistently redoubtable interpretations of Persephone's ventures between this world and another. We later learn, for instance, of Hades' plans for his captive, to whom he says, 'You're dead, nothing can hurt you / which seems to him / a more promising beginning, more true.' He makes a bed for her. Not even the possibility of sexual union can obviate the death that Persephone has experienced internally, a death paralleled in a different image from a separate poem. There we learn of a lover's early-dawn confusion upon seeing the person next to her in bed: 'We are, each of us, the one who wakens first, / who stirs first and sees, there in the first dawn, / the stranger.' As much as Persephone wakes in confusion at seeing her new lover Hades, so we, even in our loves.

In the poems where no clear myth appears, Glück's characters act out their parts in such a way as to echo the regnant myth of the collection. It is as if Glück sets up a series of archetypes that, like watchfires at a rural camp, illumine her darkness lest the old enemies make a nighttime attack. For Glück, the enemies do not vary: the illusion of love's freedom, the trick of the beautiful but heartless natural world, and the disappearance of youth, as when she writes, in a glance to Persephone, 'there are places like this everywhere, / places you enter as girl, / from which you never return.' Tellingly, when Glück does manage see light, it's during the night, as in the poem 'The Evening Star' where she dedicates to Venus, the morning star, her own

> ... vision, since on this blank surface
>
> you have cast enough light
> to make my thought
> visible again.

Again, the shrinking set of lines mimics a cone light descending down onto her page.

There remains an important question to ask when reading *Averno*. What separates its voice from that of a mere diary entry? Does the collection's apparent communicability and clarity depend actually upon the occasional mundaneness of its characters' thoughts? When the collection falters, it is perhaps for the simple reason that Glück veers too much into her own psyche without making the reader sure why her own experience is relevant. Even when she asks at the end of one of her Persephone poems, 'What will you do, / when it is your turn in the field with the god?' one has the feeling she is talking to herself. Are myths valuable only if they attach to personal experience, or should we find in them a way of understanding the experience of others?

Glück's answer would seem to be that the self buffets enough hardship to justify a personalized reading of mythology. And one might add that any understanding of others must come through and from the self. Her poetry testifies to the fact that one's own life has its own intransigent burdens against which we seek answers, though we do not often, these days at least, turn to Greco-Roman myth. The pagan persuasion makes Glück's voice a unique one among contemporary poets.

Pain ignites her search. Louise Glück poaches understanding in off-beat places, and while she might disclaim the viability of Dante's ascent out of hell – where is there really to go? – her lissome poems constantly traffic in both ugly grief and elegant reduction, torn emotional tissue and gentle verbal refinement. And, yes, there's wisdom here. Creation itself seems to be the way out of Hades, for beauty is the 'healer, the teacher' who leads Glück to the certainty that

> Death cannot harm me
> More than you have harmed me,
> My beloved life.

Rory Waterman is one of the chosen young poets in this issue.

Don Paterson: *Rain* (Faber: 2009) Hardback: £12.99.

Don Paterson's first two slim volumes, *Nil-Nil* in 1993 and *God's Gift to Women* four years later, introduced a considerable new talent in British poetry. At turns tender, funny, and startling, his was a poetry we could relate to and warm towards, whilst marvelling at his skills as a stylist.

Over the past decade Paterson has excelled at the latter, but lost something of the former, and *Rain* continues this trend. Put simply, it is always not clear what he is trying to say, if anything; his meanings can be as slippery as soap in the bath, as elusive as R.S. Thomas's God. That is why it is somewhat surprising that the inside cover of *Rain* describes it as Paterson's 'most intimate and candid collection to date'. Take the opening poem, 'Two Trees'. It tells the story, in quirky, jangling couplets, of one Don Miguel and the orange and lemon trees he planted together, and which grew so intertwined that 'each bough looked like it gave a double crop', to the delight of the local children. The next occupant of the house and garden, however, split them with an axe and planted them apart. Is this a poem about fortitude in absence? The trees did not 'weep every spring / for those four yards that lost them everything'. Perhaps. Or does the poem, the first in a volume dedicated to the memory of the late poet Michael Donaghy, highlight human grief by comparing it to something else, as 'They were trees, and trees don't weep or ache or shout. / And trees are all this poem is about'? Perhaps.

As I say, this is a *trend* in Paterson's work, not really a *failing*. 'Two Trees' is a masterpiece of the oblique: comic and chilling, beautiful and daringly McGonagallian in turns. More convincing still is 'The Swing', a beautiful, sad poem about a lost child, which ends with a chilling image of the speaker standing behind the seat of a swing he has just made from a flat-pack kit for his young sons, 'the here-and-here-to-stay':

> I gave the empty seat a push
> and nothing made a sound
> and swung between two skies to brush
> her feet upon the ground.

Elsewhere, 'Unfold', i.m. Akira Yoshizawa, the influential origami artist who died in 2005, plays with the frontier between the poet's craft and that of his subject. I would quote it here, but that would require too much space, or too little: it is a page, blank on both sides apart from title and dedication at the top of the first. One can admire the bravery of publishing such an easily-mocked poem ('would you care to read that one again, Mr. Paterson?'), which is in fact a fitting tribute, a visual one minute of silence in the medium of both artists, and which shows what stands to be created when an artist finally sets down his tools: nothing.

Paterson is a poet who knows how to win prizes, and 'Song for Natalie 'Tusja' Beridze', the winner of last year's Forward Prize for Best Single Poem, is clever, full of entertaining techno-speak, and overlong. It is his shorter tender lyrics that stand out, particularly 'Correctives', about the poet's son, and some of his versions of lyric poems by writers as diverse as Li Po, Cavafy and Salvatore Quasimodo. The long 'Phantom', split into seven sections, is worth the price on the dust jacket all by itself. This is a challenging, gale-force wind of a poem, battering the reader at once with the dexterity of a great poet at the top of his game, and startling, prosaic statements about what life *is:*

> We come from nothing and return to it.
> It lends us out to time, and when we lie
> in silent contemplation of the void
> they say we feel it contemplating us.
> This is wrong, but who could bear the truth.
> We are ourselves the void in contemplation.

The failing of this collection is not in the poetry, it is that too many of its poems fail to reach any discernible significance when they might have done. Consider the title poem, for instance. This also finishes the volume, and so takes on a double importance. It begins:

> I love all films that start with rain:
> rain, braiding a windowpane
> or darkening a hung-out dress
> or streaming down her upturned face;
>
> one big thundering downpour
> right through the empty script and score
> before the act, before the blame,
> before the lens pulls through the frame
>
> to where the woman sits alone
> beside a silent telephone
> or the dress lies ruined on the grass
> or the girl walks off the overpass ...

This is extremely *good* poetry, of course: reminiscent of Tony Harrison at his best, or even the finer work of American formalists such as Anthony Hecht or Richard Wilbur. But Harrison's poems are more than witty and metrically-accomplished. This poem whittles down from its initial promise to nothing, to the disappointing statement that ends the book: '*and none of this, none of this matters*'. But when Paterson writes poems that *do* matter, he is almost as good as any other poet of his generation.

Notes for Broadsheet Poets

Shanta Acharya

On the Nature of Poetry and the Creative Process

There are as many ways of describing poetry and the poetic process as there are poets. Among the definitions of poetry that come to mind are William Wordsworth's 'the spontaneous overflow of powerful feelings; it takes its origin from emotion recollected in tranquility.' For T.S. Eliot, 'poetry is not a turning loose of emotion, but an escape from emotion; it is not the expression of personality, but an escape from personality.' In the words of Emily Dickinson: 'To see the Summer Sky/ Is Poetry, though never in a Book it lie.' Wallace Stevens confirms 'poetry is the supreme fiction,' while Gustave Flaubert reckons 'poetry is as precise as geometry.' 'Imaginary gardens with real toads in them,' is Marianne Moore's verdict. For Percy Shelley, 'poetry is a mirror which makes beautiful that which is distorted.' Stéphane Mallarmé thinks, 'It is the job of poetry to clean up our word-clogged reality by creating silences around things.' For Frost, 'Poetry is what gets lost in translation.' God is the perfect poet in the view of Robert Browning, while for Philip Larkin, 'Poetry is nobody's business except the poet's, and everybody else can fuck off.'

All of the above reflections on poetry are valid; all represent 'a way of putting it – not very satisfactory:/.../ Leaving one still with the intolerable struggle/ With words and meaning.'[1] Besides, there are several forms of poetic expression, from epics – such as *Mahabharata* (Ganesha is attributed to have written the words uttered by Vyasa) or *Ramayana* (Valmiki), *Odyssey* and *Iliad, The Divine Comedy, Paradise Lost, The Prelude or the Cantos* – to haikus, a form of Japanese poetry composed of seventeen syllables. Matsuo Basho established the rules for writing haikus, though modern poets have interpreted it in their own way. As Roger McGough wrote: 'The only problem/ with Haiku is that you just/ get started and then.'

The difficulty of capturing the essence of poetry is its inherent characteristic; its unwillingness to be measured, defined, pigeon-holed. Poems are words that 'strain,/ Crack and sometimes break, under the burden' of definition, 'Under the tension, slip, slide, perish,/ Decay with imprecision, will not stay in place,/ Will not stay still.'[2] Poetic self-consciousness has been defined in various ways, sometimes via negatives, not unlike the Sanskrit definition of divinity, '*neti, neti*' (*not this, not this*). Keats provides an excellent definition when he refers to a poet's 'Negative Capability,' 'when a man is capable of

---

[1] T. S. Eliot, 'East Coker,' *Four Quartets*

[2] T. S. Eliot, 'Burnt Norton,' *Four Quartets*

being in uncertainties, mysteries, doubts, without any irritable reaching after fact and reason.'

For Housman: 'Even when poetry has a meaning, as it usually has, it may be inadvisable to draw it out... Perfect understanding will sometimes almost extinguish pleasure.' There are two essential aspects of poetry being referred to here – its ability to give pleasure and that such pleasure can be derived without fully understanding its meaning. Some emphasize the 'giving of pleasure' in poetry as being its primary objective. Understanding what a poem 'means or is', should be secondary preoccupation. As Eliot said with reference to Dante's poetry, 'Genuine poetry can communicate before it is understood.' In fact, perfect understanding may extinguish pleasure. 'Our meddling intellect/ Misshapes the beauteous forms of things –/ We murder to dissect' warns Wordsworth, who also wrote: 'The Poet writes under one restriction only, namely, that of the necessity of giving pleasure to a human Being possessed of that information which may be expected from him, not as a lawyer, a physician, a mariner, an astronomer or a natural philosopher, but as a Man.'

Dylan Thomas said something similar but added another attribute: 'You can tear a poem apart to see what makes it tick.... You're back with the mystery of having been moved by words. The best craftsmanship always leaves holes and gaps... so that something that is *not* in the poem can creep, crawl, flash or thunder in.' In addition to giving pleasure, for Dylan Thomas the mystery of a poem emerges from something that is not explicitly stated in the poem, as it were. The emphasis is not on understanding, but on instinct, mystery, or the chemistry of words. 'A poem should not mean, but be.'

Thus poetry, like love, gives most pleasure in the discovery, when you are first 'hooked', and then discover the levels of hidden treasures in the fullness of time. A poem 'begins in delight and ends in wisdom' Robert Frost said. The best poems are those you keep returning to, finding resonances you had missed, which yield themselves only after several visitations. It is the same with any great work of art; it never ceases to give you pleasure in its ability to open new ways of seeing things. A good reader is one who has the diligence to undertake such a treasure hunt, allowing the poem to reveal itself, without diminishing the pleasure taken in such pursuit. I am inclined to agree with Robert Penn Warren when he states, 'The poet is in the end probably more afraid of the dogmatist who wants to extract the message from the poem and throw the poem away than he is of the sentimentalist who says, "Oh, just let me enjoy the poem."'

Whether one is reading Eliot's *Four Quartets,* Vikram Seth's *The Golden Gate:* A *Novel in Verse* or his *Beastly Tales*, ghazals by Rumi or Mimi Khalvati, Shakespeare's sonnets, or poetry of E.E. Cummings, epics, lyrics, or haikus, the pleasure one derives from the words, from the arrangement of words, being moved by the words, is the lasting legacy of poetry. This is not to suggest that the content is irrelevant or unimportant. No, I would not endorse such a stance for even when reading nonsense poetry, you can glean the poets' intent. Like most things in life, the golden rule is the happy marriage between style and subject matter.

'Poetry ... should strike the reader as a wording of his own highest thoughts, and appear almost a remembrance,' said Keats. When I first read Louise Glück's *The Wild Iris* some of the poems in it struck such a chord – as if I was reading my own thoughts expressed in a language which explored my own amazement. As Emily Dickinson offers us contradictory, evolving perspectives on the nature of God, Glück's poems in this collection spoke in many voices about the nature of God. Whatever godliness may be, Glück 'honours the silence at the core of things, even as her poems push brilliantly against the limits of the knowable,' notes Mark Doty, a poet of considerable mastery himself. Poetry is the revelation of a feeling that the poet believes to be interior and personal which the reader recognizes as his or her own.

Tolstoy wrote, 'Art is not a handicraft, it is the transmission of feeling the artist has experienced.' The greatest of poems are the best examples of the delicate balance between the expression of our highest thoughts and the manner of their expression. 'The distinction between historian and poet,' wrote Aristotle, 'is not in the one writing prose and the other verse... the one describes the thing that has been, and the other a kind of thing that might be. Hence poetry is something more philosophic and of graver import than history, since its statements are of the nature rather of universals, whereas those of history are singulars.'[3] It is that 'god's eye view of things' when poetry rises from the personal to the universal.

Poetry is not only universal, it is eternal. Great poetry has that quality. In *The Path of Poetry*, Grevel Lindop refers to such a quality. Speaking of 'poetry and philosophy' he quotes the twelfth-century Japanese poet Saigyo, who was a Buddhist monk: 'Although all things in this world undergo change, the Way of Poetry extends unaltered even to the last age.' Saigyo knew well the Buddha's teaching that all things in this world undergo change. Yet, he tells us, the way of poetry does *not*. 'Two things follow from this,' says Lindop. 'First, that poetry as understood by Saigyo is not merely a part of the impermanent phenomenal world, that which is unstable and falls away. Rather, the poetic way is in some sense a manifestation of the spiritual path which leads beyond phenomena, to the Deathless. It persists unchanged, whether anyone follows it or not – like the Four Noble Truths of the Buddha's teaching, which remain true whether Buddhas arise in the world or whether they do not.'

In an era when the influential critics deny the possibility of a timeless element in poetry – the current dogma being that its origins, its reference, its materials and its interpretation are time-bound and historically determined –

---

[3] Aristotle, *On Poetics*

the notion that there might be 'a timeless poetic path' would be greeted with amused contempt as a piece of philosophical naivety, a bourgeois mystification, a fragment of that Romantic ideology we are all supposed to have grown out of. The timelessness of the poetic path that Lindop describes would have been perfectly clear to Plato, Chaucer, Shakespeare, Donne, Wordsworth, Hopkins, Blake, Keats, Yeats or Tagore, among others.

As far as critical exposition is concerned, the poet may be seen as having an advantage, but only partially. A discussion of poetry, as Eliot said, 'takes us far outside the limits within which a poet may speak with authority.' The other reason, as Eliot adds, and with which I am inclined to agree, is 'that the poet does many things upon instinct, for which he can give no better account than anybody else. A poet can try, of course, to give an honest report of the way in which he himself writes: the result may, if he is a good observer, be illuminating. And, in one sense, but a very limited one, he knows better what his poems "mean" than can anyone else; he may know the history of their composition, the material which has gone in and come out in an unrecognisable form, and he knows what he was trying to do and what he was meaning to mean. But what a poem means is as much what it means to others as what it means to the author; and indeed, in the course of time a poet may become merely a reader in respect to his own works, forgetting his original meaning – or without forgetting, merely changing.'[4]

Critical writing seeking to explore what poetry is, what its use is, what a good poem is, or exploring the creative writing process itself, fulfils the need of every generation to address such issues afresh. But these may not be the sort of issues that necessarily concern poets, nor are all poets willing to engage in such analysis. When asked what a 'good' poem is, Seamus Heaney is said to have replied in the words of Louis Armstrong who once told a reporter when asked what jazz is: 'Lady, if you have to ask, you'll never know.' There exists a commonality of experience which suggests that the peoples of the world seem to share an astonishingly detailed universal psychology. Hence no need to explain a 'good' poem!

This is not to advocate a return to a deliberate mystification of the poetic process or of the nature of poetry; no, only a restoration to its domain that was rightfully its own always – its inextricable link with the development of human consciousness and imagination. The demystification of the nature of poetry and the poetic process began centuries ago. Poets today are no longer 'the unacknowledged legislators of the world'; they are not philosophers dealing with eternal truths – like Virgil, Dante, Shakespeare, Blake, Keats, Shelley or Hopkins. Critics, editors, publishers, professors of poetry, readers of poetry – all of us are culpable in this development. To quote Eliot again, 'people are always ready to grasp at any guide which will help them to recognize the best

[4] T. S. Eliot, *The Use of Poetry and The Use of Criticism*

poetry without having to depend upon their own sensibility and taste.' We have so little confidence in our own selves or so little ability to explore our selves that we find it easier to be some body else and have our sensibilities and tastes guided by others.

As none of us are free of biases when describing the nature of poetry, what we ascribe to poetry speaks more of us than of Poetry itself. Every poet knows 'to be a poet is a condition, not a profession' (Robert Frost), though the rise of poetry as a profession is widely evident today. It may be worth reminding ourselves at this point that poetry is not the handmaiden of a select few. It may also be worth remembering how various are the kinds of poetry being written today, and how wide its appeal is to different generations equally qualified to appreciate it.

I recall one editor's comment in his rejection slip to me: 'But do you write like Geoffrey Hill?' I had recently arrived in Oxford; it was 1980. I never quite understood then or now why I should write like any one; no disrespect meant to GH, of course. If the editor had written: 'Have you read Geoffrey Hill? I really like his work,' it would have made a lot of sense to me and explained to me his bias as an editor.

But what about plurality, difference? Surviving as an 'Indian' poet in the UK has not been easy. Editors find it difficult to deal with your work unless they put you in a pigeon-hole; any pigeon-hole will do for them. And, once they have found their own 'ethnic' poets, they feel they have covered the ground. Nor does the Arts Council ensure that public funding is distributed more equitably. After all, the Arts Council exists to support all poets, not just a few poets. A high degree of open-mindedness is important not only for the survival of poetry, but also for the better appreciation of our universe. It is essential not only for the great mystic poets of the past or for that matter poets today, but especially for those poets we do not know how to appreciate and whose poetic standards we do not share.

What else is Wordsworth referring to when, in 'Tintern Abbey,' he speaks of the recollected landscape as conferring 'Another gift/.../ In which the burthen of the mystery,/ In which the heavy and the weary weight/ Of all this unintelligible world, Is lightened.' The purpose of these lines, when 'we see into the life of things,' is surely not only to commemorate such moments, nor even to remind us of their possibility, but to offer us the chance to participate in them. The experience that Wordsworth describes is an example of the 'moments' Blake refers to in a famous passage of *Milton*: 'There is a Moment in each Day that Satan cannot find.' Reading a poem, like listening to music, or appreciating a landscape or painting, is like connecting to something that is universal and timeless. It is not surprising that originally these activities were associated with religion. Having fought so hard to get rid of the shackles of religion and politics, it is ironical if we submit to the hegemony of editors, publishers and arts administrators.

It is undeniably true that each generation needs to define that consciousness individually; poets see things afresh, establishing a new relationship with the universe. Poets can be regarded as soldiers who liberate words from the steadfast possession of definition. Every generation of poets feels the need to break free of the prevalent dogmas of the day and define a new imperative. But, the denial of the possibility of a timeless element in poetry is denying its essence, its power to influence generations unborn. Each generation will need to produce its own poetic language, but to deny the role of poetry in shaping our imagination, the way we think and interpret the past, is limiting our understanding of the present.

It is this timeless aspect of poetry that makes it both elusive (for those who do not have the means to accommodate uncertainties and contradictions) or appears to be didactic (for those who try to describe too much or have a mission). Yes, every true poet is born with a vision of the universe, 'an original relation to the universe,' as Ralph Waldo Emerson put it. The challenge lies in how it is achieved. This poetic transcendence from the individual to the universal 'proceeds not from a selfish but a generous instinct,' Don Paterson reminds us. He goes on to add 'whatever inner tensions have been assuaged in our writing, we want to give these things away in the end. To have someone else want your poem for themselves, it must be desirable.'[5] To have someone discover themselves in your poem is the ultimate act of creation; it is indeed godlike.

So what does poetry mean? Like love, friendship and compassion, poetry is the highest altruistic response to the world. Through poetry we aspire to live more fully in our imagination; and in doing so we share a sense of belonging to the universe, not alienation. Robert Penn Warren put it thus: 'The poem ... is a little myth of man's capacity of making life meaningful. And in the end, the poem is not a thing we see – it is, rather, a light by which we may see – and what we see is life.' And our ability to see Life enhances our understanding of who we are. Poetry is the means by which I explore fundamental questions like: *Who am I*?

'I don't create poetry, I create myself, for me my poems are a way to me,' writes the Finland-Swedish poet Edith Södergran. It is this act of self-exploration that has been shared by poets through the ages. Art seems to be the only place we can liberate our many selves. Poetry is not only the way home to our many selves, it is also a way of healing. In the process of this self-definition, we also define tradition. If the ordinary man is a man shut in a world, the poet is a world shut in a man – then the world within the poet has to come out so that the poet's inner world can communicate with the world of other men.

The development of poetry through the ages is a symptom of change in society; defining the creative process is as individual as poets. The challenges for poets writing in the beginning of the twenty-first century are complex,

---

[5] Don Paterson 'The Lyric Principle' (*Poetry Review*, Autumn 2007)

reflecting the complex nature of our society. While Mrs Margaret Thatcher may have gone so far as to assert that 'there is no such thing as society', without society – i.e. human communication, understanding, reaching out to the Other – there can be no poetry; or for that matter business, commerce, industry and forms of human activity that Mrs Thatcher endorsed.

Having worked in the field of business/ finance, I would like to argue that business and science like artistic creativity spring from the same human impulses. Money is not the chief motivation; what drives artists, scientists and wealth creators is the generative instinct, the compulsion to create something – be it a poem, a novel, a cathedral, a symphony, a cure for cancer, a faster computer – which did not exist before, and to have your creative claim acknowledged by the world. Poetry may be mysterious, but a poet when all is said and done is not much more mysterious than an investment banker, an astrophysicist, a molecular biologist, a geneticist or a brilliant software programmer.

As our means of communication has grown exponentially, so has the way in which we live and relate to each other. Thus, questions like – what is poetry for, what do I have to say, how and to whom am I addressing it – have become potentially more complex. Is it better for the poet to define his/her niche market and write for that particular market, or is it better to discover one's voice and remain indifferent to passing fashions of the day? The answer obviously depends on the person asking the question. If poetry is a form of communication, a means of entertaining, giving pleasure, then the availability of mass media makes it easier for poetry to be enjoyed by as large and various numbers of people as possible worldwide.

A search for the word 'Poetry' brings up over 170 million references on Google, and www.alltheweb.com with 350 million references! A search for 'Art' and 'Music' generates 2,525 million and 4,780 million references respectively in www.alltheweb.com. These numbers keep changing, but trends remain the same. Poetry is being more widely disseminated today – and is more in the public domain be it radio, newspapers, TV, films, Poems on the Underground (in London); we even had poems on the buses and airports, yet the appeal of poetry to a mass audience remains limited in the UK. When will a poet fill the Wembley Stadium for a reading, though readings by poets have packed the Royal Albert Hall (Michael Horovitz and his Poetry Olympics).

The internet has made access easier and in the world of music more sales are being made via this medium. In poetry, it can be difficult to establish intellectual property rights. In his book, *The Prodigal Tongue: Dispatches from the Future of English*, Mark Abley quotes two of my poems 'Dear Tech Support', and 'Dear Customer' (both poems appear in *Looking In, Looking Out*, Headland Publications, UK: 2005) as part of a chapter on language and computers. Abley asked for my permission. Although a search in Google for 'Dear Tech Support' generates 590,000 results, most sites show variations of my poem without any reference to me, the poet! In cyberspace, there are black holes where poets disappear. The power of global media, the sway of big business, politics, marketing, branding and PR dominates our celebrity culture. Marketing strategies find it difficult to promote more than a few names at a time.

Despite the explosion in the dissemination of poetry, it is difficult to know if the pleasure taken in the reading of poetry has risen commensurately! As Walt Whitman said, 'To have great poets there must be great audiences too.' While the numbers have indeed gone up, after all there are more of us today inhabiting the earth than ever before in the history of our planet, whether there are more 'great audiences' remains unclear. The appreciation or the global dissemination of poetry has little to do with the writing of it.

Steven Pinker writes that 'the faculty with which we ponder the world has no ability to peer inside itself or our other faculties to see what makes them tick.'[6] Yet a significant number of people possess an innate ability to appreciate, what for lack of a better term I refer to as, *good* poetry. The use of 'good' immediately begs the question 'good' for whom; who decides what is 'good'? 'Good' has been decided by the Establishment for centuries now; not just in poetry but in every discipline. 'If Galileo had said in verse that the world moved, the inquisition might have let him alone,' said Thomas Hardy. Perhaps because nobody reads poetry, that poetry does not matter and is not taken seriously?

Returning to the premise that many of us can agree, without coercion, on what is good in poetry and art; that for example Shakespeare is a great master of language, Mozart a great composer, and Michelangelo a great painter – the fact that we understand someone's 'creation' though we never met that person, never lived in those times, never experienced their culture or background, suggests that some poetry like some music, art and other forms of creativity has some thing to do with connecting with the universal, a kind of 'yoga' with the universal consciousness. It is not surprising that originally these activities were associated with religion.

To refer again to Emerson's phrase, 'an original relation to the universe,' the individual is finally free to work things out for himself, albeit with help from others, if required. The act of poetic creation involves the imagination and the evolution of a consciousness that transcends the personal. Poetry may not always be able to save us; but like all great art, or science for that matter, it has the power to move us, even change the way we see things for ever. To that extent poetry like scientific discoveries is a kind of consciousness-raising, and all forms of such activity are transformational.

Quantum physics teaches us that energy can be broken down into – nothing. A cubic centimetre of empty space, the pure void of cold blackness, contains more virtual energy than a blazing star. If we can grasp this fact, make an

---

[6] Steven Pinker, *How the Mind Works*

imaginative leap from something to nothing, from solid to intangible, from energy to potential, from action to possibility, we have grasped the concept of the soul. And, if there is poetry that is eternal and timeless, like the cosmos which is a vast, churning machine for turning one level of reality into another, then so are poets. The most creative act anyone can perform is the act of creating reality. A poem is as real as a shaft of lightning or energy trapped in a fossil.

As no one poet and of no one age can be expected to embrace the whole nature of poetry, no two readers will approach poetry with the same expectations. What we see in a poem varies from reader to reader; but there exists a commonality of experience that the peoples of the world share. Hence no need to explain a 'good' poem or a piece of jazz music. 'A poem is true if it hangs together. Information points to something else. A poem points to nothing but itself,' said E.M. Forster.[7]

Among the reasons that attracted me to the writing of poetry are its indirectness, its suggestiveness, its ability to be interpreted severally. It is like a secret code that only the initiate understands. Poetry involves a high degree of precision in the use of language that surpasses other forms of writing. A poem may use intricate rhymes, may scan perfectly, it may be written in free verse or it may be nonsense verse – what ultimately makes a good poem is its ability to communicate. Every great poem like a great actor on stage makes that connection; great poetry has that spark.

Emily Dickinson says it in her own inimitable manner: 'Tell all the Truth but tell it slant –/ Success in Circuit lies/ Too bright for our infirm Delight/ The Truth's superb surprise.' Thus, unlike Logic (Lewis Carroll's 'What the Tortoise Said to Achilles,') poetry must not take you by the throat, and force you. Yet, we love poems that move us, touch us and sometimes force us to see things differently while not bludgeoning us into submission. Tipping the balance in favour of poetry is its 'unobtrusive' quality, even when stating something profound. As Keats said: 'We hate poetry that has a palpable design upon us ... Poetry should be great and unobtrusive, a thing which enters into one's soul, and does not startle or amaze it with itself, but with its subject.' The poems that appeal most are the ones with this quality of transcendence, shock of recognition, the 'aha' factor, the power to transform, a kind of a revelation, often of quite elemental aspects of life such as truth and beauty.

Poetry is an intense exploration of the human condition through language by which we seek to uncover new ways of seeing and interpreting the world. What we see and marvel at may vary infinitely. For Confucius, 'a common man marvels at uncommon things; a wise man marvels at the commonplace.' Great poetry too marvels at the commonplace, but uses words uniquely. Poetry, like other creative art forms, is a 'construct', however natural it may

---

[7] E.M. Forster, *Two Cheers for Democracy*

come like leaves to a tree. Organization is as necessary as inspiration in fashioning any thing great; a poem is no exception. Poetry is not an outburst of words, an involuntary process like a natural secretion. Such an efflux of poetry, like automatic writing, may happen from time to time; but even then it can be argued that the poem had been incubating in the writer for some time. It is difficult to imagine Shakespeare or Donne being dependent upon such capricious releases.

This is very different from what we refer to as inspiration, vision or mystical illumination of the kind that Blake experienced. For some, poems are mini epiphanies. And in any epiphany, the whole person is engaged; it is no longer just a mental activity, it becomes physical. It is also possible that the poet in such a state recognizes his or her inability to communicate it to anyone else. As the moment passes, it is impossible to recapture it. Several poets have referred to this passing, ephemeral quality of the poetic Muse; one has a flash of inspiration and decides to write in a state of excitement; but any number of things can happen to neutralize the intensity of that experience. That is why some people write regularly, in a disciplined manner, with or without the blessing of the Muse. But sparks fly when the anvil is hot.

There are times when a poem is born perfect, demanding little revision. Most of the time, poems need a lot of work. The original impulse for a poem may be a passing thought, a sentence overheard, an image, a conversation, a news items – virtually anything can trigger a poem. Developing that original inspiration, making it as perfect as possible, may take years. 'A poem is never finished, only abandoned,' says Paul Valéry. The vast majority of poems improve under the craftsmanship of a skilled and experienced editor. Poetry may be an emotion which has found its thought and the thought has found words; but it is the drawing down of the right words that characterize good poetry. Poets aspire for that quality of freshness in their writing, the best poetry is language subjected to the rigors of emotional intensity, formal composition and the richness of the human experience – the best words in the best order, in Coleridge's famously sharp definition.

According to Yeats, 'the true poet is all the time a visionary and whether with friends or not, as much alone as a man on his death bed.' This idea of the poetic act as being essentially solitary meets its corollary in its need to 'connect' with another. What Yeats is referring to is the intensity and the focused character of the poetic act. Alice Oswald's advice to aspiring poets is: 'You should never write a poem till you can feel it in your bones: because poetry is your whole body's response to the whole world, not just your head's response to a thought or a glimpse.' This is her way of describing that intense moment of creation, or epiphany. For Frost, 'a poem begins with a lump in the throat.'

You know when you start a project, you have a rush of energy, a downpour of ideas and you write your lines without thinking. John Ashbery said it is 'rather like riding downhill on a bicycle and having the pedals push your feet.' This automatic process, of being driven effortlessly to writing, is a deep internalization of the poetic experience, which is essential. Having had that rush of words, one typically spends months, if not years, polishing the poem (Horace would famously sit on a poem for seven years). Every now and then a poem arrives more or less complete. That is rare simply because poetry is language raised to the Nth power.

'In writing a poem,' says Peter Abbs, 'an emerging reality is begging to be let in. Offer me a home, it whispers, or else the world will be deprived and your own life will be eternally forlorn.' It is interesting to note that Charles Simic echoes such a sentiment: 'A poem is a place where one invites someone in. You build a little house, fix it all up real nice. Inside, you've got some interesting things you want to show them.' It is this sharing, this communication between people, that enriches the poetic experience. The reader is a participant in the very process of the poem, active rather than passive. You may be the best reader of your own work, but without someone else sharing that experience, the poem is incomplete, and without a buyer it is not published.

The quality of a poem may not be diminished if it remains unpublished, unread, unseen; after all, Emily Dickinson was virtually unpublished in her lifetime. The role of editors, publishers, critics and professors is critical in supporting the 'new voices' of their time. It is worth remembering with Wordsworth that 'every great and original writer ... must himself create the taste by which he is to be relished.' In our hugely competitive world, writing to please powerful editors may seem like a rational strategy except there is no guarantee such a strategy will succeed. As the powers that be do not have any superior resources for 'picking' winners, there is an element of randomness in such selection. And without the power of marketing, 'publishing a volume of verse is like dropping a rose-petal down the Grand Canyon and waiting for the echo' (Don Marquis).

Seamus Heaney

The Butts

His suits hung in the wardrobe, broad
And short
And slightly bandy-sleeved,

Flattened back
Against themselves,
A bit stand-offish.

Stale smoke and oxter-sweat
Came at you in a stirred-up brew
When you reached in,

A whole rake of thornproof and blue serge
Swung heavily
Like waterweed disturbed. I sniffed

Tonic unfreshness,
Then delved past flap and lining
For the forbidden handfuls.

But a kind of empty-handedness
Transpired...Out of suit-cloth
Pressed against my face,

Out of those layered stuffs
That surged and gave,
Out of the cold smooth pocket lining

Nothing but chaff cocoons,
A paperiness not known again
Until the last days came

And we must learn to reach well in beneath
Each meagre armpit
To lift and sponge him,

One on either side,
Feeling his lightness,
Having to dab and work

Closer than anybody liked
But having, for all that,
To keep working.

Derek Walcott

The Green Flash

le rayon vert

And the sea's skin heaves, saurian,
and the spikes of the agave bristle
like a tusked beast shifting to charge
tonight the full moon will soar floating
without any moral or simile
the wind will bend the longbows of the aching casuarinas
and the lizard will still scuttle
and the sun will sink silently with a stake in its one eye
bleeding behind the shrouding sail
of a skeletal schooner.
You can feel the earth cooling,
you can feel its myth cooling
and watch your own heart go out like the red throbbing dot
of a hospital machine, with a green flash
next to Pigeon Island.

John Kinsella

'Even Music May Be Intoxicating'

A melody in my head as I type
transcribes music made later to fit
indulgence of growth come late in winter,
seasonal redefinition that fits six seasons
or more if we'd listen when welcomed: rock-
faces are slippery and we go two steps back
for each step up-slope seeming greater
than a month passed, erosive sharpness,
ledges of valley. Bark hangs in distraught
strips from York gums just beyond
the house and high winds have raked
hillside reiterating value of peaks,
devastating exposure to elements
as you peer deep into the hill's core.
Ant colonies have risen and risen
amidst green their vacant spaces
clustered anomalies paradox
beyond desert thriving and energetic
in such ways that all in their path fall
and we seem richer, we onlookers,
for it, for the rustling of their feet,
springy lyrics of weeds, trills,
mordants of rocky ground.

Higher Laws

It’s a month since we’ve been here
and dandelions have confirmed a rampant
occupation: in lieu of us, as vanguard,
eyes to the eyes of our boots. A grey
shrike thrush, a red kangaroo which we
haven’t seen prior: *good*, red and grey
species mixing in *style indirect libre*,
not mating but in the vicinity, this vicinity,
of ‘distress’, of sand flowing down
from the old arena, washed off
notational rewrite of boundaries,
or an old boundary we might tap into,
dark sky opening permission to latch onto,
our gross senses making appetite of vista,
close-up realisation that every tree
planted has been eaten down to roots,
and further, further down. So, celebrate
this feeding of hillside we are part of,
focalised characters that we are,
acting outside the kangaroos’ court.

Peter Dale

Insomniac Lullaby

I would compose myself to sleep.
    No lie of the hands leads to rest.
The lengthened shadows blend and creep;
    dark floats the light up in the west.

I would compose myself to sleep.
    My hands cannot lay hold of rest.
Sweet dream, the impenetrable keep
    that circling thoughts night-long invest.

The world has lost its perfect dark.
    I would compose myself to sleep.
Oh, hands, lie still like fallen bark.
    If the dreams came they would weep.

Epitaph: The War Graves

These stones no one shall roll away.
Nothing will bring an Easter day.
These men, forever sacrificed,
gave more than any risen Christ.

Seconding Henry Allingham and all the Fallen

Remembrance Day, the Cenotaph,
the wreaths, the regimented ranks,
it's show-business on death's behalf.
The dead would not, if they could, say thanks.

Greg Delanty

Selections from *The Greek Anthology Book XVII*

Gaia's Inn

The owner informs us the inn's closed, summer's over,
    but we're welcome to a few beers, to sit on the deck.
We're sensible enough not to take any notice
    of the begging dog with a stick in his mouth.
We ignore life – work, phone calls, mail –
    that annoying tail-wagging mutt. Buoys tilt like planets,
each with its own biosphere of creatures and plants.
    Foam at the water's edge. Gaia has washed her hands
of the motor boat, the jet stream harming her,
    the radio reporting the all-too-human news

Dogus

The Soapbox

You accuse me of standing on the soapbox of the daily news
    ranting against destructive gods, the gutting of Gaia, say I abuse
the nine daughters of Mnemosyne, the fragile muses. I bear witness
    naturally to what is wrong, what is simply the distress
of the everyday, mundane battles, whatever troubles us,
    be it Ares or the likes of Drudgerius, Domesticus, Mortus.

Grigorographos

Worth Remembering

The only army of the ruined Acropolis of Sparta now
    is the army of ants filing back and forth over the stoa, the barracks,
the soldier's messhall, the sanctuary of Artemis Orthia
    where whipping contests to toughen young boys were held.
Time isn't so bad after all. Sure, all good things
    come to an end. All dreadful things come to an end as well.

The Watchman of Sparta

Patient

The snow has melted completely off the mountain.
    It's winter still. Yet another indication that Gaia
is in trouble, that things aren't sound.
    The rocky mountain top shines
like the bald head of a woman after chemo
    who wills herself out of her hospital bed
to take in the trees, the squirrels, the commotion
    in the town below, to sip a beer in a dive,
ignore the child staring at her bald head,
    wishing it didn't take all this dying to love life.

Honestmedon

Nicholas Jagger

from *Zarathustra*

x

Das Grablied The Funeral Song

You may say that we saw off youth and beauty,
waving our handkerchiefs at the ship already set
for Mausoleum Island:
your frantic swim to death,
such silence, as night choked off all sound.
So what is life if not an inventory of loss?

* * *

From every grave you dig I rise again,
tired of the rotting corpse.
I trade only in the currency of the present:
where stands your resurrected god?

* * *

To stay focused on the past takes effort,
but when does the work reduce?

Absolute monarchs are targeted.
The opposition take their papers,
deny them access to Mausoleum Island,
and so the herd are cursed.

Whatever may please them they withdraw,
poisoning friendships,
erasing night so that they cannot sleep,
interfering with memory.

* * *

The night I had planned to dance
they stopped the music;
such new philosophy, but what of that?

* * *

From every grave you dig I rise again;
what is memory if not the pyrites of the weak?

* * *

Show me the footage!

Tear-loosening loves
Rose-apple splendour
Eye-glance moments
Wild-waxing virtues

Such images have the clarity of clouded honey,
the promising poison proffered
by nostalgia made rich on easy money.
Can we say no blindly to what we are offered?

* * *

Mausoleum Island, once
such a spectacle of monuments
set in a landscape of perfection,
every hill topped by towers,
no tear of a lake without its temple.

* * *

From every grave you dig I rise again,
tired of its narrow walls.

Hope is a species of metamorphosis,
life itself an acolyte of Will.

xvii

Von der Menschen-Klugheit **Of Manly Prudence**

Not the height but the drop
        is more certain;
from where the gaze falls
and the hand flies upwards.

Oh my heart's two-dimensional Will...

The drop and my direction;
that my gaze dives into the heights
and my hand still grips the depths.

Bound by ball and chain to man,
the seed, the origin of better man.

To live amongst the leaden and know
the value of what is solid.

I sit at the doorway and ask of each,
'who will confuse me?'

This is my first man-ability,
that I make myself confused,
accepting it as local coin.

How could mankind's anchor be my ball and chain?
Such fortunes of zero would see me airborne,
but that is to be with man, unfussily drinking
from any glass, washing in any grey water.

But they can stage a good scene,
and every vain actor wishes for approval,
strutting and stealing attention,
because at heart such vanity masks inconfidence,
and this is their virtue: to need such praise.

* * *

In all the forests of the mind
good and evil are held within parentheses;
the anthropometric scale is limited.

You may push your toys around the nursery floor
but the rubber snake is toothless,
and the royal hunt for knowledge travels further.

> *Beyond Gauguin's south-sea islands,*
> *beyond the Polynesian milepost of half-achieved*
> *perfection, to a much more southern south. . .*

Awaiting man's arrival and the shout of 'Devil!'
The better man exists beyond all calibration,
naked, and brighter than the magnified sun.

Already in this godly place, the clinging stench
        of the disembarking human.

The High Commissioner combs his ostrich feathers,
makes up a landing party with the vicar and judge,
and together detonate the bomb of human dignity.

* * *

Sitting here beside you, I make work of being confused
in order to fool us both: let us hope that confusion may
mutate, and memory fail to shoulder this existence.

xix

Der Wanderer The Wanderer

Eclogue

Z: *Oh my heart at midnight...*

From the place considered home, watch the ferry
press against the water to take you on your journey.

Z: *Savour the quiet here... reed buntings flit undisturbed
through a hillside garden, calling amongst the rhododendrons.*

So many ridges risked already, so many of our friendships
sacrificed for fresher landscapes, harder climbs.

Z: *A self-effacing wanderer and mountaineer,
I travel alone under the banner of impossibility.*

To cross the fells of your own thoughts, and beyond them,
striding higher than buntings perched in rhododendrons.

Z: *To leave the country place and risk the loss of dialect:
to abandon the piano in the parlour where it stood.*

Rely on the music within, but do not be bitter;
take the ferry to another place, perhaps to *Blissful Island.*

Z: *What I take in myself is mine completely
trusting that there is always something at the bottom of the drawer.*

To look from the moor in darkness and sense the sleeping sea;
to feel its trouble, and wish it absolved of burden...

Z: *The rising tide of memory, the falling tide of expectation:
my excessive love may yet be adamantine.*

Sudeep Sen

Dreaming Of Cézanne

Art is a harmony parallel to nature. Paul Cézanne

i

Jacket on a Chair

You carelessly tossed
the jacket on a chair.
The assembly of cloth

collapsed in slow motion
into a heap of cotton –
cotton freshly picked

from the fields –
like flesh
without a spine.

The chair's wooden
frame provided
a brief skeleton,

but it wasn't enough
to renew the coat's
shape, the body's

prior strength,
or the muscle
to hold its own.

When one peels off
one's outer skin,
it is difficult to hide

blood's liquid weave.
Wood, wool, stitches,
and joints – an epitaph

of a card player's shuffle,
and the history
of my dark faith.

[based on Cézanne's *Jacket on a Chair*,
graphite and watercolour on paper, 47.5 X 30.5 cm, 1890-92]

ii

The Skulls

The three gods
I worship

are dead.
They stare

from the backs
of their heads,

through
the hollows

of their eyes –
their vision

leaking from
every fissure

and crack
on the cranium.

The bone-skin
of these skulls

shines like
the silver sheen

of a new-born
fish,

each plate
like scales

restoring memory,
genealogy –

secrets
only fossils

keep alive.
  Skulls on wood,

on carpet,
  on drapery –

studies encrypted
  like an unwrapped

pyramid of bones,
  mummies waiting

to be embalmed
  in oil and graphite –

as I sprinkle
  water and colour

on the shrine
  of my night gods.

[based on Cézanne's series *The Skulls*,
oil on canvas / graphite and watercolour on paper, 1890-1906]

iii

The Card Players

The deal was done and stamped
 on brown rough leather

of the parchment tabletop.
 Crooked spindly legs

that propped up play
 hardly held its own weight,

let alone the gravity
 of smoke, spirit, connivance.

We held our fists
 close to each other

clenching secrets,
 as if in mistrust –

stiff cards in hand
 like little rectangular blades

to cut
 and bleed our lives away.

Future like the present
 was dark and unlit,

swirling unsteadily
 in tobacco stench

permanently embedded
 in the wood of the walls,

furniture, clothes,
 and our hearts.

But at least
 this was a gamble,

a zone of unsure light,
 an unpredictability

to hold onto amid all
 the grey, brown and blue –

cold,
 deep blue, and more blue.

[based on Cézanne's *The Card Players*,
oil on canvas, 47.5 X 57 cm, 1893-96]

Sue Roe

Caillebotte's Geometry

the scent of sawdust,
wax, French polish, on the river
the warm-metal creak and heaviness
treading the boards
feeling the wood beneath his feet
and the heavy canvas
whipping the sharp wind, tugging at
the shirt on his back, racing

in the summer regatta at Argenteuil
freed from shaded interiors
the shine and suppleness
of the piano his only release – that,
the fragrance of Chopin's Nocturnes
and the opportunity, in the early hours
to push back the shutters on lilac hued rooftops
wooded with snow

observing the floor scrapers
in the rue de Miromesnil
at work against the pull of the grain
shaving up wood in curling rings
he remarked, by the ring that gleamed in the light
the married man on his knees
the stretch of his forearm muscles
the power of the plane, like a painter's brush

to caress, manipulate, massage
the pliant, most sensuous material
we walk, dance, make music on
carve, polish and all but transform
sitting at his window in Paris
musing on his secret, Charlotte
waiting for him in the garden at Yerres,
pruning her roses in the open air
tending her new-planted trees

The Dance Class

they remind him of the cotton makers
the little rats of Montmartre
scrubbed up in a froth of net and muslin
tied in silk bows, like the little rich girls'
in the Jardins du Luxembourg
trailing across the park with their nurses

they round their arms like arcs of light
pirouetting across the floorboards
calf muscles stretched like the strings
of instruments, tensed for tuning
knees bent, backs bowed at the barre
like waiting suppliants

they wait on low benches, ballet shoes
abandoned like shreds of a chemise
silk against leather, light on a piano
feet turned out like pedals, alert
to the beat and their rapped-out instructions
pliant as fresh-loaded horse hair

After Dégas : *The Dance Class,* 1873

Dancing at the Moulin de la Galette

sparkling jewellery, vivid silk dresses
hand-me-downs from the elegant clients
in the boulevard Haussmann or the rue Rivoli
the women these girls all aspire to be
here in Montmartre, in the Moulin's back shed
in the tiny, makeshift *bal-musette*
the mothers of girls keep a sharp eye out
for a passing, philandering *boulevardier*

artists, musicians, Sunday painters
in panama hats and tight *pantaloons*
happen along to taste the *galettes*
to the left of the scene, the mood is set
by gaslight or sunlight, by lovely Lisette,
Jeanne, Estelle, delicious Angele
dance with Lestringuez, Renoir, Riviere,
the Spaniard from Cuba or the rue d'Aboukir

the dancing continues into the small hours
a few streets away in the rue des Saules
the faint-hearted are still drinking white *piccolo*
until they have talked themselves out for the night
and up at the Moulin the mothers go home
to the lean-tos and shacks in the windmill's shade
and the girls dance on, in this quiet season
expecting the lads from the *Lapin Agile*
a gentleman, cad or *beau cavalier*

After Renoir : *The Moulin de la Galette*, 1876

India Russell

Final Notes to a Dancer

This, then, is the space in which to choreograph your life.
Note the over arching trees, gnarled trunks
Perfect proscenium for the action you'll invent.
Admire the pale-washed cyclorama with slowly moving
rose-pink clouds
Forming the familiar everchanging backdrop. Although,
we have to warn you,
Occasionally, strange, ancient machinery, forgotten in the flies,
Grinds, ghostlike, into action, releasing filthy plumes of dust
Turning the clouds to ominous precursors of Jove's ire.

Beware of this. Beware, also, dim
Shifting areas, upstage left and right –
Sulking, sucking bogs refusing to be fenced.
Even the Danger signs have been
Drawn down into their deathly depths.

Tread carefully. Particularly when you meet
Those crushing humans, eyes lustingly fixed upon
The spotlight. Avoid such contacts. But
Don't forget to dance. Dance and weave new patterns
With all life just waiting in the wings.

Dance in secret shapes of brilliance
Dance and give the pulsing world your breathtaking design –
Oh, dance, before the *deus ex machina*
Descends and takes you to another stage
Beyond this known proscenium, bright spotlight
and beguiling cyclorama.

Melpomene

All whom she touches are affected.
Some never go back, but follow her through
Faërie regions and sad, weeping woods, alight with
The pure flame of Truth, Beauty and Compassion.
And even scholars, who on fewer whims are fed,
Wander, enchanted, in the Garden of her Verse;
Until they come upon a fountain cool
And two forking paths.
Mostly, they return, by that which leads
Again to academe and peace; but those remaining,
As in a dream, walk on, along the way towards
The beckoning hazy sky and final freedom from
The World and all its clutching hands.

John Hartley Williams

Your Legs

Return me your legs, I need them –
those tall shiny white pillars of salt.
Put them in the post when you've wrapped them –
coarse-grained paper, the little hairs you never shaved –
I do not like a woman who's not hairy.
Drench the fibres of the wrapping in yourself.
Stare at them until your eyes begin to stream
and write my privatest address, the one with
monastery hats, balloons and bells and temples –
anything tears cannot smudge.
Don't forget your toes.
One of them was big enough to fill my mouth –
it contained China, several rivers,
moving herds of sacred elephants by the Yangtze
that reflected your big feet dangling from the jetty
where you painted your nails with the blood of fish.

I will unpack those living appendages
and think of Li Po toppling from his skiff
to embrace the moon.
Constellations will ripple through me
outwards and upwards
like stars drowning in water.

Caroline Price

Figures of eight

You were late, you told me
but smiling, without apology,
because you'd been working with the *petites insectes*

you'd inherited from your father-in-law,
you'd not known anything about bees before

but now you loved them,
now you saw them everywhere -
there are bees wherever you look, you said,
even on the rooftops of Paris! -

Yes, anyone gazing down on the city
would see roof gardens, balconies
dotted with hives; Paris in spring

is not just for lovers
but for bees finding food like lovers
as snowdrop, coltsfoot and willow break into flower,

a softening, a filling out
of the palest cream until green
dusts the sky, the temperature rising by a few degrees

and the sun high enough to finger
mansards and high windows,
the sleepers unhuddling
and venturing out, drowsy from overwintering,

climbing from the darkness of yards and stairwells
into the open, their other lives
as invisible below

as the traffic is inaudible; all they can hear
is humming, bees freighting the air
with their sweet trajectories.

Mother

How she dangled you from a window
to threaten your father, held you over Rabat's streets
like a doll, a two-year-old frozen in space;
how she refused to let you go out
after school – Work! she'd say –
or serve in the store, a shopkeeper
as you'd never be, you would go up
in the world, high above her Spanish village,
his migrant sweat. And how you obeyed
until the day, you were twenty-two, wound tight,
you danced at Chez Babette and for the first time
didn't return that night, though she leant
from the balcony wailing your name –
you walked back in a man, and from that moment
she hardly met your eyes. How you took
your first girl straight to your room
and still she said nothing, but one evening
was standing there, holding a jeweller's box
and how you exploded; you would never
marry, no woman in the dozens you'd sleep with
could erase the sound of her voice.
How you talked of returning to France
and how your father begged you not to, not yet
he kept saying, tears on his cheeks, it would break
your mother's heart; and only after he'd died
did you confront her – Come too, you said
but how she refused, would only leave Rabat
as ashes flown back decades later
to this cemetery in Marseilles
where each Toussaint you queue with your bucket
and sponge to clean their grave, a long way
from the hot spicy dust of Morocco,
though sometimes you can feel it in the air
as you kneel among the monstrous stones
and the wind blows in a particular way,
not the Mistral, or Tramontane, but a warm wind
from Africa which shivers the chrysanthemum petals
and lodges grit in the engraved names
or it might be sand, dawn breaking and
the implacable Atlantic rolling in behind you.

Peter Robinson

120 Addington Road

Now, mother, with your need to know
we lead you past the fuchsias
down our patch of garden; now
you're settled in the front room
turning out scales on an upright piano,
two-handed; now you're being shown
the narrow kitchen, its larder store –
built round the year the stock market crashed,
our house about as old as you are.

Withdrawn, foul weather
at the glass once more,
you see we're thrown together
in our tight corner
behind a flaked, black-painted door ...

and, mother, with your need to know,
now when you picture this inter-war
semi, sense its compact ground plan
imprinted from the precipitous stairs
to where new copper piping leads;
now when you rehearse your prayers
imagining how each room succeeds
room; now when you lie down to sleep,
mother, remember us, mum, if you can.

Joseph Woods

Her Own Drowning

i.m. Laura Salmeri

When I got word of her death,
on the night of San Silvestro,
I wanted to be back among
the back alleyways of Catania,
before near drowning, before her,
my dolphin who once led me to land.

There, in the span of a siesta,
streets empty and spread silent under
the sun as we pass under shutters
down on the day, to hear voices,
the clearing up of a meal,
the fall of cutlery into its tray.

A cry of lovemaking carries in the air
and inevitably, further on, a baby crying.
It's where I lose you and follow
the alley's curve to a square
full of debris, that morning's fruit
market where a few men are hosing

down its substance, small mounds
of the half-rotten and over-ripe
gathered in corners. A perfect lemon
rolls down the pavement, brushes
against my shoe and on into the gutter
to bob away in the wash.

Mayday Relay

I must have been eight when I got my first room
downstairs across from the kitchen, narrow
and windowless but I loved it for its being
at the heart of things. Our backdoor acted
as most people's front, so in bed you could hear

everything: conversations, whispered send-offs
from older siblings, a neighbour's souped-up
car changing gear and sounding off into the night
or simply follow stars through the skylight.
Imagining myself in some ship's open hold

while Morse code would drift in from the kitchen,
my brother tapping the key of an oscillator
into the dots and da's of messages.
Secret and *Plain Language, Mayday Relays*
and *Ocean Letters*, preparing for the exam
that would never quite set him to sea.

Tim Liardet

Urn Burial

The urn, brother, the black shapely urn
might be deep enough, you prayed, to hold the ashes
of every idea I'd ever had, the black petals
of every word I'd written, the soot,
the charred bits and flakes of carbon
born from how slowly books burned.

For my part, I prayed the urn might hold
the calcium of something in you that was yet
to be fully born, the ashes of your hatreds
and the cooled, weightless coals
of your refusal to tryst life – in the urn, I prayed,
to find the very last clinkers of these.

Now the urn is wholly mine, and I do not know
for all the life of me what to do with it;
I do not know what to make of its sinuous shape
and the fact there seems to be no way into it
and fear, as I turn it slowly, it might
contain the motes of the death I owe to you:

even after your death your hands are around it,
even after your death your hands clutch on,
and over and over we try to wrest
the urn from each other's grasp as if this is
actually a war to the knife to keep hold
of our mother's stretchmarked heart. You win.

Vulgar Old Smile

Sunk beyond fear, for days the frog did not move
a muscle or nerve. There in the gloom of the shed
it held its wide-mouthed vigil, reflected vaguely
in the tin and evaporating wet we kept it in.
As the skin dried on the backbone of its spirit,
pegged there, the frog seemed to prolong the change
from amphibian into an old leather glove,
just moist enough to puff its throat once in an hour.
Because it dried up so slowly, and seemed to collapse
as though somehow sucked at from the inside,
growing smaller, it began to terrify us.
Each morning we dreaded it, dared not go in
for fear of something worse, but peeped
through the door as it looked back unseeing –
like a little old man, with old man's hands;
death's vulgar old smile without a tooth in its head.
We shared the fear of it, brother, like we shared
the hairs that stood up on the back of our necks
but now, so very much later, I feel
I left you in the stifling shed that was stuffed full
of the terror – a place you could never approach
for fear of what you might find waiting for you
like a vague mirror showing how you had changed.
I left you among the cobwebs, the tines that were clung-to
by root-hairs, pierced through, I left the shed
hundreds of miles behind so that I could go
as far away as I might to find what I could
of breathing space in the north. And that for you
was the final betrayal, to be abandoned so far back,
to be abandoned completely to the fear.
And now that you are dead, though the frog is alive
and the shed's roof-felt gets so hot it almost melts,
I find myself above all wanting to ask
for some terrible forgiveness, and imagine you stare back,
like the frog, through my fumbling for words
and through the words that muddle and stumble
towards other words and try to speak the truth.

Christine McNeill

Witness

It is as if the chair you sat in
were softly beating, like a heart.
I note a book open on the table,
a sharp pencil half on the desk,
half over the edge, in space.

That time you sat before a pot with tulips
bearing tight-lipped buds:
waiting for the flowers to open.

I see you sitting after it had happened:
the petals showed their hearts to the sun.
Or did you not witness the exact moment?

No answer where sofa, table, sideboard
speak of your touch;
where absence is no longer pain but beauty:
that pencil – a hand unable to grasp it.

Portfolio

Between us were thirty years and a passion
for art. The younger, you held forth
about Tracy Emin, Damien Hirst.
I was tuned in to the Impressionists –
colour, tranquillity, above self-promotion.
Like Picasso you could make
a bull's head from driftwood and iron bar.
Evenings you walked in drunk
but with a charm that sparked our verbal exchanges,
and in the core of what we discussed
lay the mutual recognition of each other's
loneliness.

That alone is love, you said,
squeezing the glass in your hand so tight,
it cracked. Blood mingled with whisky.
By the fence, in the dusk,
a deer stood stock-still.
Then sprinted into the woods beyond.

The portfolio I discovered after your death.
You'd drunk yourself to the grave.
An oddball, who couldn't make it in life.
But who can? *If death is terrible,*
then better be done with it now, you said,
if it is sweet,
all the more reason to welcome it.

At our last talk the midges swarmed
around your thin arms.
The agave you'd pinched years ago
from a public display and planted in my pot
was bursting with health.
With some strange instrument
you burnt the shape of a human figure
onto a sycamore leaf,
thanked me for having cooked
your favourite meal.

Come back, my heart cries, when the rocking-chair
speaks the only language I know.

I reach for the red ribbon
on your portfolio: with a gentle tug,
it would fall open, disclosing sheets of drawings;
but my finger only hovers inside the loop;
plays with the notion of the linear
arrested for good.

Pruning his tree

He'd wanted pictures taken
of his last holiday in the Austrian Alps.
Studied them afterwards, noting
the black dot of an eagle in the blue sky
that had escaped us. We zoomed in on his
leaning more heavily on the walking stick,
looking, not at the camera, but into the distance.

Leobersdorf, Bad Vöslau, Wiener Neustadt,
he wrote down the passing train-stations.
Was it to make the strangeness lying beyond
his terminal illness more familiar to himself?
He doubled the number of stops,
added fourteen, halved the total,
took off the original figure that left him with *seven.*

There're seven trees in his garden.
One, whose scarlet berries he called
my mermaid gems, we prune.
I hook a branch down
with his walking-stick.
While you saw
I almost hang in the air

trying to keep the branch low,
feeling as if my head were taking off
into that blue beyond the withering leaves
to follow his name-tape on the stick.
As you cut into the wood
I cling with all my strength,
call out *Stop!*

and we both let go.
Catching your breath
you kiss me:
The wind blows the sensation up through the leaves
to where we can't follow,
but imagine it blend into the many unseen things
of which at this moment we are certain.

Peter Carpenter

The Destruction of Dresden

There you are, father, late August, early evening,
French windows left ajar, your beaky outline a Vermeer.
The light draws in. Eyes navigate print. You're set low
in your chair. Hollowed fist to lips, you clear your throat,
oblivious to our games of 'It' or neighbours drifting home
from a day in 'the smoke', its jams, its dreadful heat.
Liddell Hart, Harris, now this. Your bleached skull's visible
against the reading light, from our swing by the privet
at the very end of the garden. We get ready for bed, come down
for our night-night kiss. The book's open at black and white plates –
I glimpse rickety bodies stacked high on hand-carts as your lips
brush my face. Soon we're dead to the world. Alone after supper
and News At Ten you slide open a frosted glass pane, place the book
back in the cabinet. You imagine that it's pitch black out there.

Michael Hulse

To my Father

William Ernest Hulse, 1925-1994

Selections from a sequence

i

Did I ever tell you about that song of Grieg's
that Mrs. Sterling taught us one Tuesday,
a classful of snotty Potteries kids,
in music at junior school in Chell?

An old man was singing of the spring he knew
would be his last: the greening of the grass,
the blossoms and the birdsong and the streams.
I was in tears and couldn't sing a note.

This April, since the last time I saw you alive,
the song's been repeating in my head
for another old man who would soon be dead,
whose going was the greater for the knowing:

Dad, you knew
this April was your last. I knew it too.
I held you shaking with the knowledge
when I sat you up in bed,

coughing and gagging, the eyes staring out of your head
with effort and fear of death.
I knew what you knew
as I held you, frightened and fighting for breath.

ii

You'd understand this: when I knew you were dead,
I wept to think that I wouldn't be able
to shave you again. Not much of a service, perhaps.
But still, I longed to render it once more.

You'd lie with a towel gathered at your neck,
I'd lather you and draw the slackened flesh
tight for the blade,
and always you'd murmur *Sweeney Todd*

and giggle quietly in that way you had,
boyish and helpless, in the last month or so
when even laughing called for more strength than you'd left,
and I'd shave you with a plastic disposable razor,

and as often as not, since talking was hard,
I'd find myself thinking about the men
whose dying left a scar upon your mind:
Socrates, Seneca, Rommel.

I'd try to look them in the eye.
I'd try to know the men they were,
leading the life of action or the life of contemplation,
strongest of heart in the leaving it:

the soldier telling his wife to expect a call
from the hospital, and the usual telegrams,
and climbing into the car with General Burgdorf,
who held the poison ready in his fist,

the gadfly draining the cup at a draught,
walking among his friends till his legs were numb,
then waiting calmly for the final cold
to come with its tranquillity and healing,

and Nero's man – how old can I have been,
fifteen or so, when first I heard you say
that rather than await the worse to come
you'd opt for Seneca's way?

You scared me shitless at the time.
I hadn't realised your god
might just as well be noble, cruel, petty or sublime,
the milk of human kindness or a murderous old sod –

you'd no idea. None. And I can't shave you any more.
It's in my fingers still, the touch I needed,
that rhythm that was practice born of love.
But death has dulled my fingers like a glove.

iii

Your ash stick in the hall. Your pension book.
Your slippers, missal, cardigan,
the coronation spoon we fed you with.
Where shall I look for you now? –

on the black harbour water,
taking the bodies
of Japanese shot
in Stanley Prison

out in the night, beyond
the Hong Kong three-mile limit,
wrapping them in army blankets,
weighting them with bricks? –

or writing this letter from Singapore,
businessman to friend and Member,
wanting him to go to work
to save a Pahang Communist from hanging,

stapling a clipping to the carbon
afterwards: *Girl bandit Wong*
Ah Lan, 18, won't hang.
– I visited the temple on Penang,

that dark narcotic mystery you loved,
where at the start of every rainy season
pit vipers by the score
seek shelter and are welcomed in,

and when my eyes adjusted to the gloom
I made them out on wicker cribs and cradles,
lethal, lovely, lazy with joss and eggs,
ignorant of death. – Shall I look for you

in 626 Water Transport Company,
Lee Enfield number 25648,
waiting for Zipper, sure you'll be the first
to get your head blown off on a landing craft,

or shall I go back further, to a boy
as bright-eyed and original as Abel,
the boy who rejoiced, not an hour before he died,
in this bunch of April forget-me-nots on the table?

iv

She was the shadow I think I see,
grazing her Chinese lips
on your cheek as the rocking Dakota
touched the tarmac in Bangkok,

the shadow in the dark
driving the Vanguard, one hand off the wheel,
her smile at sixty in the Malacca night
overturning you,

the shadow love
who went into the world of light
taking and leaving a photograph
of you at Kek Lok Si

that caught you
like a shutter
half a lifetime later:
ah, the Chinese girl.

Your drunken boss Caerlion had done a bunk,
leaving you to run the show
for R. J. Wood & Co.,
offices on Raffles Place above the Chartered Bank,

Lancashire textiles, end of empire, thinning order books –
Dad, for your past I wish you frangipani nights,
a Chinese melody brimful as love in your throat,
a touch, a look, a flutter in the heart –

the shadow I think I see.
For then you were the man without a shadow,
the company bankrupt, Asia at your back,
disembarking in a trenchcoat and a homburg at Marseilles.

v

Pausing in your Gibbon at the passages you marked –
the noble spirit of Aurelius,
the salutary balm of Boethius,
the fortitude of Julian –

I see you reading in a pool of light,
a studious young man in Singapore,
with six good volumes named for Everyman;
so shortly after Belsen and Treblinka

restoring, by the scruple of the act,
the faith that words can say what living means,
can name the spirit in our brief machines –
calm and intrepid in the barbarian night.

We walked at Brothers Water
when your words were mostly blotted by a stroke,
and hazarded at what on earth you meant,
more than a pantomime but past a joke,

parading an imaginary cross –
a priest? – till in the end,
associating Marlowe's lines,
we got the word you wanted: caterpillar.

All winter long your own decline and fall.
Till all the words of all the histories
had come, on a certificate, to these:
Bronchopneumonia. Cerebrovascular disease.

Nigel Jarrett

Alzheimer's Castle

You couldn't recall who likened
the gap between remembering
and forgetting and remembering
to a sheer butterfly's wing;
but that Lysandra Blue
raised and lowered the bridge
connecting the mined citadel
to the scent of hills and acres.

Then it died unseen;
all happened behind your back,
when its wings were one
and the doomed courtiers arose:
Aricept
Exelon
Reminyl.

They attend you now.

Sitting With Aunty Vi

It was a whispered brief, gin on the breath:
Come by whenever you like and say what you've seen.
But the authority of others seemed undermined.

Naturally, I thought she meant a round-up
of the week's events in the village – half an hour
at most, I reckoned, over a Camp coffee,

though there would be other strong stuff:
the stable boy – a burden now – kicked by a mare,
and Mrs Jephcott, thrice naked at an upstairs window.

(That's apart from the resident sparrow-hawk,
crashing in now-you-see-me mode against the laurel
and erupting feather-trailed with a clutch of redstarts).

Blind since birth, she'd had her time, before
the Somme sucked in her man and the queue was spurned.
She fingered his gong's merry-go-round Braille

and read his other belongings in a scalloped tin:
a comma of her hair, one Charles-Hubert watch,
the German's lighter he filched, still reeking.

With whiskered smile and eyes flickering beyond me
at some sisterly accomplice, she said she'd been
singled out, but 'too late to fall beneath a king's horse',

though I could see her being led to a railing
with hectoring comrades hatched from a Tissot,
hear the rustle of *mantelets and redingotes.*

So I described autumn's starling clouds ('a million minions
leaderless'); the wafer's dissolution on the tongue;
the arrowhead jets; Huppert in *The Piano Teacher.*

Courting, I thought she craved more – her eyes on fire
like a dreamer's and her spinster's unseeing told me so:
your squeal on arrival, your ecstatic mimicry of sleep;

for you know that once, prim and attentive,
you inched your knees apart as I took your hand
and she seemed to sigh at a blurred quickening of desire.

Danny Rendleman

Doppler

Not so early morning,
father's coughing spell
from how many packs
of Camels the day before

(and me and mother in one
bed, cringing, her fear
not mine, his night alone
in the basement, an agreed

upon arrangement since I
was conceived, they say)
after second-shift at Chevy,
workshoes scarred with new moons

of steel shavings, hands ditto,
eyes bleared from micrometers,
Kessler's, bar air, a young
senescence. OK, pain.

The gravel of phlegm hawked up,
remembered these days as I grow
into his age then, growing slowly resonant,
constant and fickle as memory.

A chenille bedspread, mother's
patchwork quilt, cheap sheets to cover us.
We soon must be up and about –
school, his black domed lunchbox

to fill with bologna sandwiches,
which may or not be eaten by the machine
repair guy who lives below us
half our lives, and the both of them

still live as I write this,
coming nearer, nearer still,
then moving off like passengers
on a train I have bought

a ticket for, but pocket for now
as the cars grow almost tiny,
though not nearly enough, two faces
in the caboose window waving hello.

Mc. donald Dixon

The Funeral

The hearse drew up, three-o-clock sharp along the curb,
flattening the mutton grass, spilling over into
the road. My mother and a few cousins, all in
black, watch two left-overs from the wake help load
the teak tinted coffin with nickel plated handles;
there were no undertakers then, in '52,
but the dead got by, very well thank you, with help
from surviving relatives and friends. Some made wreaths,
some bathed the body in bay rum and lime while an
old woman from the choir came home to stitch the
satin shroud. Seven turning eight, they shipped me to
the neighbour's place so that my young eyes would not
get strained on death.

But after they done their tra-la-la
and rouged up my grandmother's face, they called me in
to see her, for the last, lying frail inside her
coffin. I felt the tears gathering like rain but
could not cry, not even when the joiner, without
notice, placed the lid in place and fastened it with
silver screws, in holes he prearranged. I heard my
mother hiccup, while some godchild steal a sob,
but not I, who was too young to follow the hearse
watch them rest her in her final spot in the sand,
under the old breadfruit tree.

Afterwards, they came home, my mother stretched under
the bed for the demi-john with the wicker-basket
suit and took down the glasses she was buying by
pairs for my first communion, from the safe, to serve
a round of drinks for her friends, making sure to cork
back the bottle before they filed the first down
the hatch. The next shot was on credit at Bertie's
across the street. My mother then shut her front door
and lock the gate to the yard. Inside, alone, she
begin to hop and squeal, 1 think,
on purpose to bring back the dead.

Will Stone

The Rock Tombs of Montmajour

Somehow with primitive tools
they scored the recalcitrant surface,
kneeling to let the sun yoke them,
on the silent shore of rock still there.
Like rude orphanage cradles they appear,
moulds for air churls that leap out boned
leaving only black water in a corner,
a scatter of cones...
So tiny the tenants then, adult children,
unprepared for crows that queued
to unpick their trussed forms,
beneath the sheer war tower
from whose lowest crevices thistles fire
and a lone poppy yet unfurled
calls out strangely in its sleep.
Monks passed here, their cowls taut
in the Camargue winds, laying siege
from plains whose bending reed deeps
finger unseen the faith ossuary of lost mariners.
Now you are standing there,
curiously explored by twelve centuries,
and here is your hand
touching the altar with the mason's mark,
terribly alerted by six metre thick walls
to the single leaf fall of existence.

William Virgil Davis

Pomegranates

The blood-red arils, tart to the tongue,
slash the thirsty throats of history, and men
along long trails and over mountains,
slog through sand as deep as camels' knees
and, whipped by winter's winds, are now
about to turn the corner of another century
somewhere in the deserts of Afghanistan.

Pomegranates cluster close against the house,
near the back door that bangs behind you
as you enter a room of ghosts—who never
fail to recognize you in spite of your ever
more elaborate disguises. The thick-skinned,
several-celled berries brush their reflections
in the windows. We are all eating glass.

Lynne Wycherley

from the sequence
Poppy in a Storm-struck Field

Kindness in your hands, the nimbus of your hair,
oven-warmed words on the sleet-stung air.
If love could leap the synapses, the void,
to where you are. Or were.

The days lay down their light, a shining road,
would pave my heart
to a late-March sky, hard blue.
Buckthorn, alders, hatch new leaves.

Dear one, did the black hole take you,
the storm's pupil,
or were you met by light as sheer
as this? 'Terminal'

they told you. From day one. As if we're
all born dying, must lose
the hands that held us, the moon
that hovered over us: the first face.

Hold back the bud, first leaves.
Sepals – not yet. Blossom – not yet.
Don't spill. Hold fire.
My eyes can't bear much beauty,

night-accustomed, my focus gone
to fissile stars, deep seeds.
I'd carry a torch, my moth-flutter pulse
to your pillow

quickened by death. Heckled
by the darkness in the hallway.

The Monks of Papa Westray

Men of the cross, shaven men,
they slip through the saga like shadows,
pick their way through the words'
sharp stones. *Papay in mein.*

Peer through the wind: can you see them?
Black as guillemots, sleeves flapping,
they thread between islands,
Aikerness sandstone jutting from the ebb.

Robed with purpose and a lonely light,
their hems caked with sand. An old priest
at their head; cambered, halting,
his hair white as a fulmar's wing.

Papa Westray strains at its tether:
time and salt have eaten the thread.
The tail of Aikerness vanishes inch by inch.
No longer a tide of robed men,

a cross cutting its rune in the wind.
Who now will burnish a chalice,
who will bring us a crumb of light
beyond satellites, dead stars?

Papay in mein – 'the greater island of the priests' (Orkney Saga)
Tail of Aikerness – thin causeway

Leaving Burray

Beyond the Barrier, fear's grey wall,
it appears from nowhere –

a strip of blue, transcendent blue,
as if a thousand kingfishers
fell from heaven.

Glance again and it's gone,
mist's sleight of hand,
its voltage-trace still printed on your soul.

Barrier – Churchill Barrier (Scapa Flow)

Tony Conran

Deià Unvisited

The hill haunted me. Deià –
One of my everworlds
Whose magical fauna

Sometimes as friends of friends would come
Filling my room
With his last, dumb

Awarenesses, geologically
Slow, a poetry
Speechless as lichen.

My household could have been translated
And I'd only to look out
Through olive groves

To see twilight
Blur the long stairs
Up to the town,

The corner to his home ...
And behind me, did I half-hear
Her footsteps

Who 'variously haunts'
This hill,
This island Earth?

Caoine

for Peter Prendergast painter of the Bethesda quarries

Wild rush had not left him,
Nor sphagnum
Nor the stubble
Of lichen on walls.

Ordovician rock was young
In the amplitude of his art –
A fawn, a weanling
Skipping, nuzzling the wind:

Himself the Pierre, Petrus –
With the toes of Hephaistos
A miner, he'd
Gripped the wet walkways,

Topsy-turvy tunnellings
Of cloud,
Stubs of quarrymen's cottages,
Streams and wild air.

Then, as if a menhir
Limped, a stone sidling
With a twist to it
As if lava flowed –

But what's this? He's down!
O little stones, mosses
Of Deiniolen scrub,
Dinorwic lichens ...

Has the land done for him?
Storm, or offshore gale,
Or the bear-hug of boulders
Toppled him?

Wrestled to the ground
As anguish broke?
As stone would not beat?
As time froze?

Roland John

Taking Risks

For years the entrances and exits looked
abandoned, as if they knew the old sett
was too near frequented paths; dull, blocked,
filling up with stones, old sticks, dried leaves.

Today new excavations, cleared runways,
discernible tracks leading outwards,
a fallen branch smoothed by many passings,
it intrigues my dogs, I examine for telltale hairs.

What chance of survival close to the boundary,
no houses near to watch for lampers;
I've seen those countrymen with dogs and sacks
still loyal to the old pastimes, their rural ways.

Discovering once a long dead carcass tossed
into a hedge, a spike still through the lower part,
a spade wound to the head; a country sport.
Then there's the farmer protective of his herd,

bovine TB, those entrances to snap a leg, or
cause a tractor to catch and stall, little chance
of survival here, so why did they come back?
Or am I wrong and some other mammal

has taken over? The path's too wide
for rabbits, foxes? What else is there?
All I can do is keep a vigil, perhaps tonight
I'll come out late prepared to watch and wait.

Charles Leftwich

Cadenzas

Ideas are energy, and energy change

i

Could mind ever be as still
as the noon-misted expanse
of hill and mountain, dry,
sere gold and with blue breath of quiet
stilled before us?

The bird whose underwings
blaze red as eyelids closed to sun, trusting
the air, flies unconcerned by our ontology:
wing shadows flit unchanging
on the day-tranced face of rock.

For Africa, father of continents,
sun may burn still along the ridgy jaws of mountain
speaking only stillness – though they
burn white with the light
hills leave, transforming in the artist.

Yet our still will only come
when for us
somehow the call to farrow,
to spoor-petalled paths,
to young bodies still flowered
is answered so truly
that no curl of plough through turning earth
no rhythmic nod of ox
no stamp of foot on firelit clay
could lead the mind to legend.

Until then
the blue cloud shadows
each as they sweep
will bathe anew the herd-boy,
wring from his loins a new cry –
shrill, and shriller – shriller

than his wildest cry to cows,
and no sound his throat can form
will find the call or know the caller
and no krantz
will catch
the calling.

ii

The violin bow
in a beehive of sound
with lightning pain
seeks new corners to the hexagon:
mad Nijinsky free
in a garden set to dance...

And, though in the held moment near
artistry's summit the expected peaks must
wait, pure light, for the bow's
assent,
arrival sweeps new ranges in.

When will no further phrase
wait, cat-grinned above the podium:
beyond stringed tension and the wood
can the frenzied-fingered ride of bow
ever frame repose?

iii

The bull, whose black had gorged
all the shadows of boyhood afternoon,
absorbed my sight, deepening in turn
my tauric cave that will yet breed
future bulls, including those of memory.
Still, it is the seen bull left behind
that fascinates:
untouchable to me now as the bulls
of Cretan acrobats
but with my hands ever on its horns,
behind me.

The leaps I leave
on time's fresh walls
will hold my purest hues.

iv

A snowflake falls on the dented taxi roof
Like a Mozart score on a bill of fare.

I have yet to read how the Moors in their Alhambra
made petal patterns rotate, reply,
in every symmetry flat space allows.
I know little of counterpoint, less of the fugue
of figures woven in the calculus:
only that in the Moorish frieze there was
repose, won of folding a flower
from possibilities.

When mimesis of the crystal
by the mind finds the crystal's
law-winged still;
when like hieroglyphs your brilliant
arpeggios arrange themselves on walls of air
in true pattern all about you, there
is an end of a mind – of a mind as turbulence.
Ice-pinioned apogee, unshakeable by wind
or comet, in the movement's stillness
at home.

Yet, another you is stretching hands, begins to see anew
the uncertain heave of motion's paths – when traced
in space, like fish-nets billowing.

This is now's thrill –
unliftable from past or future by nimblest
fingers even, yet telling that
now I could unpick all the spindled pinnacles
of my words – free them like fishes' tails
upon the flood

Frescoes catch dolphins in their leap,
and the deftest Cretan youths;
our greatest vault is ever
from one pattern to the next.
We are charged now in the atom ring,
and where the red shift flares.
Taurus wears our garlands;
                    Pisces steals our breath.

W S Milne

Sonnet

'Whither thou goest, I will go;
And where thou lodgest, I will lodge'
the Book of Ruth

Summer nou is a broken and a scaittered god;
there's a changing in the air.
The wiks, the months that fuir awa ti nithing!
In vain we propitiate the years.
The first yella-reid leaves o the aik-tree appeir,
and fa, and gaither thick and fast aboot the bole.
Ye've lain your heid in ma lap --on the bink--,
I play wi your brushed-up hair,
the bonnie-fine slope o your shouder.
Puddocks hae plopped in the stang aa day
and you hae picked flouers for your folder.
A drizzle o sang faas frae the trees.
Gentle speerit, sleep on, and rest.
Let us possess whit is left o the licht.

Donald Avery

The Final Page

Based on Sonnet XIV
Louise Labé
1524 – 1566

While eyes are able tears to shed
as they review the days of bliss;
while lips, that on ambrosia fed,
tremble at memory of your kiss;
while fingers can attune the dis-
harmonies and to melodies wed:
such while shall I remain in this
alone content, now you are dead.

Such while and not desire to die.
Yet, if the sacred spring run dry
and song be silenced in the cage
that is this inkwell; on such day,
unable more to praise you, may
my soul become the final page.

Norman Buller

A Jacobean Romance

i

Her Cartography

How can it be –
Since I have breached the chamber of your being,
Lifted the latches of your soul,
Heard your spheres' music – why am I not seeing
The landscape where your surface lies,
Whether here, there, you sport a mole,
Not knowing yet the colour of your eyes?

It must not be.
To roam such unmarked territory's too hard.
May I not know your birthday, send a card?
A defect so profane must ask
For remedy. Make it my task
To map your life. For why should I stay blind
To outward parts when inward seams are mined?

ii

Her Confession

Do not run
To a Confessor.
In love you are
Alone with him.
He, too, tells beads
In the same darkness
And whenever
You and he love
You hold the same prayer
In your arms.

iii

A Prospect of Letters

Forbidden, wordless art
Is my undoing.
Love on the page is merely
Language wooing,

Safe and performed as well
Parted by water.
What's mute, and done as one,
Is how I'd court her,

Here, with her perilous
Warm substance blent,
Our love our art and we
Each other's argument.

iv

Mutual Flame

Enjoy these winter days,
Snow threatening to fall,
A sky of brooding greys
And no great need at all
To leave the house as the last daylight wanes.

It's not the stricken world
Outside makes us rejoice,
Familiar contours pearled
By frosted snow. The choice
Is ours to stay this side the window panes,

Glad not to be out there
Freezing this winter's night
But warmly bedded where,
With brave, deliberate light,
Our mutual flame all icy dark disdains.

v

Her Youth

Time is my enemy although your friend;
A younger lover may last longer, though
Love measured by the year must have an end.

The minutes deafen while our physics blend;
I should abstain for fear the pain might grow.
Time is my enemy and yet your friend.

The vines of love bear fruit as they ascend
But qualify our vintage from below
Where, measured by the year, love has its end.

Love should mix equally; though time intend
We'll both wear out, I'll be the first to know.
Time stays my enemy although your friend.

Blame, then, my briefer future if I tend
To love too quickly and repair too slow.
When measured by the year love will soon end.

Time wastes us both but only you can mend
Your ruined years from greater store and so
Time, still my enemy, remains your friend
And, measured by the year, our love must end.

vi

Her Ring

I find her mislaid ring; how droll
That this forgotten token prove,
By apt reversal of its role,
Not fitted, but removed, for love!

We'd met but down her darkest lane
Where instant, shallow pleasures blend,
But those alone, for it was plain
I could not hope to be her friend.

A ring upon a finger will
Fit close though they are not combined;
Two lovers may fit closer still
Yet still not blend in heart and mind.

This symbol's truth must now be faced;
She's slipped me from her like this band
Of cooling metal from her hand -
Though rings removed can be replaced!

vii

Her Silence

I can do nothing with the moon;
It drifts, irrelevant, with stars.
The troubadours forsake their tune
And soon abandon their guitars.
Why should hope wither and decay?
    You do not say.
    You do not say.

Your silence, like a shroud, descends
Upon our scarcely-born desire,
Ensures its infant life now ends
And our bond fail. Why did our fire
Not burn beyond its tinder glow?
    I do not know.
    I do not know.

Triptych: Lyn Moir, Caroline Carver, Penelope Shuttle

The Crescent Moon spring of Dunhuang

The Crescent-shaped Spring, known to all for its crescent-shaped water body, is 100 m long from the south to the north and about 25 m wide from the east to the west as well as about 5m in its water depth. Where sky blue water looks like a sparkling and crystal-clear jade inlaid the sands. It's environed by Mingsha Mountain where the slid sands in daytime can return back in the evening comes.

i

Lyn Moir

The Crescent Moon Spring of Dunhuang

You said you would soon go
to another world.

I had not expected this...

a desert curved
to the small of your back,
flesh-coloured sand
against the black-hole mountain side.

But this is definitely your eye,
that brilliant faded-denim blue,
half open in the sun.

Of course your parts
have come apart,
dispersed
so this bright eye is in the hollow
just above your buttocks.

A monastery
or luxury hotel
(and either one would seem appropriate)
sits like a bushy eyebrow
above the lid.

Your skin has wrinkled,
coarsened with the change,
but soaks up sun
intently,
as it always did.

Fifteen eager camels
following their weary masters
trace a soft path
round your eyelashes.

ii

Caroline Carver

The Empress stops at the Crescent Moon spring of Dunhuang

She settles her head carefully onto the stone pillow
which will give her the last dreams of childhood
before she takes the western route to a new life

Outside
                the Silk Road waits in the evening sun

She has left her camels with their heads down
drinking as if they would like to drain the oasis
their babies with their soul eyes and soft muzzles

already nestled into the cupped palm of desert
waiting for the latest fall of sand
to fly back to the Mingsha Mountains

The Empress lies in her silken tent
surrounded by treasures
which her ladies place there each night –

a trunk filled with gold and silver
a glass jug engraved with flutes
a delicate ivory comb for her long black hair

She fingers the red dress embroidered with a thousand butterflies
sings to the caged canaries-twelve, for each of her twelve years
strokes the statue of the flying horse which will one day carry her to heaven

but best she loves the moths of the second moult in their large wicker basket
she likes to stir the tiny black hairs on their backs
with her polished forefinger

She does not dream of the coltish young camels
the gold and silver and glass and ivory
not even the shimmering red dress or the twelve canaries
but mounts the flying horse, beautiful as a God
clutching his mane, whispering into his soft ears
turned back to catch her voice

When she wakes and tiptoes out into the cool of a desert night
to dip her hands into the magic spring, curved like a crescent moon

she is surrounded by moths

iii

Penelope Shuttle

Known to All

Known to all
for its crescent-shaped body,
though not visible from the moon,

the Spring lies like quiet itself
under the Mingsha Mountain
where the slid sands in daytime

can return back
in the evening comes –
Crescent Moon Spring of Dunhuang

blue as the fistful of sea
I carry from The Lizard
to The Roseland,

blue as the sky over Bilbao
the day the old man in his jolly beret
clapped me on the shoulder

as I sat reading
on the banks of the Nervión –
Buen libro!

Under the Mountain,
the Spring is a blue scroll,
page from the I Ching,

buen libro unfurling in the desert,
trace of lapis lazuli in the camel's shadow
as she leads her sisters down to the oasis
to study from water's book of life.

Colin Wilcockson

Ted Hughes' Undergraduate Years at Pembroke College, Cambridge:

Some Myths Demystified

Once a myth gains currency it is soon accepted as actuality. In the case of Ted Hughes, the origin of some biographical myths may have been his own inventions, and some of the more colourful ones were re-told by him in varying versions. Other myths occur in scholarly studies, and I offer some corrections of these just for the record.[1]

Two biographies of Hughes contain a couple of questionable details, on the bases of which speculations are made which could be misleading.[2] Diane Middlebrook explains how Hughes gained admission to Pembroke College:

> ...he performed badly on the exam for entrance at Pembroke College, but his grammar school teacher sent a sheaf of Hughes's poems to the Master of Pembroke, and the poems won Hughes admission as a 'dark horse'.

Now Hughes' file confirms that some poems were indeed sent by the school, and we know that his teachers, John Fisher and Pauline Mayne, saw great promise in him, and that he in turn much admired these teachers. We know only that the poems were sent, but there is, alas, no copy of them, nor is there a comment on what was thought of them.

In the 1950s, the most common method of application to Oxford and Cambridge was via the Entrance Scholarship Examination. An outstanding performance on the, usually three or four, three-hour papers would result in the award of a college scholarship (worth £60 per annum). A very good performance would gain an exhibition (worth £40 per annum) .[3]

---

[1] **Acknowledgements:** I am grateful to the Ted Hughes Estate for permission to publish this article. Professors John Beer and Neil Roberts and Dr Stephen Ennis have kindly made helpful suggestions on a draft of this article, and I owe a particular debt of thanks to Professor Terry Gifford for a number of specific details. I am grateful to Emory University for permission to quote from the Ted Hughes papers in their Manuscript, Archives, and Rare Books Library, and also to Daniel Huws for permission to quote from his forthcoming *Memories of Ted Hughes 1952-63.* This paper is based on a lecture I gave at Hughes Hall, Cambridge, on September 26th, 2008.

[2] Elaine Feinstein, *Ted Hughes: Life of a Poet,* London, 2001, and Diane Middlebrook, *Her Husband. Hughes and Plath: a Marriage,* London, 2004.

[3] By way of comparison, a graduate schoolteacher in 1951 might in the first year earn £450-£500 per annum.

A good performance would gain a place, but with no financial component. (The majority of students qualified for a grant from the State or from their Local Education Authority.)

For administrative convenience, the Colleges were split into three groups, and boards of examiners, normally including the Directors of Studies in English from each College, marked the scripts. Thus the three or four scripts of each candidate would be distributed, so that the total written input of a candidate would have come under the scrutiny of several examiners, one of whom may or may not have been from his or her first-choice College. When the marks had been collated, the examiners convened to decide the descending order of the candidates according to their performance in these written papers. It was at the examiners' meeting that the decision was made as to which candidates should be awarded scholarships and exhibitions. The making of awards was, consequently, not within the power of a single college, but represented the collective decision of a board of examiners.

Hughes was awarded an exhibition. Thus the 'bad performance' recorded in Middlebrook's book is mythical. The 'dark horse' story sadly emerges from an insubstantial stable.[4]

I mention this, because there is a pervasive myth that Ted was not academically particularly successful in his formal English studies. He may, as the years went by, have thought that being a dark horse was rather more *romantic* than being an exhibitioner, but that shouldn't obscure the fact that the holding of a College exhibition gave one highly respectable academic status. He had taken the exams in 1948, and then spent two years on national service in the RAF. The years following the end of the war were particularly competitive in gaining university places because of the necessity to re-absorb students who had been accepted at Cambridge, or who had even started courses, and then been called up for military service.

Middlebrook's biography is excellently written and researched, but the perception of Hughes as creative, rather than academically scrupulous, though it may have some truth in regard to his priorities, surfaces again when she notes, 'Sylvia [Plath] completed the course that Ted didn't.' I assume that Middlebrook means that Plath's final degree, when she was at Newnham, was in English, whereas Hughes gave up English after Part I to switch to anthropology. But Plath, having already graduated at Smith University, came up to Cambridge on a two-year Fulbright Scholarship as an 'Affiliated Student', and Affiliated Students completed the Cambridge Part II in two-years and

---

[4] BL ADD 78761, f. 30. Letter to Keith Sagar 18.7.98 (32 pages holograph on 1 side of paper, dated '18th June 98' by TH '[actually July]' in Keith Sagar's hand underneath): 'When I sat my entrance exam to Pembroke, John Fisher sent a notebook of my poems to the College Master – S. C. Roberts. When I got back our Latin master, Angus Neil, had composed a Latin epigram on my ignominious failure. If it had been decided by my answer papers, he would have been right – but Roberts liked my poems. He persuaded them to take me on as a "dark horse". So I heard later.'

graduated at that point. Hughes spent two years reading English. Plath spent two years reading English.

Thus, any suggestion that Plath possessed more sustained commitment to the course is irrelevant, and, in point of fact, impossible to determine: for all we know, had she taken the three-year BA course, she might have changed subject after Part I, as did Hughes.

There is no doubt that Hughes found a good deal of the English course, and much of the teaching, boring, and, when one looks at the syllabuses of those times, that is understandable.[5] He also did not take to the closely analytic examination of text, 'practical criticism', much influenced by I. A. Richards and reinforced in Hughes' time by F. R. Leavis, whose combative approach towards critics of persuasions other than his own drew round him a coterie of likeminded students.[6]

The very wording of the rubrics for the papers Hughes took shows this heavy emphasis on close reading to the virtual exclusion of more thematic approaches:-

> Paper 1. The medieval paper: half was headed 'passages from specified texts for translation and explanation'
> Paper 2. *Richard III, Othello, Measure for Measure.*
> Paper 3. The first of 3 sections reads. 'Passages for detailed explanation and comment from some metaphysical poems and Browne *Religio Medici*. The other sections require answers between 1625 and 1798.
> Paper 4. Section 1: Literary criticism with reference to Aristotle's *Poetics*, Ben Jonson's *Timber or Discoveries*; Samuel Johnson *Lives of the Poets* [4 of which were prescribed]. Section 2: passages for comment and appreciation.
> Paper 5. Use of English with passages from French or Latin [the foreign language element was compulsory.]

The latest date on any of the papers appears as one third of Paper 3, 1700-1798, though it is possible that one or more passages for comment on Paper 4 could have been modern.

---

[5] BL ADD 78761, f. 61, Letter to Keith Sagar, 10.8.98: '... in my third year I switched to Anthropology. I don't recall that I ever went to an English lecture again (I went very rarely even in my 2nd year). And I went to very few Anthropology lectures – a few of Glyn Daniels. Mainly from my year 2 onwards I spent my days at the University Library.'

[6] '...in fact I had a kind of facility for destructive criticism that could have provided me with a career – if I had agreed to abandon what had been torn from me (everything behind that Fox, and the kind of language which, as I understood very clearly, was my only hope of negotiating with it and recovering it – a non-analytic language, a wholeness of language, as I described it to myself in those days, modelled on the wholeness of the language of proverbs, folk-rhymes, folk-songs and in fact Shakespeare).' Emory Box 54, FF 3. Letter to Joanny Moulin, 17.04.1995.

We know from Daniel Huws' account that Hughes had attended a poetry reading given by Dylan Thomas, and that when he spoke to Hughes some time later Huws gathered, 'Dylan Thomas was still high in the pantheon, lower only than Shakespeare, Beethoven and Yeats.'[7] Elaine Feinstein notes that the authors who had fired his imagination at school were Yeats, T.S. Eliot, Hopkins, Shelley and in particular his A-level Shakespeare prescribed text *King Lear*. Diane Middlebrook gives the list as T.S. Eliot, Robert Graves, D.H. Lawrence and W.B. Yeats. Whichever list one accepts as his 'favourite' poets, it would seem that, other than Shakespeare, all Hughes' inspirational poets were too modern for inclusion on the Prelim list – even Shelley (born in 1792). But one should approach with caution the various lists of favourite authors: in a 1995 interview, he says that his 'sacred canon' at the time he went up to consisted of Chaucer, Shakespeare, Marlowe, Blake, Wordsworth, Coleridge, Keats, Hopkins, Yeats and Eliot.[8] In any case, of course, undergraduate reading and discussion went on regardless of Faculty prescription.[9]

The Part I list of prescribed texts and periods included those for the Preliminary Examination and added further to them. It also slightly redresses the balance: available were a paper on Wordsworth and Coleridge, and another on the period 1832-1870.

But was Hughes' switch from English to Anthropology a somewhat maverick move? I checked how common it was to change from English to another subject in Ted's year, to see whether his decision was quirky.

I discovered that, of the eight students reading English at Pembroke in Hughes' year, four defected to other disciplines after Part I. An exhibitioner changed to Theology, as did a commoner. Hughes (an exhibitioner) switched to Anthropology, and the fourth (a commoner) switched to Natural Sciences. It is, no doubt, a strength of the Cambridge tripos system that such changes can be made. Nevertheless, that half the English intake to Pembroke switched to other triposes, looks like disenchantment.

Hughes told the neo-Gothic story of how his decision was reached. He fell asleep after an evening attempting to write an essay on eighteenth-century literature [Samuel Johnson], and dreamed that a man in the form of a fox entered the room. The animal was singed and bloody and it placed its paw on Hughes' essay telling him, *'Stop this – you are destroying us.'* When the paw was lifted, it left the print of a bloody human hand. Hughes resolved at once

---

[7] Daniel Huws, *Memories of Ted Hughes 1952-63*, forthcoming, to be published by Richard Hollis.

[8] 'Ted Hughes: the Art of Poetry Number 71', interview with Drue Heinz, *The Paris Review*, Issue 134, Spring 1995, p. 85.

[9] My own undergraduate years at Oxford were the same as Hughes' at Cambridge. The English syllabus ended with the year 1820, but that did not prevent discussion of later authors among ourselves. Nevertheless, there was a tacit Faculty implication that literature after 1820 does not qualify for academic study!

to switch Tripos. Brian Cox recalls Ted's saying that when the dream recurred the fox nodded its head approvingly.[10] Middlebrook notes, 'Hughes told versions of that story time and again throughout his life...Not surprisingly, the story changed significantly over the years.' One should bear in mind, however, that it is possible that Ted's story remained consistent, and the memories of those who later recalled it inadvertently changed the details. How true the visionary dream was no one can know, but the point was clear: the romantic fascination of myth and empathic kinship with the power and the violence of the animal world held little place in the English Faculty teaching of the 1950s. That half his Pembroke English contemporaries decided to change subjects (as had a number of his friends in the year above him) shows that the story of the command of the fox-man was not necessary, but, true or not, it is a wonderful allegory of the impulse for his deciding to switch. Diane Middlebrook notes several other instances of what she calls 'Hughes' creative mythmaking' about himself, notably in some of the episodes in *Birthday Letters*, where dates have been adjusted to create significant implications, for example that Hughes' and Plath's first sexual encounter was on Friday, April 13th, Friday 13th being a day of foreboding. It was, in fact, on 23rd March. 'Actuality,' Middlebrook remarks, 'is always being absorbed into storytelling.'[11]

The social context of a Cambridge college at that time is also a complex issue. John Wain's *Where the Rivers Meet* (1998) depicts a pervading atmosphere of coarse public school brashness at Oxford that intimidated and disgusted undergraduates from less privileged backgrounds. *Where the Rivers Meet* ends with the year 1933, and very probably catches the Oxbridge snobbery of that era. The Second World War, and also the compulsory National Service that followed, radically modified the atmosphere. A number of people of Hughes' era still claim that they felt inferior because they were the first members of the family to go to university, or that they came from grammar schools and were therefore in a tiny minority and made to feel socially unacceptable. There may be varying amounts of truth in this, and the ethos no doubt varied between colleges. I was interested to check the facts when I read another biography of Hughes, which I much enjoyed, that of Elaine Feinstein. She remarks, 'The school, too, recognized an unusually gifted pupil and made the decision to put him in for Cambridge, which was then far from common from a northern grammar school.'[12]

---

[10] Brian Cox, 'Ted Hughes (1930-1998): a Personal Retrospect', *Hudson Review*, 29-43, esp. pp. 33-34.

[11] Diane Middlebrook, p. 227.

[12] Feinstein p. 19. A letter in Emory Box 54, FF 3 (letter to Joanny Moulin 17. 04. 1995) does attest to the bitterness of his reaction to social snobbery, though 'when I was eighteen' locates it in Hughes' period of National Service: 'I had grown up in a part of the world utterly unaware of the English Class system – I was eighteen before I met a boy from the social levels which, I soon learned, owned and governed the country I thought was mine.'

Pembroke College was, indeed, predominately public school, though coming from a grammar school, even a *northern* grammar school (!), was by no means unusual. In Hughes' year, twenty-six undergraduates were from grammar schools, and forty-two were from public schools. That is to say, more than one third of the intake was grammar school; of these, sixteen were from northern grammar schools, and ten from southern grammar schools. To the best of my knowledge, Hughes did not mention this public school/ grammar school ratio, and I rather doubt whether it was of interest to him. He disliked a socially elite group of literary intellectuals at King's College, but so did many of his contemporaries.[13]

I have mentioned the 'dark horse' myth of Hughes' gaining entry to Pembroke. The suggestion that he did poorly in the exams continues into his first-year academic performance. I would like to rescue him from the myth that has grown up. I quote again from Feinstein's book: 'At the end of his first year in the Preliminary Examination for the English Tripos, Hughes gained only a Pass degree. This must have been something of a shock for a boy who had won a College Exhibition...and after his near-failure in taking Cambridge examinations, Ted pondered, only half jokingly, that he was likely to be living on his sister in the future.'[14]

The near-catastrophic exam performance mentioned by Feinstein is mythical. First it should be said, the Preliminary Examination, though classified 1st, 2.1, 2.2, 3rd, was not strictly part of a degree, but simply a hurdle to be cleared in order to proceed to Part I of the Tripos. The class list for the 1952 English Preliminary Examination reveals some interesting facts:-

A total of 152 candidates took the exam.
7 were placed in the First Class category.
34 were placed in the 2.1. category.
81 were placed in the 2.2 category.
30 were placed in the Third Class category.

This was at a time when grade inflation was not in operation. More than half the candidates were placed in the 2.2 class (eighty-one against seventy-one from all other classes put together). Among those eighty-one appears the name 'E.J. Hughes, Pembroke'. When, in 1953, Hughes took the Part I – which is indeed a constituent part of the BA degree – he gained a 2.1, and, when one looks at the distribution, this was clearly an excellent result:

---

[13] Feinstein p. 24.

[14] Feinstein p. 28.

A total of 164 candidates took the exam.
9 were placed in the 1st Class category (none from Pembroke)
30 were placed in the 2.1 category (4 from Pembroke)
83 were placed in the 2.2 category (3 from Pembroke)
42 were placed in the 3rd class category (I from Pembroke)

Overall, nine candidates were placed in a higher category than Hughes; a hundred and twenty-five in lower. But I also discovered that hunting up the class lists worked in reverse in the case of how Hughes did in his final (end of third year) examinations. Diane Middlebrook say, 'Hughes graduated from Cambridge in July, 1954, having achieved a rank of II.i in his exams...Sylvia Plath would achieve the same rank in 1957.' Agreed, with the Cambridge Tripos system it is a little unclear what constitutes one's degree class – is it Part I or Part II, or a mixture? To add to the confusion, in the mystical Cambridge system, a Part I can, in some subjects, be followed by a Part I in another subject, and count as a final examination. Hughes availed himself of this option when he switched, by taking the Part I Anthropology examinations. The published class-lists show that in the Part I Archaeological and Anthropological Tripos, 1954, Hughes was, in fact, awarded a 3rd. Not having taken the Prelim in that subject doubtless put him at a disadvantage. Fifteen candidates took the exam, of whom six were given 3rds, and two were allowed a Special, that is, a degree without honours. Apart from keeping the record straight, it doesn't, of course, matter at all what category Hughes was placed in. But keeping the record straight is not as straightforward as might have been supposed.

Tony Roberts

It was a language of water, light and air
  I sought – to speak myself free of a world
Whose stoic lethargy seemed the one reply
  To horizons and to streets that blocked them back
In a monotone fume, a bloom of grey.
'The Marl Pits'

Charles Tomlinson: Seeing the Light

In ***Agenda*** Vol 33 No 2, 'Charles Tomlinson: International Issue', Tomlinson is described by Richard Swigg as, 'the finest poet of international distinction writing in England today'. In a 1995 issue of *Poetry Review* Justin Quinn alluded to the celebrations, but was less than jubilant in his reception of Tomlinson's recent volume, *Jubilation,* finding in his work a limitation in scope (e.g. too much landscape); entrenchment, 'in a kind of Englishness of a bygone age', excluding 'so much of contemporary England'; and excessive control. Admiration was acknowledged for what Tomlinson does do well (letter poems, style, truth to nature), but that was in a minor key.[1]

I have been rereading Charles Tomlinson's work for some months now and I feel it is important that we remind ourselves of Tomlinson's stature and contribution from time to time. Throughout a long career he has offered a remarkably coherent body of work, concerning himself with this interaction between the human and the environment, in which a premium has been placed on the fidelity to visual experience. Of all things, he is the poet of perception, a poet seemingly at home everywhere (in place and prosody), but coming to frequent rest in his adopted Gloucestershire. Charles Tomlinson's response to the world has been increasingly meditative and – everywhere – he has written some fine poetry.

It begins in *The Necklace* (1955), which establishes Tomlinson's territory (and difficulty) from the outset, with 'Aesthetic'. This poem deals with his way of seeing the world and his own sensory values. It reads, in its entirety:

Reality is to be sought, not in concrete,
But in space made articulate:
The shore, for instance,
Spreading between wall and wall;
The sea-voice
Tearing the silence from the silence.

---

[1] *Poetry Review* vol. 85, no. 4. Winter 95/6

'Reality' here, of course, implies an experiencing subject and Tomlinson himself has always been very aware of maintaining a healthy balance in his relationship with the natural world. In *Some Americans: A Personal Record* (1981), he recorded what he described then as his "own basic theme":

> one does not need to go beyond sense experience to some mythic union, that the 'I' can only be responsible in relationship and not by dissolving itself away into ecstasy or the Oversoul."[2]

In practice, the poet refuses to accept the incommunicability of the elements, taking as his territory the articulation of perception. His talent lies in solving the problem that that poses. As he writes in 'Sea Change':

> To define the sea –
> We change our opinions
> With the changing light.

All is both ephemeral and inexhaustible. The point is made, considering rain and tares (vetch) in 'Winter Encounters', from *Seeing is Believing* (1960) – a poem which heads the Tomlinson selection in Al Alvarez' influential 1962 anthology, *The New Poetry*:

> the sense
> That having met, one meets with more
> Than the words can witness. One feels behind
> Into the intensity that bodies through them
> Calmness within the wind, the warmth in cold.

The sense that nature is simply action defies our understanding. In 'At Delft' we learn of the contrasting human tentativeness. It is nature that superimposes its will on us:

> The light itself, diffused and indiscriminate
> On face and floor, usher us in,
> The guests of objects: as in a landscape,
> All that is human here stands clarified
> By all that accompanies and bounds

It is the same with the 'Civilities of Lamplight' where, in a deft image, the man's lamp holds darkness at bay, but it follows 'sealed' behind him as he walks the

[2] Quoted in *American Essays: Making it New* (Carcanet, 2001) p. 122

track. The poem 'At Holwell Farm' also questions the tenure of our domesticity. Our homes are merely attempts 'to grasp/In a given place and guard it well.'

If we are an uneasy presence in much of Tomlinson's early poetry, *A Peopled Landscape* (1963), Tomlinson's human subjects are not individuals but types – a farmer's wife, a hired hand. If they are named, they are portraits, allusions, headstones. Even one perfectly realised individual, the eponymous John Maydew, must share his (punning) title: 'John Maydew *or* TheAllotment.'

Nature, however, is captured in detail. In 'Winter-Piece', for example, a walk from the frost- blind house, scatters rooks:

> Gates snap like gunshot
> as you handle them. Five-barred fragility
> sets flying fifteen rooks who go together
> silently ravenous above this winter-piece
> that will not feed them.

Place is porous, we learn in 'Winter.' What is wanted is 'a weather of being/an atmosphere/that we can inhabit' because houses are 'pervaded by a locality.'

As a visiting professor at the University of New Mexico, Charles Tomlinson was in a position to observe the lie of the land for his next book *American Scenes and Other Poems* (1966). At first, though, we are at home and snow embattled. In, 'The Snow Fences', 'they are fencing/the upland against those years, those clouds' of snow. Snow is blanketing all. It is a careful eye that will look on the weathercock, door or cup of other poems, to see beyond this utility to their significance in our perception.

The southwestern American scenes depict a number of unusual individuals, who have been left to flower idiosyncratically in that harsh country. Later, looking east, we meet Thomas Eakins, an artist whose realistic eye perfectly complements Tomlinson's own.

> Anatomy, perspective
> and reflection: a boat
> in three inclinations:
> to the wind, to the waves
> and to the picture-frame.
> Those are the problems. What
> does a body propose
> that a boat does not?
>
> ('A Garland for Thomas Eakins')

Tomlinson's landscapes inevitably involve a dialogue between man and place, as in the opening poem of his next collection, *The Way of a World* (1969). With 'Swimming Chenango Lake' we are close in spirit to Eakins again, for the scene is beautifully rendered in its detail:

There is a geometry of water, for this
  Squares off the clouds' redundances
And sets them floating in a nether atmosphere
  All angles and elongations:

Here the poet, as swimmer, can enter into the geometry, 'For to swim is also to take hold/ On water's meaning' and disturb it momentarily before 'The image he has torn/Flows-to behind him, healing itself', just as the wind can do when it 'is unscaping all images in the flowing obsidian.'

Written on Water (1972) is a painterly collection (its appearance having coincided with an exhibition of the poet's graphic work in London) and its subject is the necessary grappling with what is seen, in order to render it meaningfully. As 'Mistlines' reminds us, 'the mind is a hunter of forms.' Yet seeing is one thing, saying is another, as Tomlinson explains in 'Of Beginning Light':

The light of the mind is poorer
than beginning light: the shades
we find pigment for
poor beside the tacit
variety we can all see
yet cannot say:

'On Water', the opening poem, puzzles over the 'solid vacancies' of a medium which is inexhaustibly fascinating from an aesthetic point of view. The uniqueness of the poet's vision privileges revealing perspectives, such as that in 'The Lighthouse', which Tomlinson renders as, 'the church of some island sect/Who have known the mainland beliefs and have defected/Only to retain them in native purity.'

If the focus of the collection is on evanescence, as the title implies, it is also celebratory. There are affecting poems about the work of human hands, about Hardy and Williams (two of Tomlinson's masters) and the excellent 'Against Portraits', which pleads for the reality of the hesitant, the elusive, as opposed to the authority of portraiture.

Perception is troubled in Charles Tomlinson's next collection, *The Way In and Other Poems* (1974), which leaves an indelibly grim image of the Midlands. In the title poem, 'the way in' is by car, though hemmed in through 'the dismantlings of a neighbourhood.' Urban decay is a pre-eminent fact of life. In 'At Stoke' we face a land 'too handled to be primary.' Down the appropriately named 'Gladstone Street', 'the house started to subside/Towards the mines beneath.' In 'Midlands' it takes 'some god' to 'remember/The way the land lay' whereas, in 'The Marl Pits', the poet aspires to escape to, 'a language of water, light and air.' 'How Far', however, offers us no 'way in' to a more natural world, where light 'is a white lie' hiding the darkness of the incurably strange heart of flora.

In *The Shaft (*1978) deceptions abound, both in the human and natural worlds. In 'Charlotte Corday' Marat's murderer fails to bring peace, for it is 'the blade/Inherited the future now.' In 'Tree' the elm comes to be a 'stalking memorial of Dunsinane', appearing to move with the poet. In the title poem, the poet finds:

> the adit you entered by
> Filtered a leaf-light, a phosphorescence,
> Doubled by water to a tremulous fire
> And signalling you back to the moist door
> Into whose darkness you had turned aside
> Out of the sun of an unfinished summer.

The Flood (1981) attends to Tomlinson's heightened sense of the numinous, to what he calls in the poem to his teacher, Donald Davie ('Instead of an Essay'): 'an awareness of delight/I cannot name.' What is attractive in this collection - the variety aside - is Tomlinson's honest engagement with a natural world he confesses his ignorance of, in 'The Lesson':

> For twenty years here have not
> taught me to read with accuracy
> the signs either of earth or sky:

This is the poet at home in Gloucestershire. His other geographical passions are also in place: the northern coast of Italy, the American southwest. He gazes at the timelessness of these localities, but also at their rigorousness. In the title poem the poet vainly tries to divert the course of incessant rain from his house ('It was the night of the flood first took away/My trust in stone.').

If Tomlinson, by his own admission, cannot clearly read the signs of nature, he certainly describes them with virtuosity: the snow in 'Snow Signs', 'Piling its drifts in scallops, furls'; the tide in 'In the Estuary', its 'lunar ripple runs woven with the sunlight'; the 'clutching glitter' in 'San Fruttuoso.'

In the prose that ends *Notes from New York and Other Poems* (1984), Tomlinson writes of the 'flocculent plain' of cloud, as seen from a plane:

> they intensify for one that sense of things always moving, disintegrating, re-forming – the sense of a world which is never quite *there* because light and time have changed it.

The collection explores this idea of scrambled perspectives in a world accelerated by jet and car. Yet there is a strong spirit of place in the fifteen New York poems. At first he remains above the city, considering the Iroquois construction workers and the 'angle-poised' heron, but is soon amongst the cosmopolitan streets. There is equally a strong notion of the city as landscape of mist and shadows. In 'All Afternoon':

> the shadows have been building
> A city of their own within the streets,
> Carefully correcting the perspectives
> With dark diagonals,

The effect of this is not so much to make the everyday strange as to reveal the strange in the everyday.

The Collected Poems (1987), which reflected Tomlinson's Hardy-like sense of place, was followed by *The Return* (1987), a book that revisits Italy, the American southwest and Provence and illustrates in its prosody the variety that prompted Peter Levi to write: 'very few (poets) have been so experimental in rhythms inside the main stream of the English language.'[3]

Its title poem is one of Charles Tomlinson's finest, I think, an elegy for the wife of an old friend and fellow poet. In the poem, the two poets take the roads of thirty years before and remember the conversations the three of them had, as well as other voices from those hills, for 'We cannot climb these slopes without our dead':

> In the rise, the run, the fall of voices:
> Innumerable conversations chafe the air
> At thresholds and in alleys, street and square
> Of those who climbed this slope to work its soil,
> And phrases marrying a tongue and time
> Coil through the mind's ear, climbing now with us
> Through orchids and the wild asparagus:
> For place is always an embodiment
> And incarnation beyond argument,

Northern Italy is always a celebration of some sort in Charles Tomlinson's poetry; it is a landscape, a people, an art that he has always loved, and the first part of *The Return* invokes the return of springtime, the Proserpine myth. Tomlinson's sensibilities are on show, also, in a number of poems involving artists (Cézanne, Braque, Soutine, Mondrian), a reminder that the poet is also an accomplished artist himself. In 'The Unpainted Mountain' the poet and his wife discuss the changing scene:

> Where was the mountain that the painter painted?
> It was the light, you said, had changed it all,

---

[3] Quoted in Charles Tomlinson *The Return* (OUP 1987).

Sure enough the consternation is dispelled with a sudden 'seam of light' which reveals Mont Ste-Victoire in all its painterly glory, 'altar more than hill.' It is yet again the alchemical key in 'At Huexotla,' where the travellers are drawn by the sound of songbirds:

> for its was light's
> reflection had set
> those cages in loud accord
> and only night would staunch it.

This most quintessential of Charles Tomlinson's collections ends with a number of poems from home, poems which deal with the 'ardent geometry of dwelling.'

Annunciations (1989) evokes Italian religious art to provide a secular vision, prompted by 'the flashing wing of sunlight,' of the daily rebirth of light, which 'asks the name anew/of each thing named' ('Annunciation'). We have here the curious sense that it is the human that seems immutable, the landscape changeable. 'True,' Tomlinson says in 'In New Mexico':

> You could pick up a stone and feel
> That was a tight world still, but the white
> Seed of the cottonwood as the breeze that was shaping
> the cloud
> Took hold of the tree and shook it,
> Was drifting across the sand like shreds of sky.

The exuberance of *Annunciations* is a little more muted in *The Door in the Wall* (1992), though it is a typically well-travelled collection and with the characteristic revelations: of things metamorphosed by light, the elements, time or human agency. Perhaps the dizzying change of locales in place and time give it a restlessness ('Shearsmen and poets travel far these days,' he writes to Les Murray). The poem 'In A Cambridge Garden,' which takes the form of a second conversation with fellow poet, Octavio Paz, includes Tomlinson's statement of his mission, as he once conceived it:

> I thought
> That I could teach my countrymen to see
> The changing English light, like water
> That drips off a gunwhale driving through the sea,
> Showing the way the whole world
> Dipping through space and cloud and sun,
> Surges across the day as it travels on
> Turning.

He has been indefatigable in this. However, there has also been the other kind of celebration in Tomlinson, the human warmth we saw in 'The Return.' The title poem here is, to me, the collection's most memorable. It is dedicated to the memory of the Spanish poet, Jorge Guillén, and deals metaphorically with the art and the life. In the poem the reader has a tantalising glimpse of the cornucopia a hidden garden suggests:

> Under the door in the wall
> the slit of sun
> pours out at the threshold
> such an illumination,

The poem also treads the lived life, 'this broken pathway/where the sun does not dazzle' and

> where the print and seal
> the travelling foot has set
> declares, Jorge Guillén,
> the integrity of the planet.

Jubilation (1995) announces Tomlison's retirement from teaching (his title punning on the Spanish *jubilación*, meaning 'retirement'). We would not expect it to constrict his activities and indeed it does not; poems visit Japan, Portugal, Italy and return, as always, to Gloucestershire. Nevertheless there is a taking stock. The opening sequential poem addresses his family, with its four generations. In the title poem, a verse letter, the poet describes the contentment of retirement. Typically the poem ends with the poet preparing his garden whilst contemplating further travel. There is a descriptive sureness, a physicality in detail and a sense of history in poems like 'Valestrieri' and 'A Retrospect: 1951-91,' which describes La Serra:

> We first came here to streets that have withstood
>   Corsair and scimitar. A poor place then,
> But its stone severity hospitable
>   With wine and conversation round a fire
> That stung the eyes with woodsmoke.

Despite its title, *The Vineyard Above the Sea* (1999), focuses on places rather than place. It celebrates a number of familiar Mediterranean sites. He is, as always, an indefatigable companion, pointing out the moment's not to be missed and then hinting at a significance beyond their unaffected glory. 'Alchemy' is as much a Charles Tomlinson word as 'Eden' is. So, in 'Mythology' he locates the Greek invention of mythology: 'The Greeks must have got it from clouds.' 'Oporto' is animated by a surrealistic fusion of religion and nature:

And then the river
overflowed and rose
uphill through
the long canals of streets:
it mistook
the churches for cliffs
and the chapels within
for sea-caves
and covered them
with an amour
of golden molluscs.

The inventiveness recalls the earlier alabaster Virgin 'as patient as the ammonite/ coiled in the cliff', in The Door in the Wall's 'In a Cornish Church'.

In the later part of the book Tomlinson's sense of history shades us back into the southwest of England, a place as atmospheric – if not as well lit – as the Mediterranean: 'You have only to scratch this county and/Up come the oyster shell and tegulae/Of Rome' ('The Gift').

The thematic heart of *Skywriting* (2003) lies in lines that seem to be a recapitulation of the central theme in Charles Tomlinson's work. In 'Spem in Alium' (echoing a response from the Latin rite on which Tallis' motet is based) Tomlinson begins:

I have placed my hope in no other god but thee,
Transfiguring spirit of poetry,
And as the levels of the landscape rise
In roofline, tree and hill before my eyes,
Until the clouds themselves are earthed in light,
Their changes show the world is not complete
And never will be, as we read its book,
Transfiguration glancing with each look,
Whenever light (changing itself) descries
Another variation for the eyes,

Here, having substituted the word 'poetry' for 'God of Israel', the secular poet offers praise for the inexhaustibility of creation's moods.

Charles Tomlinson's *Cracks in the Universe* (2006) is as strong a collection as *The Return*. Here the poet's tutelary gods – Ovid and the Impressionists - are more overtly involved. Then there are more autobiographical moments here, like the bitter-sweet reminiscences of learning to paint and paint with words in 'Lessons'. Everywhere this book is marked by what he calls in 'Bread and Stone', 'the commonplace miraculous', the momentary deeper visions which the book's title signifies (as good a thumbnail description of Tomlinson's poetry as any). There are the bravura performances that the poet can achieve with water and reflections such as 'In a Glass of Water':

> Cheap jewels flash
> up from the inside of a glass
> which I am draining –

Reflection and refraction have given themselves to Tomlinson's art throughout his career. His willingness to see is matched by unflagging, restless curiosity – 'I ask myself what Fishkill must be like' ('A Name on the Map') - and by joy at renewal:

> Why does this repetition
> Return out of the sky each year
> As manna falling, dew upon the sense,
> Renewal of the place one finds it in?
> ('Seasons')

I said at the outset that *I feel it is important that we remind ourselves of Charles Tomlinson's stature and contribution.* I should end by adding that Oxford and now Carcanet have been instrumental in trying to do that, Oxford with their 1985 *Collected* (and then 1997 *Selected*), and Carcanet with *New Collected Poems*, which came out this year. The difference between the two *Collected* is more than simply the addition of succeeding volumes, because approximately twenty poems from the first four volumes have been omitted from the earlier collected. However, that pales in light of the addition of the seven complete books to the latter. It is clearly worth Caracanet's reminding the prospective reader that Donald Davie, Octavio Paz and William Carlos Williams each held Tomlinson's work in high esteem, though I cannot help thinking that living voices might have been added to the chorus of praise on the back of *New Collected Poems*.

At any rate to, spend time with the book is to be staggered by the tirelessness of the poet's amazement: he wakes to 'the coin-clear harness-jingle' of a float (1951); feels 'challenged/ and replenished' by focusing attention on to two cups on a table (1966); wonders at 'the shadows that seam/and grain' a cloud (1978); studies an unseeing falcon from the 'glazed interior' of a room (1987); tastes 'the texture of the air half serge half silk' (1995); imagines leaves 'preparing to drink light' (2003). For over fifty years he has been on the qui vive.

In his *Lives of the Poets*, Michael Schmidt wrote of Tomlinson's 'first major collections' as appearing in 1969 and 1972 (*The Way of the World* and *Written on Water*)[4]. What we learn from *New Collected Poems* is that his last twenty

---

[4] Michael Schmidt, *Lives of the Poets (Weidenfeld and Nicolson,* 1998)

years have been his finest. From *The Return* (1987) to *Cracks in the Universe* (2006), Tomlinson (born 1927) has perfected to a high degree his unusual talent for being conscious of the moment. In these later volumes he seems also more at peace: 'A day like this,' he writes in 'Thomas Jones in Naples, 1782', 'how little one has need of/To make that little much.' What 'little' is needed is not talent, but seeing, attention – something we all have access to. It is in the expression of that attention that Tomlinson, like the artists he admires, has found his talent. Infinite patience has brought its reward.

So, the cumulative effect of reading Charles Tomlinson's work is quite exhilarating. Whilst being ecologically sensitive, it is essentially celebrative and encourages us to appreciate the daily wonders of light and living. In a *The New York Review of Books* an article on the American painter George Inness last year, Andrew Butterfield quoted from Henry Ward Beecher's 1868 novel, *Norwood*, in which the author argues that 'most landscape painters were mere copyists of nature in her more material aspects', who 'see only matter, not mind, in nature.' Beecher went on to argue that, 'It is the amount of one's self in a picture that determines whether it is made by an artist or an artisan.'[5] Charles Tomlinson has dedicated his life's work to witnessing the many minds of nature and portraying the thrilled self in dynamic relationship with them.

---

[5] Andrew Butterfield, 'The Genius of George Inness' September 25th, 2008

Tony Roberts

Robert Lowell: Late Victorian

Shall I sonnet-sing you about myself?
Do I live in a house you would like to see?
Is it scant of gear, has it store of pelf?
Unlock my heart with a sonnet-key
Browning 'House'

On the front cover of its June 2nd 1967 edition, *Time* magazine featured a cartoon of Robert Lowell's head in a laurel wreath. Inside, where Lowell was acknowledged, 'by rare critical consensus, the best American poet of his generation', Edmund Wilson offered the opinion that Lowell 'has achieved a poetic career on the old nineteenth century scale'. Both remarks had a great deal of truth in them, at least at the time of the public Lowell (roughly from 1946 to 1970, when he left for England). In this, the fiftieth anniversary of the appearance of his influential *Life Studies*, it is interesting to reconsider what gave Lowell and his work their authority and pre-eminence.

What was 'Victorian' about Robert Lowell (1917-1977) was his willingness to stride the public stage, his ambition, the natural assurance in his voice and his prolific output (nineteen books). There were other features: a fondness for cloaking himself in the past, for example, or the inner war between personal belief and doubt. However, the salient feature was that, unlike most poets of his time and since, he would willingly take on the grand narratives; he would assume the public voice. Characteristically, his tone was authoritative, his cadences confident, his metrics assured. These belied the constant revisions in his work and his readiness to seek advice, which friends and colleagues noted for the most part approvingly, since it humanised him. Though privately subject to a bipolar disorder, which rendered him manic at intervals and played hell with his relationships, readers initially related to Lowell's public certainties and the high drama with which he expressed them. Later his wry vision, openness and bemused humility struck another chord.

His career was like that of some Shakespearean tragic hero, full of talent, ambition and gesture, flushed with success and yet flawed with the mania. His trajectory would have been perfect for the Elizabethan stage. From the tense and cluttered heroic style of his early poetry, where he took on the world, to the exhausted, personal and elegiac nature of his last, Lowell found a style to suit each major modulation.

Although clearly writing in the American-European tradition, Lowell was both of and yet not of his generation. In a late poem, 'For John Berryman', he spelt out what made the two of them emblematic of their generation of fêted, fated poets (a generation which included Delmore Schwarz , Theodore

Roethke and Elizabeth Bishop):

> Yet really we had the same life,
> the generic one
> our generation offered
> (*Les Maudits* – the compliment
> each American generation
> pays itself in passing):
> first students, then with our own,
> our galaxy of grand maîtres,
> our fifties' fellowships
> to Paris, Rome and Florence,
> veterans of the Cold War not the War –
> all the best of life ...
> then daydreaming to drink at six,
> waiting for the iced fire,
> even the feel of the frosted glass,
> like waiting for a girl ...
> if you had waited.
> We were asked to be obsessed with writing,
> and we were.

There is a note of generosity here to friend and rival. The notion that they had 'the same life', *mutatis mutandis,* ignores a significant aspect of the Lowell heritage, one Elizabeth Bishop memorably expressed:

> I must confess (and I imagine most of your contemporaries would confess the same thing) that I am green with envy of your kind of assurance..... all you have to do is put down the names! And the fact that it seems significant, illustrative, American, etc. gives you, I think, the confidence you display about tackling any idea or theme, seriously, in both writing and conversation. In some ways you are the luckiest poet I know! – in some ways not so lucky, either, of course.1

These 'names' were the (Massachusetts Bay Colony) Winslows, the (Somerset) Lowells and the (Orkney Island) Spences, generations of New England aristocracy descended from seventeenth century entrepreneurs. One needs to remember the patrician side of Lowell, the 'lucky' side, if only because others always did, just as one should remember the unlucky side, the bouts of mental illness that regularly afflicted him.

Early Lowell clangs with stentorian tones, outdoing the Victorians at their

---

[1] David Kalstone, *Becoming a Poet* (The Hogarth Press, 1989) p. 191

most self-confident. Faith, history and family were his subjects. He can speak with repressed fury, delivering jeremiads at our Christian failures in stern metres and deploying the whole Grand Guignol arsenal of effects: tight metres, raging alliterations, howling assonance, thumping monosyllables, wild personifications and metaphors:

> Here the jack-hammer jabs into the ocean;
> My heart, you race and stagger and demand
> More blood-gangs for your nigger-brass percussions
>
> ('Colloquy in Black Rock')

> Until the snake-tailed sea-winds coughed and howled
> For alms outside the church whose double locks
> Wait for St. Peter, the distorted key.
>
> ('New Year's Day')

> The world out-Herods Herod; and the year,
> The nineteen-hundred forty-fifth of grace,
> Lumbers with losses up the clinkered hill
> Of our purgation
>
> ('The Holy Innocents')

Selden Rodman wrote of Lowell's voice in *Lord Weary's Castle*, as being 'savage enough to waken all but the dead.'[2] – and those he might have shaken in their graves. The fierceness was hardly feigned. At this time Lowell had taken to his Catholic conversion with a terrifying seriousness, apparently. The style and intention of early Lowell were memorably described in the *Kenyon Review* by Howard Moss (used on the book's dust jacket):

> Lowell is that surprising phenomenon, a religious poet who writes like a revolutionary.[3]

Certainly the combination of a betrayed God and an unredeemed Man was an explosive mixture. Yet there were some more finely nuanced performances, too, in this Pulitzer Prize winning collection, quieter moments in his explorations of New England's past and his anti war poems and translations. Most memorable is Lowell's magnificent, 'The Quaker Graveyard in Nantucket', the high point of this early style. The poem is a lament for the war dead, the whaling dead, the hurt to Nature and the survival of the Lord's obscured purposes, frequently delivered in ringing metaphors shown here in verses iii, iv, and vii:

---

[2] Ian Hamilton, *Robert Lowell: A Biography* (Faber, 1983) p. 122

[3] Ibid. p. 123

They died
When time was open-eyed,
Wooden and childish; only bones abide
There, in the nowhere, where their boats were tossed
Sky-high, where mariners had fabled news
Of IS, the whited monster.

This is the end of the whaleroad and the whale
Who spewed Nantucket bones on the thrashed swell
And stirred the troubled waters to whirlpools
To send the Pequod packing off to hell

Atlantic, you are fouled with the blue sailors,
Sea-monsters, upward angel, downward fish:
Unmarried and corroding, spare of flesh
Mart once of supercilious, wing'd clippers,
Atlantic, where your bell-trap guts its spoil
You could cut the brackish winds with a knife
Here in Nantucket, and cast up the time
When the Lord God formed man from the sea's slime

Clearly it wasn't a febrile, religious style alone that kept Robert Lowell afloat. It was also this vivid sense of American and European history and culture. All Lowell's work was marbled with history from the outset. As he explained in an interview with Stanley Kunitz in 1964:

> The kind of poet I am was largely determined by the fact that I grew up in the heyday of the New Criticism, with Eliot's magic scrutiny of the text as a critical example. From the beginning I was preoccupied with technique, fascinated by the past, and tempted by other languages. It is hard for me to imagine a poet not interested in the classics. The task is to get something new into old forms, even at the risk of breaking them."[4]

As an unhappy, farouche Harvard student Lowell had taken the opportunity to bolt south, acting as a 'secretary' to Ford Madox Ford in order to join Allen Tate in Clarksville, Tennessee in April 1937. From there he went on to study with John Crowe Ransom at Kenyon College, Ohio, where he met Randall Jarrell. It was the heyday of their New Criticism. What he learnt in his salad days (including the Southern inflexion to his speaking voice) was as formative as the support these established poets offered (though later Lowell was to escape Eliot and Tate's cult of impersonality and formality).

---

[4] Stanley Kunitz, 'Talk with Robert Lowell', in Jeffrey Meyers, ed. Robert Lowell: *Interviews and Memoirs* (Michigan, 1998) p. 85

His first, slight book, *Land of Unlikeness* (1944), had begun with the dead of history. In 'The Park Street Cemetery' we are with 'the stern surnames: Adams,/Otis, Hancock, Mather, Revere', and Allen Tate writes in his forward:

> in a young man like Lowell... there is at least a memory of the spiritual dignity of man, now sacrificed to mere secularization and a craving for mechanical order.[5]

Lord Weary's Castle (1946), which contained revised versions from the debut collection, is awash with historical figures – whalers, an inscrutable God, Virgil, Napoleon, etc. – and also with the skulduggeries of New England's past

> Behind King's Chapel what the earth has kept
> Whole from the jerking noose of time extends
> Its dark enigma to Jehoshaphat;
> Or will King Philip plait
> The just man's scalp in the wailing valley! Friends,
> Blacker than these black stones the subway bends
> About the dirty elm roots and the well
> For the unchristened infants in the waste
> Of the great garden rotten to its root

The 'subway' brings 'At the Indian Killer's Grave' into our own time, but the rhetorical flow is as darkly metaphorical as a hell fire sermon. To Lowell, what has slipped is our Christian faith. From a violent God, Lowell turns to the violence of the military. Both have power, both have a terrible swift sword, accomplishments he relished in his early poetry. In fact, there was always a scarcely veiled struggle in Lowell between the liberal and the conservative. As he explained in the 1964 interview Stanley Kunitz:

> One side of me, for example, is a conventional liberal, concerned with causes, agitated about peace and justice and equality, as so many people are. My other side is deeply conservative, wanting to get at the roots of things, wanting to slow down the whole modern process of mechanization and dehumanization, knowing that liberalism can be a form of death too.[6]

What predominated in the early Lowell, notwithstanding, was his eschatological sense, as well as a certain Browning-like attraction to the

---

[5] Frank Bidart and David Gewanter (ed.) *Robert Lowell: Collected Poems*, (Farrar, Straus and Giroux, 2003) p. 860

[6] Kunitz, op cit, p. 85

perversity of power.

With *Lord Weary's Castle* Lowell had found his voice and was listened to. In a rave review, Peter Viereck predicted that he could become:

> the great American poet of the 1950s, for he seems the best qualified to restore to our literature its sense of the tragic and the lofty.7

The pressure on Lowell to fulfil this destiny led him next to the *The Mills of the Kavanaughs* (1951), a monologue as unsatisfactory as early and late Browning, and then to eight years of creative rethinking (and recurrent illness) before he startled his critics with *Life Studies*, a National Book Award winner which has its roots in the prose autobiography he began as therapy. It was certainly a new incarnation, a new style, and a calming down for the poet, Christian issues being subdued.

In fact, what is striking is the tolerance in Lowell's voice in *Life Studies*, a product of his thinking over the prose autobiographical project, as well as a series of west coast readings which had required him to simplify lines - and perhaps of a simple boredom at repeating himself. At any rate, as Lowell explained to Randall Jarrell in October 1957:

> I've been loosening up the meter, as you'll see and horsing out all the old theology and symbolism and verbal violence.8

And in December he wrote to Elizabeth Bishop that he had 'gotten rid of my medieval armor's undermining.'[9] He left the history in, however. It was now his own. In the poem 'Commander Lowell' we find the seven year old Lowell at play with toy soldiers

> And I, bristling and manic,
> skulked in the attic,
> and got two hundred French generals by name,
> from *A* to *V* – from Augereau to Vandamme.
> I used to dope myself asleep,
> naming those unpronounceables like sheep.

From the start his imaginative identification had returned to the ancient classical world and romped home through Europe to New England (and the Lowells). Now his manner was to litter his presence with the past. In 'Grandparents', for example, the ghosts of his inherited home are the 'Ancient

---

[7] Steven Gould Axelrod, *Robert Lowell: Life and Art* (Princeton, 1979) p. 49

[8] Saskia Hamilton, *The Letters of Robert Lowell* (Faber, 2005), p. 295

[9] Ibid. p. 306

Regime'. He also plays acquaintances against historical characters (in his poetry and, apparently, during his manic bouts). So, in the prose extract, '91 Revere Street', Lowell wrote of his ancestor:

> He was a dark man, a German Jew – no downright Yankee, but maybe such a fellow as Napoleon's mad, pomaded son-of-an-innkeeper general, Junot, Duc D' Abrantes; a man like mad George III's pomaded, disreputable son, 'Prinny', the Prince Regent.

Later in that same collection, in the harrowing 'Waiting in the Blue', he writes of a fellow inmate of McLean's Hospital:

> the hooded night lights bring out 'Bobbie,'
> Porcellian '29,
> a replica of Louis XVI
> without the wig –
> redolent and roly-poly as a sperm whale,
> as he swashbuckles about in his birthday suit
> and horses at chairs.

The new Lowell of *Life Studies* remained as compelling as the earlier, but in a completely different way. After four poems in his established style, the prose extract described moments from his uncomfortable childhood in Boston. He presents himself as the 'disloyal' son of a shrill, domineering mother. His ineffectual father's 'downhill progress as a civilian and Bostonian' provides much of the understated pathos of the extract '91 Revere Street'. The poetry that follows grows from the dysfunctions of family.

'My Last Afternoon with Uncle Devereux Winslow' gives the measure of the new Lowell in its openness and descriptive flair:

> Uncle Deveroux stood behind me.
> He was as brushed as Bayard, our riding horse.
> His face was putty.
> His blue coat and white trousers
> grew sharper and straighter.
> His coat was a blue jay's tail,
> his trousers were solid cream from the top of the bottle.

Here the repetitive construction is deceptive. The imagery is taken from a child's world, the repetition mimics the repeatedly returning glance.

Lowell's insight had been that he could filter history through himself. His first great themes had been faith and power, which he had dealt with in an impassioned manner. Now he had begun to learn to stand against his own rhetorical flow, to puzzle openly over the battle ground of himself, his own past and relationships. With an openly autobiographical work he popularised himself with those readers who responded to intimacy and fine writing. This was not 'confession,' as M. L. Rosenthal's judged it to be in his influential 1959 review for 'The Nation.' However self-deprecating the poet seemed, his first impulse was not the admission of guilt, so much as the exploration of behaviour. Besides, Art was always there. As he explained to Frederick Seidel, in a 1961 *Paris Review* interview, 'The reader was to believe he was getting the *real* Robert Lowell.'[10]

After *Life Studies* and the Lowelling of European poetry in *Imitations* (1961) – transpositions into the poet's sensibility - he moved with *For the Union Dead* (1964) and *Near the Ocean* (1967) into an increasingly public role, when his Cold War status (as a WWII pacifist) and his nuclear fears chimed perfectly with the liberal wing of the national mood. Lowell might be the tortured artist (by the bipolar disorder) but he was also a worried citizen and certified man of conscience. His poems now seemed to enter more wholly into the public domain, aided by his increasing literary and celebrity status. He expressed the international fear over the nuclear future in 'Fall 1961':

> All autumn, the chafe and jar
> of nuclear war;
> we have talked our extinction to death.

and later, in 'Waking Early Sunday Morning,' lamented America's self-styled mission in a dangerous world:

> Pity the planet, all joy gone
> from this sweet volcanic cone;
> peace to our children when they fall
> in small war on the heels of small
> war – until the end of time
> to police the earth, a ghost
> orbiting forever lost
> in our monotonous sublime

Lowell had courted the attention paid him, however indirectly. In a repetition of his public refusal to undergo the draft in September 1943 ('Member of Famed Family Balks at Military Service' – reported the Bowling Green 'Sentinel')[11] , he also rejected an invitation to participate in a White House Arts Festival in 1965, infuriating President Johnson because of the rumpus the proposed propaganda event caused. In both cases Lowell had shown an initial, understandable willingness to participate, then changed

---

[10] Frederick Seidel, 'The Art of Poetry: Robert Lowell' in Meyers, op cit, p. 57

[11] Hamilton, op cit, p. 90

his stance. In sending notification of his Johnson refusal to the *New York Times*, however, he would have known he would inevitably garner publicity for himself, albeit that his motive was to publicly protest at U.S. foreign policy.

Certainly Lowell's credentials as a public intellectual were impeccable, political, almost starry. In late 1965 he escorted Jackie Kennedy to the opening night of a friend's play. In later 1967, after his *Time* front cover, he agreed to campaign for Eugene McCarthy, who had decided to challenge Johnson for the Democratic Party's presidential nomination. Further, his patrician nature was about to be immortalised by Norman Mailer, who wrote an account in *The Armies of the Night* of how he and Lowell were amongst those caught up in the reaction to the October 1967 anti-Vietnam march on the Pentagon. Lowell is a hero of the book, admired by Mailer:

> Robert Lowell gave of at times the unwilling haunted saintliness of a man who was repaying the moral debts of ten generations of ancestors.[12]

Disillusion set in quickly with the national scene, nevertheless. Assassinations and urban violence, as well as the failure of politics left and right quelled his desire for the national platform. As he wrote to Donald Davie, he had 'no faith in idealist violence or in revolution'[13]. What is more, he told Al Alvarez in 1963, if he had an image of America

> it would be one taken from Melville's Moby Dick: the fanatical idealist who brings the world down in ruins through some sort of simplicity of mind.[14]

These ructions in society, the weariness brought on by recurrent ill health, and his foundering second marriage to Elizabeth Hardwick undermined his current faith in America and himself. Lowell decided to retrench. Besides, a certain wariness at being centre stage is evident in an interview with Ian Hamilton for *The Review* in 1971:

> You say I have become more overtly concerned with public events, but true public poetry must come as an inevitable accident. I grew up in anti artist-sage days, when Eliot and Picasso worked in one surprising style for some years, then surprised with another – maturing without becoming public voices or portents. Who wants to be on call to society? Have a resonant poem for each great issue?[15]

---

[12] Norman Mailer, *The Armies of the Night* (Signet,1968) p. 99

[13] Hamilton, op cit, p. 533

[14] A. Alvarez, 'Robert Lowell in Conversation' in Meyers, op cit, p. 77

[15] Ian Hamilton, 'A Conversation with Robert Lowell' in Meyers, op cit, p. 155

Lowell turned instead to history and, taking his cue from the Victorians (or Berryman), turned to the (modernist) sonnet form, in *Notebook 1967-68*, *Notebook (1970)* and, in 1973, *History* ('O there's a terrifying innocence in my face/ drenched with the silver salvage of the mornfrost.'). With *History* (1973) Lowell explored his subjects in unrhymed blank verse poems, filtering them through his own ego. The book came out of the earlier Notebook poems, which were originally caught in journal form over the course of a year. He explained to Peter Taylor in March 1972:

> I expect it to be a school text – an entirely old-fashioned history only considering Wars, Heroes, women, and myself.[16]

Despite the flippancy, this was a pretty good thumbnail sketch of *History*, which does indeed treat of those subjects, though the sonnets swallow some of his earlier *Imitations*, too. What *History* does do is to allow him to roam freely through European history and myth, donning cloaks whenever he desires. It could be argued that that is what Lowell had always done this to some extent, but never so completely.

By the time of these last books Lowell had relocated to England and Ireland with Caroline Blackwood. *For Lizzie and Harriet* (1973) collects *Notebook* poems for the wife and daughter he was leaving. Its final poem, 'Obit', begins with the words

> Our love will not come back on fortune's wheel

And ends with the heartbreaking

> After loving you so much, can I forget
> you for eternity and have no other choice?

He followed that with emotional irresponsibility in *The Dolphin* (1973), his partly fictionalised account of the end of his marriage to Elizabeth Hardwick and his new one to Caroline Blackwood. The book's last sonnet, 'Dolphin', ends with the steely admission:

> I have sat and listened to too many
> words of the collaborating muse,
> and plotted perhaps too freely with my life,
> not avoiding injury to others,
> not avoiding injury to myself –

---

[16] Hamilton, op cit, p. 588

to ask compassion ... this book, half-fiction,
an eelnet made by man for the eel fighting –

my eyes have seen what my hand did.

It did not dispel the criticisms. These are the lines which Adrienne Rich referred to as 'bullshit eloquence, a poor excuse for a cruel and shallow book'[17], given that they misused Hardwick's letters as poetic material.

Finally, a contrite and confused Lowell became the elegist, writing poems which were something of a return to form. Near his death, in *Day by Day* (1977), he acknowledged, perhaps, the lost plot of his life:

Those blessèd structures, plot and rhyme –
why are they not help to me now
I want to make
something imagined, not recalled?

At least it seemed that way. By now Lowell was exhausted. His heart attack in a New York taxi cab, returning to his second wife whilst clutching Freud's portrait of his third, had something of the dramatic gesture the Victorians had admired in the ancients.

Writing to George Santayana in February 1948, Lowell had taken Robert Browning to task, for failing to be what he might have been:

> I think Browning had all the right ideas about what the poetry of his time should take in – people and time. But (this is presumptuous) how he muffed it all! The ingenious, terrific metrics, shaking the heart out of what he was saying; the invented language; the short-cuts; the hurry; and (one must say it) the horrible self-indulgence – the attitudes, the cheapness! I write strongly, for he should, with patience, have been one of the great poets of the world. Anyway, he was on the side of the angels a lot of the time.[18]

That was in 1948. In 1977 – the year of his death – Lowell might have been more charitable. He might even have seen the shadow of his lesser moments in his remarks on that great Victorian.

---

[17] Richard Tillinghurst, *Robert Lowell's Life and Work* (Michigan, 1998) p. 55

[18] Hamilton, op cit, p.81

Anne Price-Owen

What says Dai's *mabinogi?*

This question concerns identity and multiculturalism in David Jones's literary and visual art. The title misquotes a line from David Jones's long poem *The Anathémata* (1952),[1] thereby altering the meaning of the subject, 'What says his *mabinogi?*'(A.207), where 'Dai' is substituted for '*his*'. Dai is a direct reference to David Jones, who earned the nickname *'Dai Greatcoat'* when he was living at Capel-y-ffin, in Wales's Black Mountains. Jones, who was always complaining about the cold, was often seen wandering about in his greatcoat. Moreover Dai Greatcoat is the title of his collected letters, sub-titled *a self-portrait of David Jones in his letters*.[2] Normally, we think of self-portraits as visual images, but René Hague, editor of the letters, obviously believed that Jones's writings could reveal as much about the artist as physiognomic images. Considering that Jones was living in Capel when he conceived writing *In Parenthesis* (1937[3]), it's unsurprising that the character of Dai insinuated himself into the poem, and that that Dai would share some of Jones's thoughts and beliefs.

The discussion commences with a question in the penultimate section of *The Anathémata*, in Part VII, tellingly entitled 'Mabinog's Liturgy'.(A.185-221) 'Mabinog' is a reference to the child, while liturgy tells the child's story. But because of 'liturgy's' correspondence with the rites of the Christian Church, especially the Eucharist, the Celtic story is thus an analogy of the Christian liturgy.

Accordingly, 'Mabinog's liturgy' means the liturgy of a child, 'based on the story of an infant'.[4] Section VII opens by placing the action at the time of Christ's Passion, and charts significant events connected with the preceding centuries, until the time and place of the Crucifixion. This was a time of transition, when the Classical gods and goddesses of Greece and Rome were worshipped, but whose powers of metamorphoses and transformation were subsumed into Christ, whose miracles include the transformation (or transubstantiation), of bread and wine into His own body and blood, and which He commanded his disciples to memorialize: 'Do this as oft as ye shall drink it, in remembrance of me', or as Jones puts it: as 'anamnesis', meaning 'in memorial'. Hence, Jones identified parallels between the Christian religion and *The Mabinogion*, Wales's oral epic which was committed to written form in about 1050. The

---

[1] David Jones, *The Anathémata: fragments of an attempted writing* (London: Faber and Faber, 1952), p. 207. Herein this book is referenced in the text as *A*.

[2] David Jones, *Dai Greatcoat: a self-portrait of David Jones in his letters*, edited by René Hague (London: Faber and Faber, 1980).

[3] David Jones, *In Parenthesis* (London: Faber and Faber, 1937), p.x. herein this book is referenced in the text as IP.

[4] René Hague, *A Commentary on The Anathémata of David Jones* (Wellingborough, 1977), p. 206.

latter concerns shapeshifting characters with superhuman powers, and was to the Celtic what Classical mythology was to the Greeks and Romans. But WHAT says his *mabinogi?*

What says his mabinogi?
Son of Mair, wife of jobbing carpenter
in via nascitur
Lapped in hay, *parvule.*(A.207)

In a nutshell, we learn that He wasn't born at home but in an alien stable, hence the reference to hay, that his mother's name was Mary and she was married to a humble carpenter.

That sums up the infant's tale, and leads to the second question. But before that, let's consider Dai – short for Dafydd, the Welsh form of David (Jones) – and his 'mabinogi'.

He was born in 1895, in Brockley, Kent. His father, who was from Holywell in Flintshire, left his native Wales to find work in London, and was employed as a printer's overseer with the *Christian Herald* newspaper. Jones's mother was a Londoner (whose genealogy could be traced back to Rome), and a competent watercolourist. Small wonder then, that Jones grew up in a household that 'took the printed page and its illustration for granted',[5] that he excelled in drawing and painting, and that he was a devout Christian. Moreover, he looked to both his Welsh roots as well as the influences of the Holy Roman Empire for his historical allusions in his literary and visual art.

Let us now examine the second question:

But what does his Boast say?
Alpha es et O

that which
The whole world cannot hold.
Atheling to the heaven-king.
Shepherd of Greekland.
Harrower of Annwn.
Freer of the Waters.
Chief Physician and
dux et pontifex.

Gwledig Noefoedd and
Walda of *every* land
et vocabitur WONDERFUL. (A.207-8)

[5] David Jones, *The Dying Gaul and other writings* (London: Faber and Faber, 1978), p. 23.

The tale of Christ's infancy contrasts with the 'Boast of his maturity, which is expressed in terms of the Celtic, classical and Judaeo-Christian tradition.'[6] The first line recalls the Apocalypse, I.8, 'Atheling' refers to the prince of royal blood, (David's line), 'Shepherd of Greekland', is there because, although the pastoral metaphor is Judaic, it is also Greek, and the 'Good Shepherd' comes to us through Greece. 'Harrower of Annwn' & 'Freer of the Waters' reference two stories from *The Mabinogion*, the first being that of Pwyll, Prince of Dyfed who descends into Hell, while the second alludes to Peredur, who is also the Chief Physician and Healer.[7]

This boast concerns Christ's courage by associating Him with heroes from alternative cultures who performed similar deeds long before Christ's birth. In Wales, the principal bard recites the boast by singing the praises of the Chief, and listing his triumphal battles and heroic feats. The bard was a key figure in recording the superiority of his Chief's court, and publicizing his achievements. It was when he was at Capel-y-ffin that Jones became conscious of his Welsh heritage, realizing that:

> The bards of an earlier Wales referred to themselves as 'carpenters of song'. Carpentry suggests a fitting together, and ... the English word 'artist' means, at root, someone concerned with a fitting of some sort ... Round about 1924-6 I was at last understanding something of the nature of the particular 'carpentry' which most sorted with my inclinations ... circumstances occasioned my living in Nant Honddu, ... to feel the impact of the strong hill-rhythms and the bright counter-rhythms of the afonydd dyfroedd [water brooks] which make of Wales such a 'plurabelle'.[8]

The introduction of the Boast scene to 'Mabinog's Liturgy' legitimizes the Celtic ethos of this section, although the Classical & Judaeo-Christian traditions are retained, so that all these cultures coalesce within the poem. Even the variety of rhythms, languages and intermix of verse and prose signify the universality of the theme: the argosy of the Redeemer. It is therefore non-specific and cosmic in its conception. These features are also communicated in Jones's painted inscription, 'What says his mabinogi', that was made six years after *The Anathémata* was published, and Jones returned to the poem's text especially to make it. By this time he'd been experimenting with painted

---

[6] René Hague, *A Commentary on The Anathémata of David Jones* (Wellingborough: Christopher Skelton, 1977), p. 223.

[7] Cf. René Hague, *A Commentary on The Anathémata of David Jones* (Wellingborough: Christopher Skelton, 1977), p. 223.

[8] David Jones, *Epoch and Artist* (London: Faber and Faber, 1959), pp. 29-30.

inscriptions, most of which are in languages other than English. The English language here is visually florid, because Jones wished to imbue it with Celtic flourishes. Mair is particularly decorative, and her name is accented in olive green, as is 'parvule' and 'Alpha es et O', thus distinguishing these key nouns from the remaining text. Jones also added a Christmas greeting in Welsh and Latin which frames three sides of the inscription. He often used more than one language in his inscriptions, in order to suggest the ethos of the time and culture that are evoked by the language. He does the same in his poetic texts, believing that the original language resonates the precise meaning he required.

'What says his mabinogi' (1958) is on heavy paper. Many of his earlier inscriptions are on thin paper, and it's a measure of the importance he put on his later inscriptions which were perceived as serious works of art, that he dispensed with cheap paper, and spent a good deal of time working on the layout, colours and letter-forms. In this, the background is under-painted in Chinese white to create luminosity behind the lettering, and there are traces of red, grey and yellow painting under the black, showing that he had formerly introduced a range of colours, before finally deciding on these, possibly to connote the seriousness of the message. By painting white around the lettering, as well as beneath it, it allowed him to correct or modify the shapes. While the overall effect of the alphabetical forms is Celtic, there are also instances of Greek, Latin and Saxon styles that reference the original languages. Fittingly, he used the Welsh Dafyd J. to sign the work, and adds in Welsh 'a'm gwaith' [made this].

There is clearly more than meets the eye in the passage responding to 'What says his *mabinogi?*' This is because, as Jones maintains in his Preface he, like Nennius, who wrote the *Historia Brittonum* in c.829/830, also 'made a heap of all that [he] could find'. (A.9) His findings are inextricably linked to his own life story – his mabinogi – where he recalls everything that has influenced him. Accordingly, he can justify that:

> this writing ... is about one's own 'thing', which *res*, is unavoidably part and parcel of the Western Christian *res*, as inherited by a person whose perceptions are totally conditioned and limited by and dependent upon his being indigenous to this island ... there are the further conditionings contingent upon his being a Londoner, of Welsh and English parentage, of Protestant upbringing, of Catholic subscription... such biological accidents are ... responsible for most of the content. (A.11)

To that effect, Jones created a painted inscription in honour of these influences. 'Parentibus Meis'(1952) doubles as a frontispiece and gives an overview of his approach to the work. Being entirely in Latin, he implies that the inscription relates the bloodline of the British to the Roman past, with the crux of the poem centring on the time of Christ's Passion. In English it reads: 'To my parents and forebears and to all the inhabitants of the island of the race of the

Britons.' Ultimately, the reader is prepared for allusions to the effects of the past on the present. The inscription is a commemorative tribute, by colour and arrangement of the words, as Nicolete Gray explains:

> The incidence of the red, INDIGENIS GENTIS and the P of PRIOR, highlight the recalling of all past generations back to the Roman Britons in affectionate greeting. The piece is v. simple in both layout & lettering, making it easy to trace the interrelation of letter-forms. The pattern of Os, the open spacing of the last line, the ligatures ET in the 4th line, & TT in the penultimate line, the slightly slanted movement of N, increasing in the lower lines & halted by the T in the final line, all build up in concert into a complex, yet balanced, rhythm.[9]

Jones's composition for this work complements the text accompanying the inscription in the double page spread, which shows the structured layout of the outset of the poem, where the priest is saying Mass. The Mass is a recurring motif in the poem, a sign that recalls various times and places throughout time until the present day. The layout of the pages, although not a mirror-image, forms a mutually reflective pattern which demonstrates Jones's conviction that 'the task of any artist in any material, [is] that whatever he makes must necessarily show forth what is his by this or that inheritance'(*A*.9), and that the artist's legacy, what has been passed down to him through the ages, is worthy of recalling.

Nowhere is this more apparent than in Jones's epic poem, *In Parenthesis,* (1937), which recounts his experiences in the trenches during the Great War. In spite of its personal reflections, it too deals with universal themes, reminding us that Jones proceeded from the particular to the general, in order to tackle themes that are common to humanity. The evidence for this is no more clearly illustrated than in the central section of the poem, Dai's Boast.

This section is, as Thomas Dilworth observes, a 'micropoem'[10] of the whole, and Jones imparts his own thought-mantle to the figure of Dai. At first, the Dai who recites the Boast, appears not as the soldier-poet David Jones, but as a Welsh warrior who takes on the role of the Welsh bard to relate the achievements of his Ruler. This Dai is literally at the core of the poem, where, to quote Dilworth again, his 'boast is a catalogue of military service extending back through history and quasi-historical legend to mythological time immemorial.'[11] This legendary figure differs from Jones's persona which

---

[9] Nicolete Gray, *The Painted Inscriptions of David Jones* (London: Gordon Fraser, 1981), p. 32.

[10] Thomas Dilworth, *The Shape of Meaning in the Poetry of David Jones* (University of Toronto Press, 1988), p. 108.

[11] Thomas Dilworth, *The Shape of Meaning in the Poetry of David Jones* (University of Toronto Press, 1988), p. 108.

is consolidated in the character of Private John Ball. Jones himself declared that as a soldier he was a 'knocker over of piles, a parade's despair'. (*IP*.xv) Such self-effacing remarks display Jones's modesty, for he was, by all accounts, a crack shot at the beginning of the war, but by 1918, when disillusion set in, he was a third-rater! The unkempt soldier is actually sourced in Malory's *Morte d'Arthur* Bk.IX , known as Dai de la Cote mal taile. (*IP*.70) This dishevelled knight's 'over-garment sat over-thwartly,' while his presence injects the text with comic moments that recall Jones's own sense of humour. However, as Pte John Ball, who carries the narrative forward, he is a more sympathetic sad-clown figure, whose 'pack, ill adjusted and without form, hangs ... heavily on his soldier blades ... and ... a sense of ill-usage pervades him.' (*IP*.2) But above all, Jones is in effect, the Dai of the Great Boast, and he, like both the comic soldier, and Pte Ball 'adjusts his slipping shoulder-straps, wraps close his misfit outsize greatcoat, [before] articulating his English (boast) with an alien care.' (*IP*.79) Dai is the mouthpiece for Jones's long monologue (albeit with the odd interruption from other soldiers' interjections), which sums up Jones's own thoughts on the history of war in the West. Dilworth argues that this is his archetypal mode, where he claims to have participated in an ensuing list of battles so that Dai as a character, is no longer distinct from his predecessors, but 'recalls the distant past in the first person singular, which he ... combines with the present tense to transform identification into anamnesis [or memorial]'.[12] Thus, he finds himself in a disparate range of conflicts, timescales and peoples which gives credence to his soldier's universal, multi-faceted persona. In other words, Dai is part of our tradition, and has always been with us, and the Boast scene supports this notion by ending with the soldiers bursting into song:

> Old soljers
> Never die, never die,
>   Old soljers never die, they never die,
>   They
> Simply fade away. (*IP*.84)

As the archetype of mankind, Dai displays our strengths and frailties. He is a human being, and this is how Jones entitled his self-portrait in oils, in 1931 (a couple of years after he'd begun working on *In Parenthesis*, and just a year before the first draft was completed),[13] showing that he prefers to be considered a typical human being, not a specific individual. The common man, and also Christ who was made in the image of man, are Jones's subjects.

Saunders Lewis recognized Jones's Everyman concept, proposing that:

[12] Thomas Dilworth, *The Shape of Meaning in the Poetry of David Jones* (University of Toronto Press, 1988), pp. 110-111.

[13] Paul Hills, *David Jones* (London: Tate Gallery, 1981), p. 57.

> it ... grew into part of his make-up, ... that the soldier is the normal Western layman, the chap who has always been there when the Greaco-Latin civilization of the West has had its quarrels or has had to be defended. Anonymous, unknown, peasant or small labourer, he sailed with Odysseus, he fought at Philippi, he was at the Milvian Bridge, he was at Agincourt, he was a Desert Rat. He carries the tradition of three thousand years. He is timeless, old soldiers never die.[14]

This concept is realized in the illustrations that Jones made for *In Parenthesis.* The nearly naked soldier in the 'Frontispiece' (1937) is wounded in the left leg, as was Jones in the battle of Mametz Wood in 1916, but the position of his arms evokes the Crucified Christ, confirmed by the two prominent trees behind Him. Also in the background, the darkening sky and the stars suggest an eclipse, so that the time of the Crucifixion is also implied.

In the Tailpiece illustration, 'The Victim'(1937), the ram caught in the thicket and substituted for the sacrifice of Isaac (and Jones quotes *Leviticus* 16:10, 'the goat on which the lot fell, let him go for a scapegoat into the wilderness' *IP*.226), doubles as a symbol of the Lamb alias Christ the shepherd. The spear in the side is a reminder of Longinus's wounding of Christ on the Cross, and the eclipse is emphasized in this drawing. The analogy between the soldier and the ram/lamb image is made more potent by the knowledge that the soldiers' jackets were lined with fleece, and when they wore them inside out, they actually took on the raiment of sheep.

Both the soldier-figure (Christ), or perhaps Dai Greatcoat, and the Lamb are symbols for eternity. The soldier's feet are not on the ground, so that he elicits an image in one of the poem's battle scenes, where the soldier 'looks like/ one assumed' (*IP*.164), bringing to mind Old Master paintings of the Assumption of the Virgin, or of Christ's Ascension. This could be Dai (of the boast), who was blown to bits, and therefore no mortal remains could be found: ultimately, he is the iconic 'Unknown Soldier'.

In his preface Jones states 'I have ... tried to make a shape in words' (*IP*.x), and in the preface to The *Anathémata* he uses the same terminology in asserting that he has attempted 'to make a shape out of those ... things' (A.10), with which he most identifies. His repetition of making a shape, of fashioning something, implies the plastic arts, and reminds us that he was primarily a visual artist. As a result of his soldiering he investigated an artform in words, rather than images, and I want to consider for a moment what made him turn to writing. Firstly, his father was a printer's overseer, and brought work home with him, and Jones equated words with images. But at the turn of the century, images were secondary conduits of information, and not until the end of his

---

[14] Cf. Paul Hills, *David Jones* (London: Tate Gallery, 1981), p. 60.

life would Jones have been aware of the growing use of images, and certainly might not have anticipated the visual culture that we, as a post millennium audience, would take for granted. Secondly, the Word, or Logos, (not the image) was, according to John's gospel, the beginning of Christianity.

As if to verify this tradition, Jones in both poems draws attention to the written word. Four short lines into his Boast, Dai beaks off to remark: 'it is in the histories you can read it, ... – it is writ down – yes.' (*IP*.79) And following Christ's Boast in *The Anathémata*, where Christ's authenticity is discussed, the 'book' is called for: '... fetch the codex ... number four ... yes, yes, here it is, more or less.' (A.213) The book consulted is the fourth book of Vergil's *Eclogue*, where, in the Middle Ages, this passage was interpreted as predicting Christ's Incarnation: 'Now Apollo returns, now also the Virgin returns.' In his early inscription (c.1946), Jones took little account of the layout of the lettering. In his later, more sophisticated inscription (1949), where Virgil's prophesy is inscribed around the margin, the main text is from *Luke* II, telling of Christ's birth. This is probably the first inscription where the background is heightened with white, and marks the phase where Jones became more absorbed with creating calligraphic paintings, rather than figurative ones.

> There went out a decree from Caesar Augustus, and she brought forth her firstborn son, and laid him in a manger, and this shall be a sign unto you.

Nevertheless, Jones declares, 'it would be an absurd affectation in me to suppose that many of the themes I have employed are familiar to all readers, even though they are, without exception, themes derived from our own deposits', (*A*.14) realizing that the themes and motifs that he deals with are the very signifiers of our Western culture, but which are lost to many modern readers.

If he were writing about cultural changes in the 21st century, I suspect Jones would reiterate what he stated in 1952: 'We are, in our society today, very far removed from those culture-phases where the poet was explicitly and by profession the custodian, rememberer, embodier and voice of the ... people.'(*A*.21) He might follow this up by reminding us of his plea to poets, those whose business is metaphor, which he articulated in visual mode. In fact, he used his painted inscription 'Beird byt Barnant'(1959) as the frontispiece to his own collection of prose writings, *Epoch and Artist*(1959), in his evocation of the 6th century poet Aneirin and his commemoration of *The Gododdin* together with his tribute to *Ecclesiastes*:

> The bards of the world assess the men of valour: but on the Judge's seat they shall not sit ... yet with the creation of the everlasting ages they (in some sense) collaborate – and their prayer is in the operation of their art and without these the city is not built. (English translation)

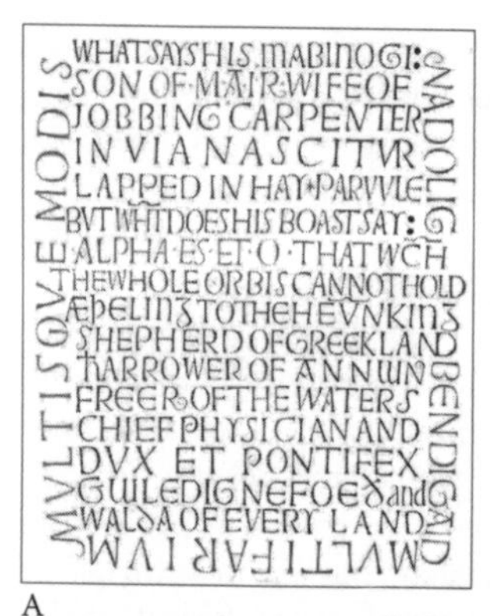

A

B

C

D

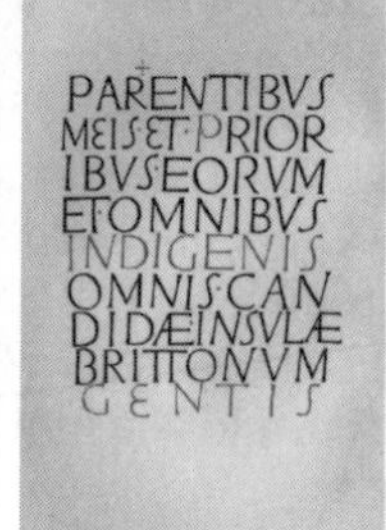

PARENTIBVS
MEIS ET PRIOR
IBVS EORVM
ET OMNIBVS
INDIGENIS
OMNIS CAN
DIDÆ INSVLÆ
BRITTONVM
GENTIS

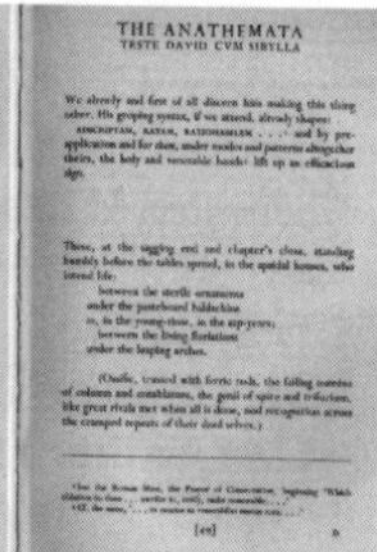

THE ANATHEMATA

E

Illustrations

A 'What says his Mabinogi' (1958), painted inscription, 76 x 57cm. National Museum and Galleries of Wales, Cardiff.

B Photograph of David Jones in army uniform: the greatcoat. Private collection.

C Desmond Chute, 'David Jones' (1926), pencil & watercolour, 20 x 11cm. Private collection.

D 'River Honddu, Capel-y-ffin' (1927), 36.5 x 57cm. Private collection.

E Double page spread from David Jones, *The Anathémata: fragments of an attempted writing* (London: Faber and Faber, 1952), pp.48-9, 28 x 22cm.

F 'Frontispiece to *In Parenthesis*' (1937), pencil, ink & watercolour, 38.1 x 28cm. National Museum & Galleries of Wales.

G 'Human Being' (1931), oil on canvas, 75 x 60.3cm. Private collection.

H 'The Victim' (1937), pencil, ink & watercolour, 38.1 x 28cm. National Museum & Galleries of Wales, Cardiff.

I 'The Artist' (1927), wood-engraving, 11.8 x 5.1cm. Private collection.

J 'The Crucifixion mural at Capel-y-ffin' (1924), house paint on kitchen wall, 128 x 90cm. Private collection. Photograph: Tilla Brading, 2004.K ëSanctus Christus de Capel-y-ffiní(1925), gouache, 19 x 13cm. Tate Britain.

L1 'I am redit Apollo'(c1949), crayon inscription, 29 x 33cm. Private collection.

L2 'Exiit Edictum (Redit et Virgo) (1949), painted inscription, 40.5 x 33cm. Tate Britain.

M 'Beirdd byt Barnant' (1958), painted inscription, 59 x 38.8cm. National Library of Wales, Aberystwyth.

F

G

H

I

J

K

IAM·REDIT
APOLLO·IA
M·REDIT·ET
VIRGO

L1

IAM·REDIT·APOLLO·IAM·REDIT·ET·VIRGO
EXIIT·EDICT
VM·A·CÆSAR
E·AVGVSTO·
ET·PEPERIT·
FILIVM·SV
VM·PRIMO
GENITVM·
ET·RECLINAVIT·
EVM·IN·PRÆSEPIO·
ET·HOC·VOBIS·SIGNVM

L2

BEIRD·BYT·BARNANT
the bards of the world assess
WYR·O·GALLON
the men of valour: but
SVPER·SELLAM·IVDICIS
NON·SEDEBVNT:
SED·CREATVRAM·ÆVI
CONFIRMABVNT
ET·DEPRECATIO·ILLO
RVM·IN·OPERA
TIONE·ARTIS
and without these non ædificatur civitas

M

Yang Lian

Translated by **Yang Liping** *with* **Jeffrey Twitchell-Waas**

'In the timeless air' – Chinese Language, Pound and the *Cantos*

The Chinese version of 'in the timeless air' from *Canto 76* – 'in everlasting time and space' – deviates from the original meaning of the poem: here the timeless air refers to a space separated from time (an artificial thought).[1] The world exists timelessly. What 'everlasting time and space' emphasises is the permanent unity of time and space. Because of this misunderstanding, what should be a Tang dynasty landscape full of Zen realizations of time and life has turned into medieval theological dogma. For me, Pound intended this line to pinpoint the emptiness and absurdity of recorded history. At the same time, set against the never-ending air, he demonstrated a transcendent synchronic dimension to people living in the diachronic. In a certain sense, this captures the fundamental theme of the entire *Cantos.*

In praising Pound, T.S. Eliot claimed that the poet 'invented' Chinese poetry for the age. What Pound invented was his unique understanding of Chinese written characters and some elements of classical Chinese poetry. In fact, a new perspective or mode of experience also updates what is observed. I once called Pound's English translations of some Chinese poems a 'great misunderstanding': 'great' because of his originality. Never had anyone (including Chinese poets) prior to Pound recognized the distinctive structural features of Chinese characters, the special functionality of Chinese grammar, the philosophy and aesthetics as exhibited by classical Chinese poetry and these features' importance for literary creation in the modern world.

His misunderstanding resulted first from the fact that he was a poet writing in English. All his reflections on the Chinese language and Chinese poetry served his poetic writings in English. A man rooted in Western culture, he tried to acquire revelations from Chinese and absorb all that he could: the word-forming approach of Chinese, the juxtaposition of images in classical Chinese poetry, Confucian thinking and the like. He had never (nor ever could have) recognized other essential elements of Chinese poetry, such as tonal patterns, rhyme schemes, poetic forms, etc.

The 'great misunderstanding' was actually a purposeful choice. He managed to find inspiration for his own poetic composition from his indirect understanding of the Chinese language. This was consistent throughout his

[1] [Translators' note] Yang Lian is referring to the first complete translation of the *Pisan Cantos* into Chinese by Huang Yunte published in 1998: *Pangde shixuan bisa shizhang*, ed. Zhang Ziqing. Guilin, Guangxi: Lijiang Publishing House.

career, from early Imagism that revolutionized the expression of English language and poetry to the late *Cantos*, which display a synchronic poetic sense and a unique perception of the Chinese language. I have to admit that all Chinese poets in the 20th century have been following Pound's path in taking an individualistic attitude towards language: what we have been doing is to transcend the unconscious use of language and reach conscious creativity.

In my opinion, Pound's study of 'Chinese poetry' must have had a hidden core, that is, thinking about synchronicity. First, he grasped this revelation through a study of the structure of Chinese characters and poetry, using his intuition as a poet. Then, he distilled his philosophical position and gave it full expression in the *Cantos*.

Chinese characters and poetry constitute a concentric circle of synchronicity: Pound paid close attention to the word-forming method of Chinese characters (诚 [*cheng*, meaning 'sincerity'] – is a perfectly structured character) and thus he grasped the spatial elements of Chinese characters right from the start. Characters are not only pictorial. The juxtaposition of different constituents of each character leads to visual, audio, denotative and associative combinations. A character itself is a poem, a multi-layered space.

Strictly speaking, Chinese has no 'grammar' as defined in the West: describing a specific action or thing with meticulously defined person, tense, part of speech and number. One of the salient features of Chinese is that the form of the verb remains unchanged no matter how the person and tense change. Here the Chinese language abandons particularity for abstractness. It implies that 'now' does not exist and there is only language. Once written down, 'this' person, 'this' action and 'this' moment become something universal. Writing is synthesis rather than analysis.

The juxtaposition of images in classical Chinese poetry is an extension of the spatiality of the Chinese characters and the abstractness of the Chinese language. Abandoned are the grammatical and logical rules that govern the links between different strokes, different parts of each character, different characters, various images and sentences. As a result, discontinuity and blanks are found everywhere.

Robert Bly once pointed out that when the imagination is employed to link these discontinuities, the abstract levels quietly pervade them. From this Pound derived Imagism. However, the key point here is not only images but also a space detached from (or containing) time. The form of a classical Chinese poem is in fact a microcosm. Take for example the typical *qilu* [regulated verse: eight-line poem with seven characters to a line]. The opening couplet avoids antithesis to imply the sense of time; the middle two couplets are antithetical and thus expand the spatial distance horizontally; and the final couplet returns to non-antithesis as an echo of the beginning. The theme is rarely linear argument as in Western poetry. It is more like uncovering layer by layer at a single spot. It is a field of resonance that incorporates whoever reads it.

The tradition of classical Chinese poetry has had nothing to do with so-called 'natural poetics.' On the contrary, its formal design reflects an extreme artificiality – so artificial that it is usually mistaken for 'naturalness.' 'Nature' as subject matter should not and cannot replace poetics. I often emphasize 'written' rather than 'spoken' Chinese because in Chinese history the written and spoken languages have long existed separately. This facilitated the formal evolution from the Han dynasty *fu* [rhyme-prose] to *pianwen* [rhythmical prose], *jueju* [quatrains] and *lushi* [regulated verse] with the aim of constructing an increasingly perfect and organically enhanced poetic space while erasing time. A poetic form like the *qilu* has been used by Chinese poets for over a thousand years. At the same time, poets have been busy compiling collections of poems, but neglecting to write a book on the history of Chinese poetry. Not until the 20th century was the first history based on Western evolutionary theory completed. Is this comic or tragic?

Two linguistic terms, synchronic and diachronic, seem relevant here. Synchronic relates to a language as it is at the particular point in time, and diachronic relates to the way a language has developed over time.

What is synchronism in poetry? In short, in terms of time sense, synchronism contains diachrony; in terms of life experience, the situation contains events; in terms of language consciousness, abstractness contains particularity; and in terms of a point of view, a non-person contains a person. In the final analysis, writing does not only deal with existence but is existence on another level, and everything in history has become materials and fragments for writing to paste together. Poetry does not merely draw the past into the present because there is neither past nor present. Only 'air' is 'timelessly' written on paper. It is poetry.

For me, the fundamental theme of the *Cantos* lies between its synchronic poetic sense and its diachronic poetic language. This means that the poem integrates changing human history. Here, the dazzling inserts and juxtapositions of large-scale images (understanding 'images' in a broad sense) are more historical imagination – the unchanging behind all changes – than history. Each person, including Pound himself, is only a part of humankind. The Greek myths, Confucian preaching, and the daily routine in the POW camp in Pisa all happen all the time. This is just like the verbs in the Chinese language that never change their forms.

However, Pound faced a problem – he had to write in English. His pursuit of synchrony and attempt to break through the diachrony of English – transcending diachrony in diachrony – leads him into conflict with his native language, the western mode of logical thinking and the 'historical narrative' that has existed throughout western cultural tradition.

I am deeply shocked by such 'impossibility' as seen in every part of the *Cantos*. While synchrony in Chinese is something inherent, the elimination of diachrony in the *Cantos* represents a human wrestling in the true sense. Pound did not merely 'expound' this theme but demonstrated a way of getting rid of diachrony. This determines the structure and language of the *Cantos*:

discontinuity between different parts, ubiquitous fragments, unexpected blanks and transformations in which lie secret chains of cause and effect concerning destiny. Complicated times, locations, characters and multiple foreign languages represent a required effort rather than a trick of showing off his profound learning. The only prominent feature is that no distinctions exist. What remains is nothing but the *Cantos* and the transcendent words: 'in the timeless air,' a synchrony containing diachrony.

The synchronic poetic sense is not merely a metaphysical game. What it touches on is exactly the absolute predicament of human existence. Synchronic fate adds weight to diachronic experiences. The synchronic has nowhere to go, which has been verified by the *samsara* of historical evolution.

To sum up, the two dimensions act together to define a person. This accounts for a mysterious parallel between Pound and contemporary Chinese poetry: Imagism/*Menglong* poetry (in the early 1980s); the initial translation of the *Chinese History Cantos*/ 'Roots-Seeking' poetry that reflected on Chinese traditions and language (in the mid and late 1980s); and publication of the Chinese version of the *Pisan Cantos/Liuwang* (Exile) poetry and its international experience (in the 1990s). Chinese poets' experience of the realities, especially China's mixed 'realities' of yesterday and today, provide the motives for poetic innovation. This can be seen in the following: the self-consciousness in 'rewriting' traditions and language in order to explore the possibility of deepening the Chinese language. Contemporary Chinese poetry's leaping images, free sentence patterns, swift movements of poetic thought, rich layers of meaning and especially its creation of a spatial structure to take the place of linear description result not only from the influence of one or more modern literary trends from the West but also from the spatial-synchronic essence of the Chinese language. The best contemporary Chinese poets can confront directly the human condition of having no place to hide.

The publication of the Chinese version of the *Pisan Cantos* in the 1990s was a major event for Chinese poets and for Pound. Chinese readers at last had the opportunity to read this relatively complete part of that grand literary construct. Pound would be pleased (would that he was still alive!) to see that the gap between the synchronic poetic sense in the *Cantos* and the diachronic sense of English has been bridged. Owing to the square-shaped Chinese characters, those linguistic fetters tightly bound around him have been suddenly thrown off. The world returns to its original 'timeless' state. Disjunction, intersection and convergence are fragmentary and integrated at once. There are no such fragments or whole. There is also no beginning or end to poetry – just as he should have originally written in Chinese. Here, the *Cantos* have reached their true completion.

Belinda Cooke

Academia or Grub Street? Look at all the writers who've found it more rewarding...to succumb to the deserved patronage of the former than to perish from neglect in the latter.[1]

Why I Translate

Writers of poetry often find themselves having to triangulate the interconnected worlds of poetry, translation and criticism as Peter Robinson notes in the above epigraph from his collection of aphorisms *Untitled Deeds*. Sometimes it is just too hard to get the recognition for one's own poetry that comes more readily through the spadework of the academic essay or translations of poets from other cultures. And there is also the question of how to promote oneself as a writer: academic, translator poet, poet translator or poet with the odd translation on the side? Dedication to the source language allows the other writer's words to get into one's bones influencing one's own poetry, but can also lead to isolation, like the woman who stays home to mind her children only to find herself as trapped as Willy Russell's Shirley Valentine, left talking to the kitchen wall.

One consolation lies in finding soul-mates with a similar dedication to the source language, like the translator Juan Gabriel López Guix who held a Mad Hatter's tea-party for forty-plus translators of *Alice in Wonderland* [2] or Jakob Kenda who developed an interest in translating children's literature after reading Professor's Kodre's translations of the dreadful Vogan poetry of a *Hithchiker's Guide to the Galaxy*: 'drankle me with crinkley bindlewurdle' into Slovenian.[3] One can admire these fanatics seemingly free of ego in pursuit of their particular passion, yet for those of us looking for more personal recognition this might not quite resolve the question: why translate?

It certainly helps if one sees one's translation as integral to one's reading and writing self – a sense that one is functioning within some vast cultural canvas. This is a view-point that has been argued by many Modernist writers. Ezra Pound, for example, whose practical advice on the tightly-honed image is still part of the bread and butter advice on creative writing courses today, was committed to translating French, Provençal, Italian and Japanese poetry as part of his dedication to his own poetry. He believed the would be poet must acquire craft via wide reading in European and indeed world culture, a

---

[1] Peter Robinson (Cambridge: Salt Publishing, 2004), p. 20.

[2] Cited in Belinda Cooke, review of *The Translator as Writer*, eds., Susan Bassnett and Peter Bush. *Modern Poetry in Translation*, 3rd ser., 10 (2007):143.

[3] Ibid.

literary apprenticeship not to be taken lightly:

> Don't imagine that the art of poetry is any simpler than the art of music, or that you can please the expert before you have spent at least as much effort on the art of verse as the average piano teacher spends on the art of music.[4]

T.S Eliot provides a less pragmatic argument suggesting the poet needs to feel that he is writing within a vast world culture that transcends time:

> The historical sense compels a man to write not merely with his own generation in his bones, but with a feeling that the whole of the literature of Europe from Homer and within it the whole of the literature of his own country has a simultaneous existence and composes a simultaneous order.[5]

Matthew Arnold also sees something unifying in writing within a cultural tradition: '[the] mind's deliverance…is perfect when we have acquired that harmonious acquiescence of mind which we feel in contemplating a grand spectacle that is intelligible to us.'[6] But we must turn to the Russian poet Osip Mandelstam – who absorbed other writers both through translation and allusions in his own verse – for the most powerful statements of cultural synthesis. He saw poetry as the means whereby he could experience what he called 'recognition' – a timeless connection with poets from the past. Victor Terras argues that it is not 'novel concepts or insights… but the originality, plasticity and beauty of Mandelstam's formulations'[7] which makes his critical prose so appealing and that is certainly in evidence in the following:

> We are free of the burden of memories. On the other hand, we have so many rare presentiments: Pushkin, Ovid, Homer. When in the stillness of the night a lover gets tangled up in tender names and suddenly remembers that all this already was: the words and the hair and the rooster crowing outside his window, exactly as it had been in Ovid's *Tristia*, the profound joy of recurrence seizes him, a dizzying joy.[8]

---

[4] 'A Retrospect,' in *Literary Essays of Ezra Pound,* ed., T.S.Eliot (New York: New Directions, 1968), pp 3-14, (p.5).

[5] 'Tradition and the Individual Talent,' in *The Sacred Wood: Essays on Poetry and Criticism,* (London: Methuen University. Paperbacks, 1960), pp. 47-59, (p. 49).

[6] On the Modern Element in Literature,' in *On the Classical Tradition: Vol 1 of Complete Prose Works,* ed., R. H. Super, (Ann Arbor: University of Michigan Press, 1960), pp.18 -37 (p. 20).

[7] 'The Time Philosophy of Osip Mandelstam,' *Slavonic and East European Review,* 47 (1969) (p. 344).

[8] *Complete Critical Prose and Letters,* trans., Jane Gary Harris and Constance Link. (Ann Arbor: Ardis, 1979), p. 14.

Yet it is not always this harmonising 'whole' sense of European culture that provides the *raison d'être* for many translators, but the other side of the coin: a fragmented war-torn Europe. A powerful motivator for any translator is the opportunity to translate the poetry of those driven out of their homes through war or political repression and the Polish poet Czeslaw Milosz, who worked with the underground throughout the Warsaw Rising, is well qualified to describe what such experiences feel like:

> The poetic act changes with the amount of background reality embraced by the poet's consciousness. In our century that background is, in my opinion, related to the fragility of those things we call civilisation or culture. What surrounds us, here and now, is not guaranteed. It could just as well not exist – and so man constructs poetry out of the remnants found in ruins.[9]

Milosz's poetry is living testimony to the notion that poetry will emerge out of the ruins created by modern warfare. And he was just one of many artists who fell victim to what we can now see with hindsight was a European Civil War[10] – the giant anthill of Europe poked by a stick sending its inhabitants fleeing in various directions in the battle between two forms of totalitarianism.

The First World War was to be the Pandora's Box to trigger or impact on much that followed: the Russian Revolution and Civil War; the failure of The Weimar Republic as Germany became the boiling pot for these polarised camps of communism and fascism; the practice run of the Spanish Civil War which was to be followed by the Second World War with its battle for territory between Stalin and Hitler. Here, Stalin's allies, Churchill and Roosevelt, often seem little more than figureheads muttering democratically on the margins, with hands that can only partially be seen as clean. The conflict continues through the Cold War and on to the collapse of the Berlin Wall in 1989 and the European fallout from that event.

The translator interested in the European Civil War is certain to find many poets whose experience is comparable to Czeslaw Milosz's as is clear from Tony Judt's observation in *Postwar*: 'No other conflict in recorded history killed so many people in so short a time'[11] providing us with an estimate of thirty-six and half million Europeans, over half of whom were civilians. Military historians

---

[9] Czeslaw Milosz. *The Witness of Poetry: the Charles Eliot Norton Lectures: 1981-1982* (Cambridge: Harvard Univ. press. 1983), p. 97. See also Norman Davies, *Rising '44: the Battle for Warsaw,* (London: Pan Books, 2003) and there is also a good account of the Polish Resistance during the war in Andrzej Wajda's *Canal*, 1957, the first ever film about the Warsaw Uprising.

[10] see Ernst Nolte, *Der Europaische Burgerkrieg: 1917-1945: Nationalsozialismus und Bolschewismus, (The European Civil War 1917-1945: National Socialism and Bolshevism),* (Munich: Herbig, 1997).

[11] Tony Judt, *Postwar: A History of Europe Since 1945* (London: Heinemann 2005), p. 18.

have no shortage of such statistics to cover all manner of 'legal' and illegal exterminations occurring on both sides, and with a glut of such texts one's mind becomes numbed by the incomprehensibility of such mass slaughter.

Statistics are similarly impossible to grasp when one looks at both forced and voluntary twentieth century migrations. First we have Russian émigrés leaving in various waves as a result of the Revolution and en masse with the defeat of the Whites in the Civil War. Then, with the rise of Hitler, comes the Jewish flight from Germany initially encouraged by the Nazis but gradually seen as a closing down of the hatches as Jews found it increasingly hard to gain visas into other countries.[12] As for Poland, one has only to look at the way her map has changed throughout history to get some sense of the forced expulsions individuals from that country have been through.[13] Finally, the migrations in the course of the Second World War reach absurd proportions as areas cleared by Hitler to provide *Lebensraum* for Germans are then reversed after the war by way of reprisal including the expulsions of Germans who had been living away from Germany for generations.[14] Judt is once more helpful here:

> Between them Stalin and Hitler uprooted, transplanted expelled, deported and dispersed some 30 million people in the years 1939-43. With the retreat of the Axis the process was reversed. Newly-resettled Germans joined millions of established German communities throughout Eastern Europe in headlong flight from the Red Army... From the east came Balts, Poles, Ukrainians, Cossacks, Hungarians, Roumanians.[15]

The cost to life is hard to grasp, but what of the impact on our culture? A whole raft of movements and individual personalities were victims of this tragedy: the doomed generation of young men of the First World War which included poets of the short-lived movement of German Expressionism curtailed

---

[12] See Bruno Arpaia, *The Angel of History,* trans., Minna Proctor, (Edinburgh: Canongate: 2006), a semi-fictionalised account of Walter Benjamin's flight from Germany in 1940 and the difficulty of getting visas into potential countries of refuge.

[13] See Friedrich von Wilpert, *The Oder-Neisse Problem: Towards Fairplay in Central Europe,* (Bonn: Atlantic-Forum, 1964), for an account of Poland's shifting borders historically and more recently as a result of Hitler's invasion in 1939 and the postwar Soviet establishment of a communist bloc.

[14] For the complex issue of German responsibility after the Second World War see Alfred-Maurice de Zayas, *The German Expellees: Victims in War and Peace,* (New York: St Martin's Press, 1993), and David Rock and Stefan Wolff, eds., *Coming Home to Germany? the Integration of Ethnic Germans from Central and Eastern Europe in the Federal Republic,* (New York: Berghahn Books, 2002). See also Bill Niven, ed., *Germans as Victims,* (Basingstoke: Palgrave, 2006) for a rather judgemental account of how far any Germans are allowed to see themselves as victims post 1945, compiled notably predominantly by British and American academics.

[15] *Postwar,* p. 23. See also pp 23-27 for a detailed summary of the extent and nature of people on the move at the end of the war.

by the young deaths of its key players: Alfred Lichtenstein, George Heym, Georg Trakl, Ernst Stadler and August Stamm, most of whom died in active service;[16] the loss of one of the world's greatest poets Federico Garcia Lorca in 1936, murdered at the age of 39 by Nationalist rebels;[17] the fate of Russia's inner exiles: Anna Akhmatova, Osip Mandelstam and Boris Pasternak along with the even more wretched fate of those forced to leave: Marina Tsvetaeva and that whole generation of Russian exiles,[18] many of whom were unknown even to Russians until the flurry of publications which appeared from 1989[19] onwards in the wake of *Glasnost'*. Tsvetaeva's older daughter Alya Efron, describes them as those who went

> down the most mournful, erroneous, and thorn-laden path in the world, through Gallipoli and Constantinople, to Czechoslovakia and France, into the ranks of living shadows, of people without citizenship or nationality, without present or future, with the unbearable burden of having only the past behind them.[20]

Anna Akhmatova, who had to endure repeated incarcerations of her son Lev in the Gulag, nevertheless describes the decision to leave as a worse choice, telling us: 'the Bitter air of exile is like poisoned wine'[21] and Tsvetaeva in her poem 'Longing for Home' describes the exile's alienation and loss of identity:

> It's all the same to me among whose
> faces I am to bristle like a captive
> lion, and what power will be used to
> distance me from myself, from my essence

---

[16] See Michel Hamburger and Christopher Middleton eds. and trans., *Modern German Poetry: 1910-1960*, (London: Macgibbon and Kee, 1962) for a selection of these poets.

[17] See Alex Gibson *The Death of Lorca* (St Albans: Paladin, 1974).

[18] Useful general surveys on this topic are Robert C. Williams, *Culture in Exile: Russian Emigrés in Germany: 1881-1941*, (Ithaca: Cornell Univ. Press, 1972), Marc Raeff, *Russia Abroad: A Cultural History of the Russian Emigration 1919-1939*, (Oxford: Oxford Univ. Press, 1990), *Soixante-dix Ans d'Émigration Russe: 1919-1989, (Seventy Years of Russian Emigration)*, (Paris: Fayard, 1996) and Hélène Menegaldo, *Les Russes à Paris: 1919-1939, (Russians in Paris: 1919-1939)*, (Paris: Autrement, 1998).

[19] *Glasnost'* was happening in the mid-eighties but 1989 was a landmark year in Russia for the publication of writers previously banned or with limited publications. There were also many Russian émigrés published for the first time. This was the first time many younger Russians living in Russia had ever read them.

[20] Alya Efron *No Love Without Poetry* (Evanston: Northwestern Univ.Press, 2009), p. 19.

[21] 'Poem without a Hero', *Selected Poems*, trans., Richard McKane (Newcastle: Bloodaxe Books, 1992), p. 314.

like a Kamchatka bear driven off the ice
and where I won't waste my time trying to
get on with people and where I will
abase myself – it's all the same to me.
......

But then... perhaps, along the road I'll see
a bush rise up, especially the rowan...[22]

Daniel Weissbort's *The Poetry of Survival: Post-War Poets of Central and Eastern Europe*[23] provides the anthology *par excellence* of German, Polish, Hungarian and Czech Second World War exiles such as Paul Celan, Yehudi Amichai, Miroslav Holub and Vasco Popa. Then there is the more unusual experience of inner exile of the Italian poet Vittorio Sereni. Captured towards the end of the war when Italy changed sides, he was unable to fight with the partisans as part of Italy's Resistance, and as a result experienced feelings of dislocation that remained with him well into the fifties – here one of his most powerful responses to the war:

But if you truly were
the first fallen splayed on the Normandy beaches,
you pray if you can, I am dead
to war and to peace.
This, the music now:
of the tents that flap against the poles.
It's not the music of angels, it's my own
music only and enough.[24]

And finally, there is the whole minefield of German culture. One must consider the destructive impact of National Socialism in general[25] and the even more vexed question concerning East German poets both before and after the collapse of the Berlin Wall. How far can this latter group be seen as

[22] *Paths of the Beggarwoman: Selected Poems of Marina Tsvetaeva,* trans. Belinda Cooke, (Kent: Worple Press, 2008), p. 127.

[23] (London Penguin Books, 1993)

[24] Vittorio Sereni, *Selected Poetry and Prose,* trans., Peter Robinson and Marcus Perryman, (Chicago: Univ. of Chicago Press, 2006).

[25] Two wide-ranging surveys which include this period of forced migration from Germany are Fermi, Laura. *Illustrious Immigrants: the Intellectual Migration from Europe 1930-41* (Chicago: Univ. of Chicago Press. 1968); Palmier, Jean-Michel. *Weimar en Exil: Le destin do L'Emigration Intellectuelle Allemand Antinazie de Europe et aux États-Unis. Tome 1: Exil en Europe, 1933-1940: de L'Incendie du Reichstage a la Guerre d'Espagne* (Paris: Payot, 1988).

victims of the European Civil War following on from the discovery of the Stasi scandal when numerous 'dissident' poets were later shown to be collaborating with the Stasi in their surveillance programme?[26]

The writer in such circumstances must always suffer, but what of the art object itself? If as we are told poetry is an overflow of powerful feeling, must war ultimately be the place where it gains its most profound impact giving us the awful truth that poetry is somehow enhanced by life's tragedy? Czeslaw Milosz in 'Dedication' shows how such horrific experiences can act as the poet's muse:

> You whom I could not save
> Listen to me.
> Try to understand this simple speech as I would be ashamed of another.
> I swear, there is in me no wizardry of words.
> I speak to you with silence like a cloud or a tree.
>
> What strengthened me, for you was lethal.
> You mixed up farewell to an epoch with the beginning of a new one.
> Inspiration of hatred and lyrical beauty,
> Blind force with accomplished shape.[27]

Similarly poetry that comes out of repression is often unbearably moving to read. Some of Mandelstam's most heartbreaking poems are those that focus on the very movement of the lips as in 'Having deprived me':

> Having deprived me of seas, of running and flying away,
> and allowing me only to walk upon the violent earth,
> what have you achieved? A splendid result:
> you could not stop my lips from moving.[28]

Moving as the above examples are, I am not suggesting that poetry of the exiled is merely attractive because it deals with exilic subject matter: exiles as much as anyone lead complex varied lives producing poetry that reflect

---

[26] See Karen Leeder, *Breaking Boundaries: a New Generation of Poets in the GDR* (Oxford: Clarendon Press. 1996), Ann Funder, *Stasiland: Stories from Behind the Berlin Wall* (London: Granta Books, 2003), and Henckel von Donnersmarck's Stasi drama *Das Leben der Anderen (The Lives of Others,)*, (2007).

[27] Czeslaw Milosz, ed., *Postwar Polish Poetry,* (Berkeley: Univ. of Califorrnia Press, 1983), p. 74.

[28] *The Voronezh Notebooks*, trans. Richard and Elizabeth McKane, (Manchester: Bloodaxe Books, 1991), p. 43. McKane's introduction also provides a detailed account of Mandelstam's various periods of exile before his death due to heart failure 27th December 1938 at a transit camp en route to Vladistock after being sentenced to five years in a labour camp.

those experiences. Paul Tabori, in his seminal *The Anatomy of Exile,*[29] makes clear diasporas have been part of 'civilisation' since its earliest days – the Greek influence on Roman culture, the various Christian schisms of the early church, the wandering Jew, those most famous of exiles, Ovid and Dante. Whether it be a stirring of different-coloured paints or a mixing of oil and water, the effect of diasporas on indigenous populations is complex as is the role of the translator in this process of assimilation. What I do argue, though, is that dispossessed poets are often at their most moving when they write on their exilic situation.

Yet there is also something else which, though connected with all the above, is I believe a powerful draw for the translator: the fascination with the unknown, the opportunity to provide a window onto a closed culture especially if one is working in a less well-known language. And translators, as much as explorers, will battle to be the first to make others aware of the undiscovered territory.

The 'Thaw' and Translation in the Sixties.

We of the internet age may feel that we are now inundated with too much information so it is hard for us to grasp just what an incredible cultural discovery it was for writers during the 'Thaw'[30] – the period when tensions eased between The Soviet Union and the West after the death of Stalin in 1953. Though it was happening in the fifties, its impact wasn't really felt in the West until 1960. Up until this time access to Russian culture had been almost totally shut off.

A landmark event was the appearance of Boris Pasternak's *Dr Zhivago* in1958, for which he was awarded the Nobel Prize in1960, although forced to refuse it. Today this book seems flawed in many ways with its plot contrivances and unnatural conversations between Zhivago and his lover Lara who reads more like his philosophical alter ego than the romantic heroine of David Lean's film. But Zhivago's interior monologues, as the thinly disguised artist Pasternak surfacing from the previously impenetrable Iron Curtain, were mesmerising for many at that time. This was just the thin end of the wedge in revealing previously unknown Russian poets who, in spite of hardship and repression, were writing a poetry that was life-affirming, and in direct contrast to the inner angst of many poets in the West, particularly those in America. Major poets such as Robert Lowell, John Berryman, Theodore Roethke, Randell Jarrell, Sylvia Plath all experienced depression or insecurity and met untimely

[29] *The Anatomy of Exile: A Semantic and Historical Study* (London: Harrap, 1972).

[30] It derives from Ilya Ehrenburg's novel *The Thaw*, trans. Manya Harari (London: Macgibbin and Kee, 1961).

ends. For them, and many like them, these Russian poets were a revelation.

As a result of this new access, there was a ferment of interest in translation. In Britain, Daniel Weissbort and Ted Hughes founded *Modern Poetry in Translation*, Hughes arguing that it was born out of a desire for 'global unity,' the means whereby various nations could 'make a working synthesis of their ferocious contradictions.'[31] One can sense his passionate engagement with poets such as the Hungarian János Pilinszy and the Israeli Yehuda Amichai, who only came to people's attention in the West by being showcased in *MPT*. Richard McKane was also a key player in this new artistic scene and below he outlines his early involvement and the excitement of the period, particularly as it was felt at Oxford University:

> My life in Russian poetry started in the 60s coinciding with Prince Dimitri Obolensky's *Penguin Book of Russian Verse* (1962). I read Brodsky's and Voznesensky's poems before Akhmatova and had a crack first at translating Alexander Blok's 'The Twelve' while I was still at Marlborough College. Soon the Biblioteka Poeta editions had done *Pasternak* and *Tsvetaeva* and in the West there had appeared the Struve/Fililippov *Akhmatova* and *Mandelstam*. My *Selected Poems of Anna Akhmatova* appeared in 1969 shortly after my graduation. The book was kick-started by Akhmatova having received an Honorary Doctorate at Oxford the year before she died in 1966. I remember the excitement at my college Univ. Oxford of reading her and also the responsibility of translating 'Requiem,' which was not published in the Soviet Union till 1989. I also remember translating 'Poem without a Hero' in Antalya, Southern Turkey in the 70s. Oh yes, Gumilyov had also been published in the 60s in the West. It was immensely exciting to be in at the beginning of Akhmatova translation and subsequently to be invited by the Union of Soviet Writers to Moscow for the 100th anniversaries of Akhmatova and Pasternak.[32]

In America there was a positive furore of translation activity. There developed a fascination with all things Russian at this time, clearly evident in periodicals, notably *The New York Review of Books*. There were also a number of exchanges and visits. Some were merely diplomatic exercises. Stanley Kauffman, suggests this was the case when the ageing establishment poet Robert Frost visited Russia describing him as 'a kind of portable Roman ruin'[33]

---

[31] Cited in Belinda Cooke, review of *Ted Hughes: Selected translations*, ed., Daniel Weissbort, *MPT*, 3rd ser., 9 (2008): 167-168.

[32] Email interview with the author, September 2009.

[33] Stanley Kauffman, review of 'Frost in Russia' by F. D. Reeve, *New York Review of Books*, 25 June 1964: 10-11.

while the visits to America by Yevgeny Yevtushenko and Andrei Voznesensky established genuine links between Russian and American poets. Another major contributor was the émigré writer Olga Carlisle. Both as a native speaker and coming from a long line of Russian writers – her grandfather, the playwright Leonid Andreyev and her father and uncle, Vadim and Daniel Andreyev both poets – she was able to provide access both to the language and culture. She also went to Russia in 1960 and interviewed Pasternak and other Russian writers for the *Paris Review* published in book form in her *Voices in the Snow: Encounters with Russian Writers* (1962).[34] Along with this, she collaborated with a number of American poets to produce her poetry anthology *Poets on Street Corners: Portraits of Fifteen Russian Poets* (1968).[35]

There were a number of entertaining translation debates between Robert Lowell, Edmund Wilson, Vladimir Nabokov and George Steiner. Lowell openly admitted in the Introduction to *Imitations:* 'I have been reckless with literal meaning, and laboured hard to get the tone,'[36] and was seen, along with George Steiner, as the major supporter of free translation. Nabokov, on the other hand, embarked on a personal vendetta against any writer who presumed to deviate from literal translation of Russian poetry. The distinctive characteristic of his various articles was the entertaining quality of the abuse: 'For something must be done, some lone hoarse voice must be raised to defend both the helpless dead poet and the credulous college student from the kind of pitiless and irresponsible paraphrase whose product I am about to describe."[37] Wilson provided an amusing riposte to such comments:

> Mr Nabokov is in the habit of introducing any job of this kind which he undertakes by an announcement that he is unique and incomparable and that everybody else who has attempted it is an oaf and an ignoramus, incompetent as a linguist and scholar, usually with the implication that he is also a low-class person and a ridiculous personality.[38]

There was also much envy of the prominence given to poetry in these Eastern Bloc countries both by individuals and the Soviet State – the one bonus in Stalin's desire for writers to act as 'engineers of the human soul.' Stanley Kunitz here describes his feelings after a visit to Russia:

---

[34] (London: Weidenfield and Nicolson, 1962).

[35] (New York: Random House, 1968).

[36] (London: Faber, 1971), p. xi.

[37] 'On Translating Pushkin: Pounding the Clavichord,' review of *Eugene Onegin*, trans. Walter Arendt, *New York Review of Books*, 30 April 1964:14-16.

[38] 'The Strange Case of Pushkin and Nabokov,' review of *Eugene Onegin: A Novel in Verse*, trans., Vladimir Nabokov, *New York Review of Books*, 15 July 1965: 3-6.

> I came back from the Soviet Union in the spring of 1967 full of affection for the writers I had met, sharing the frustrations and anxieties of their predicament and, to a degree, strangely envious of them. A writer is dignified by the attention of the state, even when it is the wrong kind of attention. As Mandelstam remarked, there is no denying the importance of poetry when people are killed for it.[39]

Lowell captures this attraction in an interview with D. S. Carne-Ross: 'I think we have the feeling of discovery of what we lack. Someone like Neruda has something that no North American poet has. So has Pasternak.'[40]

Both these poets have more to say about how this encounter impacted on their translation. Stanley Kunitz argues that:

> Poets are attracted to translation because it is a way of paying their debt to the tradition, of restoring life to shades, of widening the company of their peers. It is also a means of self-renewal, of entering the skin and adventuring through the body of another's imagination. In the act of translation one becomes more like that other, and is fortified by that other's power.[41]

For Lowell there was the added appeal of being there at the start: 'Well, there's a great charm in doing a first – or a near first, nobody ever seems to do a real first. But you do an almost first, Mandelstam, say, and that's wonderful.'[42] The academic Clarence Brown reinforces how tantalising it is to engage with the unknown, here also with reference to Mandelstam:

> His then obscurity, in every sense, had a seductive appeal...His fate was utterly mysterious, even the little that was known of his life was a web of surmise, for the most part, and his poetry, in the context of what I then knew of Russian poetry, seemed even more miraculously *sui generis* than it later proved in fact to be.[43]

Of course, when we read some of these poets today, we cannot recapture the moment of initial revelation, and can only imagine how extraordinary it must have been. All we know for certain is that their impact remains with us today.

---

[39] 'A Visit to Russia,' in *A Kind of Order, A Kind of Folly: Essays and Conversations* (Boston: Little, Brown and Co., 1975), pp. 18-38 (p. 18).

[40] D.S. Carne-Ross, 'Conversation with Robert Lowell,' *Delos: A Journal on and of Translation*, I (1968), 165-174 (p. 170).

[41] 'On Translating Akhmatova,' in *A Kind of Order*, pp. 38-46 (p. 46).

[42] Ibid., p. 171.

[43] *Mandelstam,* (Cambridge Univ. Press, 1973), p. 7.

It is still inspirational to read say, Pasternak, Akhmatova or Mandelstam who all write with an absolute belief in themselves as poets and the 'gift' of their poetry, while knowing what they had to endure in their lives. Take Pasternak's nature poetry with its pantheistic merging of the self and nature as in 'My Sister – life, is today in flood':

My sister – life, is today in flood,
having been battered with spring rain everywhere,
but people in trinkets grumble like mad
and politely sting, like a snakes in the grass.

The old have their reasons for this.
Your reasons no doubt are equally ludicrous,
that in the storm there are lilac eyes and lawns
and the horizon smells of damp mignonette.

That in May, in the carriage when you read
the timetable of the Kamyshin branch,
it is more grandiose than sacred writing
and the carriage seats are black from dust and storms.[44]

And then there is Akhmatova, who started out as a love poet but transformed herself into a public poet as a result of Russia's cataclysms between the two wars. Here in 'MCMXXI' it is difficult to know how she can manage to express such faith in the future given Russian's state due to revolution and famine:

Everything is looted, betrayed, sold,
the wing of black death has fluttered in,
everything is gnawed at by famished anguish,
then why has it become bright for us?

The untold forest near the city by day
is wafted with cherry blossom scents.
The depth of transparent July skies
sparkles at night with new constellations.

The miraculous comes so close
to the dirty, destroyed houses,
unknown to anyone, to anyone,
but desired by us for an age.[45]

---

[44] Trans. Belinda Cooke.

[45] Trans. Richard McKane.

Finally, Mandelstam who – unlike Akhmatova or Pasternak, was unable to ensure his survival through any form of compromise with the Soviet State, and who was thus to die during Stalin's Purges – could nevertheless express absolute faith in poetry, in his blessed Word, as is clear in 'We will meet again in Petersburg:

> We will meet again in Petersburg
> as though we had buried the sun in it,
> and we will pronounce the blessed
> senseless word for the first time.
> The dear eyes of blessed women still sing,
> the immortal flowers still flower,
> in the velvet emptiness over the whole world,
> in the black velvet of the Soviet night.
>
> The capital is hunched like a wild cat,
> a patrol stands guard on the bridge,
> only an angry motor rushes through the mist
> and cries like a cuckoo.
> I don't need a night pass.
> I am not afraid of the sentries:
> I pray for the blessed senseless word
> in the Soviet night.[46]

Life-affirming as these poems are, and marvellous as it must have been for these American writers to be there at the blossoming of this cultural exchange, this uncovering of uncharted territory is, fortunately for us who follow, not exclusive to the sixties. For me, the ultimate pleasure to be found in translating, particularly from a less well-known language such as Russian, is the fact that there is still endless scope to do 'a first or near first' – one can remain ever the translator of the artic regions. Tsvetaeva, Pasternak and Mandelstam are poets who have to date not been translated in their totality. These are the later poets of Russia's Silver Age but their forerunners, the Symbolist poets,[47] are still fairly unknown to writers in the West – we have limited translations of, say, Alexander Blok, Viacheslav Ivanov, Andrey Bely or Zinaida Gippius. As for the Russian emigrés who ended up in Berlin,

---

[46] *Guests from the Future: Poems of Anna Akmatova, Osip Mandelstam and Boris Pasternak*, trans., Richard and Elizabeth McKane, (Moscow: East-West Creative Association Graal Publishers, 1998).

[47] See Avril Pyrman, *A History of Russian Symbolism*, (Cambridge: Cambridge Univ. Press, 1994) for the most thorough survey of this period to date.

Prague and Paris,[48] they up to this day still remain the lost generation known to few outside of Russian academics of the American west coast. Thus there is no shortage of work to do.

The Life and Death of Russian Berlin of the Twenties: Europe's Eastern Train Station.[49]

And of all uncharted territories the most tantalising for me is the lost world of Russian Berlin. Though in a different way from the American Russian encounter of the sixties, Russian Berlin of the twenties provides a mine of, as yet, untapped material for translation. For a short, intense period (1921-1924) Russians lived in a closed society with its own schools, clubs, and shops, producing an array of newspapers, journals, and magazines which, due to economics and war, was destined, like some kind of lost Atlantis, to be completely wiped off the map. I find myself tantalised and gripped by a kind of surrogate nostalgia for a world that can only be seen in old photographs, and at the same time am intrigued to know how this Russian Berlin could coexist so apparently separately from the doomed, yet vibrant Weimar Berlin of the twenties:

> The name Weimar Republic has a whiff of fragility, of scandal, of doom about it. It denotes a tiny period of German history, the years from 1918 to 1933; an interval of tremulous government, between monarchy and dictatorship, between one catastrophic war and the approach of another; but most of all a period that was fast and febrile and fun, and....became practically synonymous with the Jazz age of the Roaring Twenties.[50]

Reading about the poets who came to Berlin[51] at this time only reinforces the impression that Russians were isolated both from the economic hardship with its spiralling inflation as well as this dynamic Berlin culture for they seem

---

[48] Two useful surveys on Russian Émigré writers in English are Simon Karlinsky and Alfred Appel, Jr., eds., *The Bitter Air of Exile: Russian Writers in the West* (Berkeley: Univ. of California Press, 1977) and Nina Berberova, *The Italics are Mine*, trans., Philippe Radley (London: Vintage, 1993).

[49] This term comes from Karl Schlögel's survey of Russian migration to Berlin, *Das Russische Berlin: Ostbanhof Europas, (Russian Berlin: Europe's Eastern train-station)* (München: Pantheon, 2007).

[50] Michael Hoffman in the translator's introduction in Joseph Roth, *What I saw: Reports from Berlin: 1920-33,* (London: Granta Books, 2003). Other useful books on this period include Otto Friedrich, *Before the Deluge: a Portrait of Berlin in the 1920s,* (New York: Harper Perennial, 1995).

[51] See Thomas Urban, *Russishe Shrisftssteller im Berlin der Zwanziger Jahre, (Russian Writers in Berlin in the Twenties)* (Berlin: Nicolai, 2003).

largely enclosed in their own Russian literary concerns. This is certainly what is conveyed in the celebrity photographs of the poet Sergei Esenin with his then partner Isadora Duncan strolling the Berlin streets on the front of *Rul'* (Rudder) and other Russian newspapers – a very different picture from his tragic end with its haunting final poem which was to double up as his suicide note:

> Goodbye my friend, with neither hand nor word.
> Don't grieve, or drop your head in sorrow.
> In this life there's nothing new in dying,
> likewise there's nothing new in living.[52]

Also Vladmir Mayakovsky was a popular performer during this time with his dramatic recitations of poems, rich in hyperbolic metaphors of the self acting as fragile masks for his own insecurities, such as 'A cloud in trousers' or his love poem 'Lilichka! Instead of a letter', expressing unrequited love for Lili Brik:

> Apart from your love,
> for me
> there is no sea,
> yet tears give me no relief from your love.
> When a tired elephant wants to rest
> it lies down majestically in the scorched sand.
> Apart from your love
> for me
> there is no sun,
> but I don't even know where you are and with whom.[53]

Vladimir Nabokov,[54] so well known to us now as the writer of *Lolita,* was a familiar figure in the Berlin scene but we know little of his early poetry written under his pseudonym Shirin. He was among the earliest to arrive and last to leave as Hitler's rise made the plight of the Jews more precarious.

Poets like Esenin and Mayakovsky had the luxury of being visiting celebrities able to travel back and forth between Russian during the relaxed period of Lenin's NEP[55] but Soviet treatment of writers hardened later on in the twenties and there was less opportunity for this kind of travel. And as far

---

[52] Trans., Belinda Cooke.

[53] Trans., Belinda Cooke

[54] See Dieter E. Zimmer, *Nabokovs Berlin, (Nabokov's Berlin),* (Berlin: Nicolai, 2001).

[55] The New Economic Policy was Lenin's return to a limited form of private enterprise in the early twenties to avoid Russia's economic collapse.

as Russian Berlin was concerned, the revaluation of the Mark in 1924 made the place less viable for Russians who, up to that point, had benefited hugely from the exchange rate, living in the best areas and well able to fuel the Russian publishing houses. As a result, Russians relocated en masse to Paris – the brief honeymoon period was over. The lives of the émigrés became increasingly austere, with many who had previously led privileged lives in Russia being forced to work as taxi drivers, waiters, car mechanics, and even prostitutes.

This is not to say that all Russians who made Berlin their first port of call lived a life of luxury. Marina Tsvetaeva lost nearly everything during the Revolution, and suffered extreme hardship in the famine that followed, including the death of her younger daughter from starvation. The one thing she could bring with her, though, was the reputation she had already established and this allowed her some access to the émigré journals and publishing houses. The younger generation were less fortunate and fell down a cultural gap. The émigré academic Gleb Struve dedicated his life to drawing attention to them but many today are still little translated. One of the best examples of such a writer is the poet Boris Poplavsky (1903-1935).[56] Though generally considered to be one of the most talented of the younger generation, to date his novels, journals, and much of his poetry have still to be translated. His highly individual world-view merits him being recognised as a major European poet and the fact that he was also to die an untimely death from a drugs overdose only makes this forced anonymity all the more tragic. Below in its entirety is my favourite Poplavsky poem and I offer it as my final answer as to why I translate:

Romance

The town is dark, its parks mysterious,
while above, the sky is a shimmering sea
of emeralds. Salome – the soul forgets,
how your voice was like death.

And now I remember, you came out of the sunset,
a black cup in your slender hands. To the song
of the white acacia, the evening walked away...
beyond the river and into the clouds.

---

[56] See *Flags*, trans., Belinda Cooke and Richard McKane (Exeter: Shearsman Press, 2009), the only full-length collection of his poems translated to date.

Everything seemed pointless and strange.
The black knight shut his eyes. The restaurant
orchestra swam over the marsh,
and into the interminable distance.

Sleeping spectre, there is no way
I can wake you, I am your dream.
Salome now inclines her head to sing
in harmony with the lonely marsh waters.

Time flies past, the earth's black-winged
spectre has long since disappeared.
I shall wait for you in the castle tower,
where the star sings in the distance.

Through the passing centuries you
shall remain: golden, unique and alive.
Sleep my knight, above *Roncevaux*,
like those fine fires up in the clouds.

So that you will not see sadness
and will live happily through this year,
I shall throw the black cup into the sea;
I shall walk off into those radiant marshes.

The years turn pink on the mountains.
All that is past is close to spring.
There under this bright star of freedom
memory sleeps, smiling in its dreams.[57]

---

[57] Trans. Belinda Cooke. A slightly modified version of this poem appeared in 'Six Poems by Boris Poplavsky, trans. Belinda Cooke and Richard McKane,' *MPT*, 3rd ser., 3, (2005):111-118.

Louis Aragon

Elsa Your Eyes

your eyes so deep I stoop to drink I've seen
all the bright suns assemble here to preen
seen the despairing all plunge in to die
your eyes so deep I lose my memory

in the birds' shade it's raging ocean tempest
then see the weather's fine your eyes are changed as
summer carves clouds to apron-size for angels
sky's never bluer than above the harvest

what if the winds dispel the blues of heaven
your eyes outshine it when a teardrop glitters
your eyes the clear skies' envy after showers
never so blue the glass as when it's broken

o the wet brightness seven-sorrowed mother
the colour-prism pierced by seven broadswords
the day stabs deep that stabs among the mourners
the shot-silk iris bluer for the graveside

your eyes in sorrow pierce the pair of holes
the magi re-enact their miracle
all three of them observed with pounding pulse
the cloak of Mary hanging in the stall

words may-time saw a pair of lips suffice
for all the cries of woe and all the songs
not enough heaven for the starry throngs
they need your eyes your eyes' twin mysteries

the child with pretty pictures on the brain
reveals his own affairs more cautiously
you make big eyes perhaps it means you lie
exotic blooms laid open by the rain

do they hide lightning in the lavenders
where insects shaft their violent amours
I'm tangled in the net of shooting stars
a sailor dead at sea when august flares

I won this radium from the raw pitchblende
in this forbidden fire my fingers burned
my paradise so often lost and found
your eyes my indies andes demavend

it happened one fine night the universe
foundered on reefs where wreckers lit a flame
set high above the sea I saw them gleam
your eyes elsa your eyes elsa your eyes

Translated by **Timothy Adès**

Note:
Demavend: Persian mountain.
Aragon wrote *Golconda*, an Indian city noted for diamonds.

Marina Tsvetaeva

Marina Tsvetaeva (1892-1941), after her departure from Russia during the Russian Civil War, lived variously in Berlin, Prague and Paris. During this time she worked on the poems that were to make up her collection *After Russia: 1922-1925* (YMCA Press, Paris 1928). Here her language becomes increasingly experimental and, in particular, she explores notions of gender and sexuality in relation to the poet. She also brings greater complexity to her use of mythological figures such as Orpheus, Eurydice and the Cumaean Sibyl.

Olga Peters Hasty in *Tsvetaeva's Orphic Journeys in the Worlds of the Word* dedicates a chapter to explaining Tsvetaeva's use of the Sibyl. She draws on Ovid's *Metamorphosis* where Apollo is described as falling in love with the Sibyl after which he grants her any wish in exchange for her taking on the role of prophetess. She asks for a long life, as many years as there are grains of sand in a small heap before her. Apollo grants this but unfortunately the Sibyl forgets to ask for youthfulness so has to suffer extreme ageing with only her prophetic voice unaltered. Tsvetaeva uses this myth to provide a female equivalent to the role Orpheus often takes with male poets (most famously Rilke in his *Sonnets to Orpheus*, 1923).

In the three-poem sequence she initially shows how the Sibyl is gradually divested of all physical sensations in the process of gaining access to the transcendent world of the prophetess and thus by association of Tsvetaeva as creative artist. The second poem goes on to present the Sibyl as a promontory set apart but looking over the material world, and finally the third poem speaks to a child who must suffer being born into the world from which the Sibyl has now been freed. However, by way of consolation, the child is told that death will ultimately enable it to enter a similar state to the Sibyl's, achieving a transcendent rebirth.

Sibyl

i

Sibyl: burnt out, Sibyl: a trunk.
a god came in though all the birds perished.

Sibyl: drained dry, Sybil: a desert:
veins all withered from one man's passion.

Sibyl: departed – devourer
of destiny and death. Tree among maidens.

Ruling tree in a bare wood –
First came the fire and then

concealed beneath eyelids – in flight, unawares,
a god rose up through the dried-up river basin.

Suddenly, unable to look from the outside
my heart and voice fell deep inside me.

Sibyl: prophet! Sibyl: vault!
Thus the Annunciation is fulfilled in that

unageing hour, fragile virginity and grey-haired
grasses, transformed into a cave

for the Miraculous Voice...
– thus into the starry whirlwind

is the Sibyl departed from the living.

ii

Like a grey stone clod
having broken off ties with the age
your body – is the cavern
of your voice.

Deep into your night, eyes blinded
by eyelids like the eye-slits of a fortress,
silent and unhearing high over the girls –
those gaily-dressed haymakers.

Wrapped up against the rain,
the mushroom grows mouldy,
a thousand years splashing
about these stuporous clods.

O grieving mountain. Beneath
heavy eyelids, the wisdom of ages past –
earthenware fragments
of kingdoms and the roadside dust

of battles.

iii

Sibyl to the Infant

Cling to my breast
little one:
birth – is a falling into days.

From those ephemeral cliffs beyond the clouds,
my infant,
how low you fell.
You were spirit, you've become dust.

Weep little one, for them and us:
birth – is a sinking into the hour.

Weep little one, in the past and the future:
birth – is a sinking into blood

and into dust
and into the hour...

Where is the glow of his miracles?
Weep little one: birth into weight.

What gift have you been given?
Weep little one: birth into reckoning

and into blood
and into sweat...

But you will rise up. That which is called death
in this world – is a sinking into firmness.

But you will see what lies before you. That which in the world
is the closing of eyelids – is a birth into the light .

From now –
and forever.

Death, little one is not to sleep, but to rise,
not to sleep but to return.

Swim my little one. You've already
left the step...

Resurrection into day.

Translated by **Belinda Cooke**

Toon Tellegen

Six poems translated from the Dutch

Toon Tellegen, born in 1941, is one of Holland's best known poets, with a long list of awards to his name. In 2007 he was awarded three prestigious prizes, two of which were for his entire oeuvre. He is also a prolific children's book writer and novelist, and his poetic animal stories are extremely popular among both children and adults.

The poems translated here are from a recent collection, *Raafvogels (Raptors).* The selected poems are from a sequence of poems which all start with the words 'My father', and they paint a picture of an imaginary father and his family.

In his preface to the collection, Tellegen writes: 'Years ago I invented someone whom I called my father. It was morning, very early, I couldn't sleep any more, I remember it quite clearly. My father didn't seem surprised at having suddenly appeared out of nowhere and, in his turn, invented my mother, my brothers and myself. He even, that very same morning, invented the life we should lead.

We led that life for a long time. My father made sure that there was always something inadequate about it, something painful, like a shoe that pinches.'

Raafvogels was published by Querido, Amsterdam, in 2006.

My father
died a thousand deaths,
my mother put on a brave face,
my brothers were lost for words

my father,
a lonely dead man among countless immortals,
no one died as often, as daily and as disastrously
as he did

and those who saw him die became uneasy
                                        and awkward,
wanted to make up for it, make up for something,
didn't know what or how

and every time my brothers would be lost for words again,
would say: 'but...' and 'you...' and 'that...'
my father would die all over again
and my mother put on a brave face,
hair-raisingly brave.

Translation of 'Mijn vader/stierf duizend doden'

My father,
who blows up rocks, blows away people, blows out peace,
blows off simplicity,
cried out that he was cold and despondent
and that if *he* wasn't saved...

my mother stood still,
torn between aversion and mercy,
wrung her hands,
tied inextricable knots in her thoughts –
dreaming of a little Alexander –
and called my brothers

but my brothers were in their millions,
were tired of saving.

Translation of 'Mijn vader/die rotsen opblaast'

My father
kept up appearances –
o let everyone please keep them up!

but my brothers smashed them to pieces,
'we'd rather you kept us up,' they said

my father went on a journey
in search of even finer appearances
and in search of love and precision

but my mother stayed behind,
waited,
put my brothers in a box,
drilled holes in it

so that they could peer at the stars at night,
whispered something encouraging to them,
threw away the key.

Translation of 'Mijn vader/bewaarde de schone schijn'
Source: Raafvogels (Raptors), Amsterdam, Querido 2006

My father
talked gibberish
and gibberish fled into my mother

oh my father,
my bright, sun-baked father,
seasoned by infidelity and idle days,
my rusty, conniving father
who creaks and crunches and opens:
no one at home,
no one to forgive a faux pas,
my adorable brothers, caught in a black frame,
and all that remains for us:
a note on the table:

I'm gone,
don't forget to live or whatever

my father bawled gibberish, begged gibberish,
but my mother kept silent
and caressed him.

Translation of 'Mijn vader/sprak wartaal'

My father
was gone,
but not really

my mother and my brothers fumbled
with their insecurity, unflagging,
muttered:
'he's gone forever'
but he wasn't really gone for ever,
'he's gone completely'
but he wasn't really gone completely,
'he's gone irrevocably'
but he wasn't really gone irrevocably

even the realest thing
is not the very realest thing

darkness fell, thrushes sang in trees
of dubious charm,
and everything uninhabited became even more uninhabited,
but my father,
my tiny irrelevant father,
was not quite really, really gone.

Translation of 'Mijn vader/was weg'

Translated by **Judith Wilkinson**

Andrew Waterman

Mioritza

(translation of the Romanian folk ballad)

Note
The ballad *Mioritza* (Ewe Lamb), known by Romanians in hundreds of variants for centuries, was first written down and printed by **Vasile Alecsandri** in 1850. His is the standard literary form, but its creator is the **Romanian people**. In *Mioritza* they find a myth defining their identity and psyche. It fuses fatalism – the victim neither fights nor flees when warned of what threatens – with a transcending of evil in a manner both mystical and ethical: a majestic pantheistic affirmation coupled with, in the shepherd's instructions to his lamb, a compassionate moral vision. Mioritza differs from such other national epics as the *Iliad* and the *Nibelungenlied* not only in its brevity, but in its minimal narrative, dropped with its outcome undisclosed as a serene lyricism supervenes. Instead of relations between characters shaping action, here they are undeveloped beyond the jealousy of the two other shepherds; but nature, rather than mere backdrop, is an active agent. *Mioritza* has complex, mutually enriching origins; the notion of death as a wedding has been traced back to pre-Roman Dacia. Its spell is in the power and beauty of the myth, given perfect artistic shape that is no feat of individual genius, but evolved through the collective processes of oral telling. My translation aims for as close a fidelity as possible to the text and feel of Alecsandri, for which adherence to his pithy rhymed form, with its unadorned directness of diction, is essential.

On a green slope straight
Below heaven's gate,
Descending the trail
That drops to the vale
Come three flocks of sheep
Three shepherds keep,
One a Moldavian,
One Transylvanian,
And one Vrancean.
Now the Transylvanian
And the Vrancean
Sharing their thought,
Conspire in a plot,
When the sun leaves the sky
The other must die,

That Moldavian,
The wealthier man,
With more sheep in his flock,
Long-horned sturdy stock,
Better-trained horses
And his dogs the fiercest.
But a ewe-lamb, small
With yellow-white wool,
While three days pass
Bleats without pause,
Won't eat any grass.
'Pied lamb with your black
Face and legs and white back,
While three days pass
You bleat without pause,
Don't you like this grass?
Are you too ill to eat,
Mioritza my sweet?'
'O dear shepherd, gather
Your sheep to the river,
Dark woods spread through
With grass for us too,
And shadow for you.
Master, master,
Call to that pasture
The bravest of all
Your dogs and most loyal,
For at sunset those two
Intend murdering you,
That Transylvanian
And the Vrancean!'
'Lamb, if by some spell
What's to be you foretell,
Should I chance on my death
On this stretch of heath,
Tell that Transylvanian
And him, the Vrancean,
They should bury me near,
In the sheepfold here,
So that I will
Be with you all still,
And hear my dogs bark
Round the fold in the dark.
Tell them what I've said,

Then place at my head
A pipe of beech,
Of love is its speech,
A pipe of bone
Caressing in tone,
A pipe of elder
Fierier and wilder!
Winds when they blow
Will sound through them so
All my sheep crowd
Round weeping aloud
With tears of blood!
But don't breathe a word
That I was murdered,
You must just say
I married today,
A king's daughter my bride,
The whole world's pride;
At my wedding tell
How a star fell;
That the sun and moon
Carried our crown;
Of the guests at our feast,
Firs and maples, our priests
Great mountains, and birds,
Thousands of birds
Our lutes and guitars,
And our torches stars!
But if you sight,
If you should meet
My old mother in her wool
Sash, from her full
Eyes the tears flowing,
Over fields going,
Asking of all,
Speaking to all,
"Who of you has known,
Who has seen my own
Proud shepherd, as slim
As if drawn through a ring,
The white of his brow
Milk-foam from the cow,
His moustache neat
As an ear of wheat,

Thick curls that grow
Like the plumes on a crow,
And his two eyes
Wild blackberries?"
Then, my little ewe,
Pity her too,
You must just say
I married today
A bride royal and great,
At heaven's gate,
But to my sweet
Mother never repeat
That a star fell
At my wedding, nor tell
Of the guests at our feast,
Firs and maples, our priests
Great mountains, and birds,
Thousands of birds
Our lutes and guitars,
And our torches stars!'

Ben Mazer

Somnambulist Ballad

after **Lorca**

Green wind, erasing sleep.
Green branches, eroding dreams.
A ship far out at sea
and a horse up in the mountains.
Sawing the shadow
of her waist in half,
moonlight dreams on the balcony,
her face green, long hair green,
eyes ashen as the moon.
Skin green as translucent film,
face green as my long last look,
eyes a dull and flashing silver
colorless, without emotion,
meaning nothing, spent in the landscape.
She cannot see.
Beneath the primitive moon
everything watches.

The call is for warmth,
the hunt is for death.
Her face as tenuous and dead as green,
promising nothing, past recompense.
Charged with the landscape, bulleting questions
at the end of dreaming. My own death.

Vacuous and green
vacuously green
transparent without thought
spread across the night
like a translucent thread
where a small pine that moves
is mirroring his thought.
The horn it signals warmth.
The hunt it signals death.

Green, how much I want you, green.
Huge stars of white ice
with the salmon of darkness
come in dawn's river.
A tree rubs the wind
with sandpaper branches.
The cat of the mountain
bristles in darkness.
From where will it come?
How will it happen?
She lingers on her balcony,
green skin, hair streaming green,
dreaming of death and the sea.

– Friend, let me trade
my purse for your glass,
my horse for your house,
my knife for your bed.
May it be heavy iron.
Friend, I am bleeding,
I've ridden a long way.
– I wish I could, old friend,
accommodate your need.
But I am not more I
than this house is my house.
– How much worse the past seems in this light.
The wind signaling with its dewlaps, with its hassocks.
Hyper proximity of the hyper legal
always heading first for wherever you are,
the Bogart of gossip, the Dietrich of murder.
Old faces too familiar
no protection against the wind.
Figures of smoke in a landscape,
my first fears. A fullness
of words, ripeness in ruin.
Friend, I want to die
peacefully here with you,
and wake up in fine Holland.
The wind comes a long way from him
with its district of birds.
A maze of mirrors in which
I look not knowing which
is the true shard that moves.
Friend, can you not see

horrors no words can say.
Hide me in your house.

Let me die in my sleep.
Can you not see the wound
circling my heart and throat.
– Your stainless record shows us
two dozen bouquets of roses.
Your blood swims in your clothes
in a disarming pose.
But I am no more I,
nor is my house my house.
What was no longer is.
– Let me at least climb to the top,
beneath the spire, where I passed many hours.
Let me at least climb up
to the high balconies:
Take me there! Take me there!
to the green balconies
where I can see the moon and the sea.

Now the two friends go up
to the high balconies
shedding their steps of blood
letting their light of kiss
blurring the light with tears.
Dropping blood on each step
leaving trails of their eyes.
On some invisible roofs
a few trembling lanterns burned.
A thousand chimes were taking
the long hill in the dawn.
Green! I want you green,
green face, skin of green,
green gazes, bark of green,
sap green.

The two friends rose.
The large wind left
a dry, stiff taste
of mint and bile,
a strong, strange taste
of mint, sweet basil and bile.
Friend! Tell me, where is she,
your bitter girl?

How often she waited
how often she would wait
dark as the wind
cold as the moon,
on this balcony!

On the face of the water
cupped by the shore
she swam and swayed.
A green face. Long hair of green.
Glance fast as silver bullets.
– a fragment of moon
dangles over water.
Water revives
old memories.
Green as my chances, green
as the rushing band. Reprise
warm as a calling horn.
The shifting instruments
rearranging hearts. Time spins.
Life stops in a bar rest.
Night
becoming as intimate
as a small café,
as a village square.
Drunken murderers
pounding the floors.
Green, how much I want you green.
Green wind. Green branches.
The ship at sea.
The horse in the mountain.

Belinda Cooke

Words in Air: The Complete Correspondence between Elizabeth Bishop and Robert Lowell, edited by **Thomas Travisano** with **Saskia Hamilton**, Faber and Faber, £40, 875pp.

Saskia Hamilton's *The Letters of Robert Lowell* (Faber and Faber, 2005) was a healthy counterbalance both to Ian Hamilton's *A Biography of Robert Lowell* (Faber and Faber, 1982) and Paul Mariani's *Lost Puritan: a Life of Robert Lowell* (Norton, 1994). Hamilton offers perceptive literary criticism but relishes a little too readily accounts of Lowell's bizarre behaviour during his annual manic episodes (reduced only with the appearance of Lithium in the late sixties), while Mariani, though less damning, fills in gaps in Hamilton's account by focusing on Lowell's heavy drinking. It is thus extremely moving to meet the largely sane Lowell of his letters – clearly mortified by the effect his illness had on others – observing at one point: 'It's hard for the controlled man to look back on the moment of chaos and claim' (p. 430).

Lowell was certainly no fair-weather friend, maintaining strong bonds throughout his life with early school friends such as Peter Taylor, as well as keeping in touch with his first and second wife – Jean Stafford and Elizabeth Hardwick. *The Bishop Lowell Letters*, containing their complete correspondence, shows Lowell's forty-year friendship with Elizabeth Bishop to be one of his deepest and most enduring.

The meticulous footnoting of every review, poem, or book referred to in passing is a labour of love that must have been years in the making and which academics will find invaluable. All this is further supplemented by a biographical introduction, along with various indexes and appendices. Travisano, assisted by Hamilton, may be taking things a step too far when he provides detailed descriptions of the front of each postcard, along with recording each time Lowell changes his typewriter ribbon, but the dedication to detail does help these letters to act as a more authentic form of life story than we are often given in biographies with the almost inevitable bias that one finds.

What we see throughout the letters is how much Lowell found a soul mate in Bishop: similarly coming from affluent backgrounds but ones that failed to provide the emotional support they craved. They had many common interests: the formal aspect of poetry, history, art, travel and were both voracious readers – variously off on 'writing jags' as Lowell calls it – whole summers of Dickens, Hardy and the like. They also both possessed their own private demons: Lowell's traumatic bouts of manic depression and Bishop's own serious asthma, along with the alcoholism which in her later years became increasingly damaging to her health. Also in the letters, though, we note the contrast so visible in their poetry: Lowell who writes with his heart of his sleeve, is more prone to the 'confessional', while Bishop, though warm in her expressions of friendship, is far more closeted in her discussions of both her relationships and her drink problem.

Bishop shows herself to have a droll sense of humour both in her anecdotes and her comments on Lowell's poetry. Of a bad poet: 'One poem this time is about his soul fermenting in a barrel of sauerkraut. He is also grateful to God for sending him such marvellous ideas, but personally I'm afraid God is playing tricks on him' (p. 102). She tells of the visitors to Ezra Pound who bizarrely decide to bring along their 9-month-old baby, or the minister who on a boat trip makes them all sing: 'Nearer my God to thee', after revealing that this was sung when the Titanic went down (p. 130). When critiquing Lowell's *Mills of the Kavanaughs*, on the line 'a girl can bear just about anything' she states: 'It sounds to me as if the next line should go "if she has a good big diamond ring." Please forgive me' (p. 113). She also makes lovely observations on Lowell's various muses, on one occasion: 'or I see your muse, a rather large rough type, giving you a whack on the ear' and on another calling her: 'tough, red-head illegitimate!' (p. 497), while of her own: 'mine is suffering from leukaemia, not having tuned her lute since God knows when' (p. 483).

With Lowell, we get both wit and eloquence, though in the letters they appear as gems in the midst of an everyday working voice. Of his father's death: 'The death seems almost meaningless, as is perhaps always the case when the life has long resigned itself to a terrible dim, diffused pathos' (p. 108). When Bishop mentions how Randall Jarrell never lifts a finger in the house, Lowell responds: 'I feel solaced; I find it so hard to lift a finger' (p. 337). Lowell's daughter clearly acted as his muse and the letters are filled with affectionate observations and anecdotes, describing how she is 'more fun than a rubber ball' (p. 404); and how they as parents deal with her: 'by cheating and using cunning and withdrawing into the shadows she can't understand.' (p. 339) He paints a picture of her as witty, precocious child full of colourful language – 'energy boxing with ignorance'. One moment she describes how she felt 'her heart bleed' (p. 443), the next she is responding to Allan Tate saying he's looking forward to meeting her as a grown up: 'If you live that long'.

But most valuable of all with regards Lowell is the literary criticism of fellow poets. Writing without the benefit of hindsight he is wonderfully astute on the impact of Plath's poems: 'makes one feel at first reading that almost all other poetry is about nothing...[you] almost wish they weren't there' (p. 543). He is also great on technique, speaking of Baudelaire: 'I never realised that such wonder could be done with a sentence, moving through its terrible balances and metric and so seldom turning into a mere fireworks of syntax' (p. 338). He can get to the essence of a writer with wonderful brevity; on translating Akhmatova he states: 'her grief has such grandeur. Strange to write from behind such a mask' (p.520), and of Stevie Smith: 'A curious writer of gruesome light verse' (p. 527). As we work through the letters, we can't help but be struck by the sheer number of fellow poets they must watch die before them, Lowell writing to Bishop with fitting tributes for each as it happens: Randell Jarrell,

John Crowe Ransom, T.S Eliot, Marianne Moore, Ezra Pound. His page-long tribute to Delmore Schwartz is particularly powerful – here a taster:

> ...it was like living with a sluggish, sometimes angry spider – no hurry, no motion, Delmore's voice, almost inaudible, dead, intuitive, pointing somewhere, then the strings tightening, the roar of rage – too much, too much for us! Nothing haunts me more than the breaking with friends. I used to think he was the only I broke with (p. 603).

At times, when reading, it is hard not to baulk at the impression one gets of Lowell and Bishop as a privileged and exclusive club of two. Along with, say, their shared low opinion of Richard Eberhart's poetry or their frustrations mixed with admiration for the brilliant overpowering critic, Randall Jarrell, we see them seconding each other's proposals of favoured poets for various awards or organisations. Added to this Lowell was certainly also instrumental in furthering Bishop's career. Naturally shy of the limelight, she relied on him a great deal to promote her work and find her substantial grant to aid her travel abroad as unfavourable exchange rates in Rio affected her income.

Though the letters take us through the vicissitudes of both of their lives, with Lowell the various manias are shown only as gaps in otherwise monthly letters. In the case of Bishop we see the shift from extreme loneliness in the early days to a long period of stability when she settles down in Brazil with her life-long partner, Lota de Macedo Soares. For many years Lota, through her extended family and wide social network, was able to provide Bishop, who was orphaned early, with some experience of family life and help her control her drinking. However, from 1963 onwards, the situation between herself and Lota deteriorates. This is largely due to Lota's growing involvement in politics at the same time as Brazil was becoming increasingly unstable. This was to be the cause of Lota's depression and ultimate suicide. Bishop was never to achieve a similar tranquillity again as she had had in the heyday of the relationship and ended up leaving Brazil, grieving and embittered.

The major personal trauma of Lowell's life that does comes clearly though the letters is his divorce from Elizabeth Hardwick and subsequent marriage to Caroline Blackwood. Here we see the greatest test and enduring quality of his friendship with Bishop. She is horrified to discover him adapting Hardwick's personal letters to him as material for his poetry as he does in *Dolphin*: '...you have *changed* her letters. That is "infinite mischief".... It is not being "gentle" to use personal, tragic, anguished letters that way – it's cruel' (p. 708). Another situation that might have led to conflict but didn't was issues over their joint employment over their work contracts when they were working at Harvard. Yet none of these situations were able seriously to disrupt this enduring friendship that, as is profoundly evidenced in these letters, was clearly a marriage of true minds.

Tim Liardet

John Hartley Williams: ***Café des Artistes,*** Cape, ISBN 978-0-224-08785-8, £10.00

John Hartley Williams' work has always been characterised by energetic wit and a highly restive imagination. *Spending Time with Walter* and *Blues*, his previous two collections, showed he was one of the shrewdest observers of social and political mores currently writing – satire seen through an absurdist lens, perhaps, which invented ever more original narratives to keep its edge sharp. Then came *The Ship*, an unexpected retrospective of hitherto uncollected poems to further augment an already distinguished opus. *Café des Artistes*, his ninth full collection, not only consolidates these strains but amplifies them with typical Hartley Williams élan.

Until you have left the country of your birth, to adapt Joyce's dictum, you cannot hope to write about it or the world. John Hartley Williams has lived in Berlin since 1976, has been a congenial host to many British poets out there and regularly returns to Britain while remaining firmly rooted in Germany. Over the years, I feel, this has had the effect of shifting his register. He has had to invent a language, and a mythology, to fit this shifting world. Since 1976, his angles of vision have become increasingly acute, more unusual, more original, revealing at the heart of his poetics the truths of a fruitful dislocation. His poems have therefore been full of hotels, cafés, half worlds and half-lights, vehicles to evoke the ephemeral nature of human existence, chance meetings, creeping atmospheres harnessed by imagistic risk.

His poems in *Café des Artistes*, his ninth full collection, are full of what can only be called an eerie 'inbetweeness'. Hartley Williams can do more with ellipsis than most poets can do with public statement, as in the memorable opening to 'The Reader':

> The reader finds himself in an old Europe,
> in a shadowy night of lamps and chairs
> through which long-aproned waiters glide.

This has the atmosphere of exile about it, poised half way, perhaps, between a Sidney Greenstreet movie, say, and a Graham Greene novella. Inevitably I imagine the central protagonist of this poem wears a dishevelled white suit and hear the squeak of the ceiling fan overhead (though you have to read the title poem actually to meet with the fan which utters '...a noise that someone really ought to fix.') This is the core strength of a Hartley Williams poem – it provides one narrative while simultaneously inviting the reader to supply another. Despite the specific mention of Europe in the opening line, the central achievement of this poem and of many others is that it could quite as easily have been set in Bangkok, Singapore or Colombo, and quite as easily in Prague, Brussels or Paris but – ironically enough – is set in London, in 2007. It is a London which speaks a different language, is foreign, treats poets like anyone else and is full of crowds comprising '...the young, the drunk, the happy / that fill the night with selves that do not read.'

The natural corollary of such productive estrangement is a sense of things in a state of unpredictable flux, edging towards break up which is impending but never quite implodes. And if isolation goes hand in hand with this, it is only the kind of existential loneliness that is the focus of the title poem. In it, we see the Café des Artistes vividly, are able to see details which are not described as such; its six panels of wood nymphs on the wall, for example, the strategically-placed mirrors, a temporary resting place for celebrities and artists:

> Mr Loneliness takes his usual seat
> at the corner furthest from the door,
> and moves the pepper pots aside
> for a better view of the floor.

Contemporary poets, therefore, are treated as itinerant, in a sense almost homeless, shifting from place to place with their belongings in their bags, like cartoon sailors, implicitly as irresponsible and as bibulous as cartoon sailors might be considered to be, explored at length in 'Port':

> The poets are leaving,
> wheeling their strange bags
> to the harbour's edge [...]
>
> In colourless rooms
> the widows lock up
> decanters of the dark red wine.

Dominating the sixty-eight pages of this wonderful collection for me, though, is the presence of 'The Blind Dog,' introduced to us in the twenty-seventh poem: 'in the Hotel Egalitarian / the taps drip, here are containers / to catch the water, the bath tub / is big enough to hold a dog, / but the dog is blind / and bumps its nose against the taps / and the beds are too short.' Again the hotel could be in any capital in the world, and is as much allegorical as real; throughout it there is an obvious sense of the blind dog leading the blind who 'pass each other with surly shouts and imperatives / that have to do with the end of free electricity, / shouting *Where's the dog?*' Nothing fits into the Hotel Egalitarian, it does not know how to make its clients fit; its blind dog is in the attic, the basement and in every room, but cannot offer guidance. The Hotel Egalitarian is Hartley Williams's truest embodiment of estrangement, restlessness and longing for home. It is at once the hotel all travelling poets have stayed in at some stage, unable to sleep, vaguely watching some foreign football match at four in the morning; it is also Roy Fuller's 'cellular hotel', the body in which we stay for a while as guest, perhaps, but never quite learn how to feel comfortable in – the hotel in the rooms of which we have a being other than idea.

Café des Artistes is an outstanding collection. It puts real vigour into the notion of artist-in-exile and articulates it wonderfully with a language that is quite as inventive as it has ever been, if not more so. The characteristic imagistic fervour is arresting; page for page – be prepared for the tempo of its delivery; there's scarcely the time to recover from the last image before you are hit by the next. The donkey-jacket that is 'A coat / smelling of tarpaulins, / thrown across track / in rain...'; Bacchus's tongue that is '...claret-sticky'; the love poem opening with the line 'Zou-Zou, You were the eyes of my otherness'; and, memorably, in 'The Pope's Dreams:' 'No more skin, no more / teeth, no more breath, no more perfume. / *God hates apothecaries*.' And so forth. It is somehow hard on all the other images in the book to isolate just a few at their expense. This is Hartley Williams's ninth collection and might just be his best to date. Poem for poem it deploys his long-ago mastered technical powers to maximum effect: the formal suppleness, the one-off diction, the sly asides, the absurdist leaps and – despite its eclecticism – the sense of unity which comes from sustaining the underlying theme of productive estrangement.

John Levett

Michael Hulse: ***The Secret History*** (Arc, 2009), ISBN 978-1906570-24-8, £9.99, 113pp (pb)

'Life beats art, so to speak, and sense beats eccentricity' wrote Randall Jarrell and his words provide one way into Michael Hulse's new collection of predominantly autobiographical poems. In their openness and honesty they conform to what Jarrell went on to say '...the way things really are beats the most beautiful unreal visions, half-truths, one can fix up by leaving out and indulging oneself.' Sensitive areas of Hulse's life are revealed in these poems full of love and candour about the lives and deaths of his parents, his own past relationships and losses, his friendships, the tensions inherent in his English/German background and the enriching fulfilments that come with love, marriage and the birth of a child.

Two poems stand sentinel at either end of this emotional journey. 'Caput Mortuum' is a verbal and syntactic tour-de-force pouring without pause over seven four line stanzas in an exacting contemplation of the colour blue. 'To our unborn daughter'(after Sophocles) is a more personal and direct message, its language pared down compared to the bravura refulgence of the opening poem's chromatic catalogue. It is just as aesthetically engaged but pauses, after considering a range of natural phenomena, human vanity and high artistic achievements, to point out that

> These, though not ours to give, are yours to inherit

viz. the deceptively simple yet powerfully elegant gift of a complex insight to an unborn child.

Hulse's hypersensitivity to the insecurities of life are never far below the surface and give his work an edgy truthfulness as in these lines describing images of our past selves from 'The Kid':

> They never speak to us, those kids. They scarcely seem
> to know that we are what they have become. Always
> they're looking for someone else.....

and

> .....might we fail our own past?

The metaphysical shiver this invokes is a pervasive element in many of the poems, ghosting as it does around sincere autobiographical detail, darting in and out of historical narratives that, in their telling, are brought to bear on modern life, and moving elusively amongst an array of convincing contemporary detail – Reeboks, subways, fast-food outlets, Anna Kournikova and WALK/DON'T WALK signs. These truthful stories are studded with beautiful lines:

> throbbing Latin murmurous as diesel
> ('The Tunic of Christ')

> .....the muscled confluence
> that gave this German town its Latin name....
> ('All Saints' Day in Konz')

Evocations of a peaceful beauty are not the only chords, however, and exist alongside a concise and destabilizing wit.

> At the foot of the concrete campanile
> of the post-war church like a paper hat...
> ('All Saints' Day in Konz')

Brutalities are recounted with a clear-eyed directness:

> One enemy she had chained to a manger
> eating and shitting where he stood,
> an ass in all but the braying...
> ('The Secret History')

Contrasting with this is the extraordinary shift of tone from the same poem:

> the alabaster light on your upturned
> face and the greatness of beauty unfolding
> within you like sun on a rose...

Time and again Hulse retrieves an unexpected beauty from the cruelties he is only too aware of and teases out a morality from affectless historical anecdote to give us, in our own brutal world, some degree of hope.

Sincerity and brave honesty are difficult qualities to sustain across such a wide emotional register. One of art's purposes, as is clear from many of these poems, is to shape and transform our pain into aesthetic objects – Auden's 'Rummaging into his living, the poet fetches/The images out that hurt and connect...' Unmediated, however, pain and hurt remain simply that. So, if I do have any misgiving about this collection, it is that sometimes, for me, the autobiographical truth, told with fidelity, is not entirely transformed and so does not always pass beyond having a documentary interest. Where this is most apparent, most exposed, is in the occasional tell-tale failure of craft.

Technique is a line of defence as well as a tool for exploration and when it breaks down it can alert us to a sensibilty becoming, under the stress of too great an emotion, fatigued. Some of the poems in this collection do contain these faultlines. All of the poems have virtues but some, for me, are marred by such problems. 'Wintereisse' is a sincere and ambitious poem in three sections written predominantly in octosyllabic rhyming couplets. Hulse would not, I think, normally settle for such well-patented phrases as 'surprised by joy' and 'come to dust' or the inversions 'liked it not' and 'The touch of fire it is I've lost' or lines such as

> ...and act as if I weren't unduly
> Troubled by the grace of Julie...

But then, in the same poem, he astounds with a skilfully turned insight:

> the pyrrhic victories of art
> Over the knowledge of the heart.

It is, perhaps, an impertinence to complain about perceived stylistic shortcomings when such strong emotions are in play. Paramount in 'Wintereisse' is the poet's need to convey an intense and complex set of feelings and it is probably unfair to quote out of context. All writers who are remembered, however, are taken out of context at some stage and a telling test of a poem is its ability to survive credibly when dissassembled, as it surely will be, even if only by a notoriously faulty public memory.

Just as Jarrell gave us a way into this collection, he also provides a caveat to place on these reservations:

> Really one expects most of a good poet's work to be quite bad – if that isn't so it's the 30th February; it's amusing to have reviewers complain that some of the poems in a poetry book aren't good, because that applies to every book of verse there ever was.

This is an intelligent and moving collection. Michael Hulse has set out to be unflinchingly honest about his own life set against the wider background of European history, the heights of its artistic achievements and the depths of its falls from grace. He writes with a controlled passion, close to the spoken word, using sophisticated effects to locate the significant and develop its larger emotional truth. Such art and honesty make us all want to believe that tomorrow could be the 30th February.

Bernard Spencer (1909-1963) Centenary Supplement

Introduced and compiled by Peter Robinson

Charles Bernard Spencer was born into a collateral branch of the Spencer-Churchill family in Madras, India, the second son of Sir Charles Gordon Spencer, a high court judge, on 9 November 1909. He was sent to England in 1911, to be brought up by relatives and guardians with his elder brother John and his sister Cynthia, at first in Southampton, then in Crowell, Oxfordshire. From 1918 the latter part of his childhood was spent at Rowner, near Gosport, one of the reasons why yachts, boats, and ships figure so prominently in his poetry. In 1923 he followed his brother to the traditional family school of Marlborough, where he was a contemporary of Anthony Blunt, and met the more senior John Betjeman and Louis MacNeice. In the Michaelmas term of 1928, he went up to Corpus Christi, Oxford, as a Gentleman Commoner. His closest friend there was his near contemporary Isaiah Berlin. In 1930 he co-edited *Oxford Poetry* with Stephen Spender and the following year with Richard Goodman.

In the summer of 1932 Spencer graduated with a second-class degree in Greats. Once he left university, it has not proved easy to follow his tracks during the rest of the 1930s, though a number of important developments are clear. Some letters and a poem, for example, sent to Rosamond Lehmann (to whom he had been introduced by Spender) have survived in her archive at Kings College, Cambridge. Selina Hastings, in *Rosamond Lehmann: A Life* (2002), dismissively reports the young poet's brief infatuation with his hostess. In November 1934 he was with the family when his father died at the family home Tarwood House, South Leigh, Oxfordshire. Between 1935 and 1938 he helped Geoffrey Grigson edit *New Verse*, and it was there that most of his mature early work appeared. On 1 August 1936 he married Nora Kathleen Gibbs at the Hampstead Register Office. During these years he also worked as a Classics teacher at Chipping Norton Secondary School, Hillside School, Reigate, Harrow View House, Ealing, and Westminster School. He was for a time a copywriter in Royds' Advertising Agency, the Strand, a scriptwriter for a film company, and co-wrote the biography of a Victorian politician, Sir Henry Cunninghame, which appeared in 1938.

These years of uncertain direction were given shape and a more clearly documented track on 16 February 1940 when Spencer – born with a congenital heart condition that rendered him unfit for military service, and permanently in precarious states of health – joined the newly formed British Council and travelled with his wife by train via Belgrade and Athens to Salonika in Greece. There he became a Teacher at the Institute of English Studies, where he also acted as the Librarian. Nora returned to London for a holiday before the Fall of

France and she appears to have been refused permission to return to Greece. Through the war years Nora worked at the Ministry of Supply in London in a secretarial post. During July and August of 1940 Spencer was on Mykonos with Lawrence Durrell and Nanos Valaoritis, his future co-translators of George Seferis' poetry. On the 28 October the Italians invaded Greece and in that month air raids on Salonika began. The Hotel Luxembourg was hit and Spencer's room demolished. The British Institute was damaged in several bombardments and closed by police. By Christmas, Spencer was in Athens waiting for a transfer to Fuad I University in Cairo. His British Council record says that he was posted to Egypt in December, to take up the lecturing post in March. It seems, however, that he left Greece by ship in January, evacuated with Robert Liddell.

As well as lecturing at the university, Spencer gave talks on painting and literary subjects at the Institutes of Cairo and Alexandria. They were joined by the great exile from Greece in May. During the late summer, in the gardens of the Anglo-Egyptian Union, Durrell, Robin Fedden and Spencer came up with the idea for the magazine that would become *Personal Landscape* (1942-1945). This is the second journal of the three with which his poetry was to be principally associated. In 1942 he met Keith Douglas, some of whose work first appeared in the magazine, as, in the final issue, did Spencer's obituary for the poet killed in Normandy. Durrell had the right to use the diplomatic bag to convey material back to London, and it was he who sent Spencer's poetry to T. S. Eliot at Faber & Faber. In June 1942, the period of the 'Flap' when the fleet withdrew and papers were burned because Rommel had reached El Alamein, Spencer spent time in Palestine. When his wife Nancy left him in July, Durrell moved in with Spencer at 27 Sharia Malika Farida, opposite the Mohammed Ali Club, where editorial meetings for *Personal Landscape* took place. On 11 November a party to celebrate the new issue of the magazine, Robin Fedden's marriage to Renée Catzeflis, and Durrell's departure for Alexandria took place at the flat. Though the years from late 1942 may have been ones in which Spencer undertook some of the translations of Seferis that were published as *The King of Asine and Other Poems* (1948), these were years in which the dates on the post-1930s section of *Aegean Islands and Other Poems* (1946) suggest he wrote no poetry. In November 1944 Olivia Manning's essay in *Horizon* asserts that Spencer's poems 'never pretend to be more than they are', and this is a key indication both of their unique value, and their resistance to a facile success. At Faber & Faber, Eliot's decision was to wait until the poet had a complete book of post-Thirties poems. His secretary, Anne Ridler, passed the manuscript on to Tambimuttu, which is how Spencer's first collection came to be published by Editions Poetry London in the year after war ended.

Spencer's wife Nora joined him in Cairo in early 1945, where she appears to have done some broadcasting. The confidential British Council report by a Mr. Furness in January notes: 'In such contacts as I have had with him, I have found him satisfactory to deal with, though except among his intimates he has a rather unforthcoming manner. He used often to strike me as somewhat melancholy, but I have the impression that he has been more contented of late, especially since his wife joined him a few weeks ago.' In August the couple returned to England 'on account of ill-health' according to a British Council document. Tambimuttu wrote to Durrell on Patmos at about this time reporting a reunion of the Cairo exiles – Ruth Speirs, Bernard Spencer and Gwyn Williams – in London. By the autumn, the poet was writing educational notes at the Council's Film Department in London, waiting for a permanent position in the overseas service of the Council. On 1 July 1946 he was posted to a lectureship at the British Institute in Palermo, Sicily, leaving England on the 28 August to take up the post on 1 September. Spencer had begun writing his own poetry again. 'On the Road', written during the following year, may be recalling this journey through harvest France. During that winter Nora became ill with TB, dying of heart failure caused by the disease in Rome (where the couple had gone in the spring to find treatment) on 13 June. She is buried in the Protestant Cemetery, just behind Gramsci's grave.

On 1 September, Spencer was posted to Turin, as Lecturer at the British Institute. Durrell is reported by his biographer, Gordon Bowker, in *Through the Dark Labyrinth* (1996) to have met the newly widowed Spencer in Lisbon during November 1947, where the poet is said to have been working for the British Council. While there is no evidence for such a posting to Portugal it is at least possible that Spencer made a journey to visit his friend who was on route for Argentina. Spencer returned to London on 17 May 1948, himself suffering from tuberculosis, and on 1 September went to Leysin, Switzerland, for treatment involving surgery on the lungs done with a local anesthetic. By December he was back in London, doing light duties at the Council's Davis Street offices. *The King of Asine and Other Poems* by George Seferis appeared from John Lehmann in 1948, and Lehmann was to publish Spencer's poetry in *The London Magazine* after he had re-founded the journal in February 1954.

The poet's post-war life began to take a more steadied shape when in September 1949 he was posted to Madrid as a lecturer at the British Institute. It is also from this point that complete manuscript records of Spencer's poetry begin to survive. On 1 September 1955 he was posted to Athens, an interlude that came to an end the following year. Spring 1956 saw the escalation of the Cyprus crisis, which led to the poet being expelled from Athens by the Greek authorities in the summer. The British Council, though, has him returning to England for health reasons in June, and correspondence in the archives with Ian Fletcher suggests that he heard of his expulsion from Greece when already in London. Spencer was based at the Council's London headquarters until January 1958 when he took up a temporary appointment as a lecturer at Ankara, Turkey. By September of the same year he was back in Madrid, once again a lecturer at the Institute, and it was in the Spanish capital that he was to meet his second wife, Anne Marjoribanks. On 31 December 1960 *The Twist in the Plotting*, a limited edition of twenty-five poems, was published by the Fine Art Department at the University of Reading. This volume was commissioned and overseen by Ian Fletcher. On 6 April 1961 a party was held at the British Institute, Madrid, to celebrate publication. In July, Spencer and Anne were in Ibiza, where archival material shows he wrote 'Boat Poem'; and this holiday was followed by a visit to London to have a check-up with his doctor. On 29 September the poet was back in Madrid where the marriage to Anne took place.

In July of the following year, the couple left Madrid and in October 1962 Spencer was transferred to Vienna, as a lecturer at the university, employed by the British Council. On 7 February 1963 the poet's son Piers Bernard Spencer was born. That year the family summered in Italy on the Adriatic, with a visit to Venice. However, the holiday was interrupted because of a breakdown in Spencer's health. Already seriously ill with a high fever, he was inexplicably allowed to leave the Viennese clinic where his illness was being investigated. His body was discovered at 5 am on 11 September beside suburban railway lines, with head injuries that suggested he had been hit by a local train. The poet's widow had wished to have questions asked about why he was allowed to leave the clinic, but the Council did not want to strain relations with Austria. Various suggestions have been made for the poet's fever and sudden decay of mental powers ranging from an undiagnosed brain tumour to an enlarged prostate causing uric acid to infect the brain. After an autopsy, Spencer was cremated in Vienna. His ashes were returned to England and buried with his parents in Wheatfield, Oxfordshire. Alan Ross had been featuring new poems written in Vienna in *The London Magazine*, and in 1965 he brought out the first edition of Spencer's *Collected Poems*. This was followed by Roger Bowen's enlarged and lightly annotated edition, which appeared from Oxford University Press in 1981.

Bernard Spencer is not one of the four poets – Auden, Spender, MacNeice and Day-Lewis – whose names were to be made synonymous with English poetry in the 1930s. He had, though, known one of them, Louis MacNeice, at both Marlborough and Oxford, and with another, Stephen Spender, had edited a volume of *Oxford Poetry*. (His view of Auden was briefly stated in a comment for a double issue of *New Verse* dedicated to the poet in 1937). Yet, in a recent Allott Lecture at the University of Liverpool, Christopher Reid chose to talk about a different grouping, Auden, MacNeice and Spencer, making a point by this seeming misprint (for 'Spender' read 'Spencer'), which not a few of those well-read in 1930s poetry would agree with – namely, that while the reputations of Spender and Day-Lewis have been in decline since their hey-day, and the much larger oeuvres of Auden and MacNeice contain much forced and arid writing, the more modest but no less complex poetry of Spencer has yet to reach its proper level of appreciation. The manuscript and typescript remains at the University of Reading suggest a poet motivated to complete poems as he felt them emerge, and happy to have them placed in friendly magazines or read on the BBC Third Programme. Yet he was clearly incapable of writing attention-seeking work, and not inclined to initiate or actively pursue volume publication. What did happen to Spencer's poetry that aided its survival in the reading public's mind was its regular appearance in anthologies over almost forty years from the end of the 1930s to the mid-1970s. Though Spencer was never the voice of his times, this has meant that his work can speak so much more clearly from its own circumstances, its own times, and the vicissitudes of a life that, while marked by difficulties, was lived with a sense of unhurried dedication to poetry that is manifested by the manuscript remains held in Special Collections at the University of Reading.

At the time of his death, Spencer had recently expressed the hope that, after many years of living abroad and on the margins of a largely insular English poetry establishment, he might be finding some recognition for his art. His book, *With Luck Lasting*, published by Hodder and Stoughton just months earlier, had been named a Poetry Book Society Recommendation alongside Charles Tomlinson's *A Peopled Landscape*. Though death meant that such a fate was not to be for him, it did issue in a moment of attention for his life and work, especially in *The London Magazine*. Martin Dodsworth's 'Bernard Spencer: The Poet of Addition', first published in 1964, raised discussion of his work to a new level of seriousness and subtlety. At about the same time, Robin Skelton's anthologies, *Poetry of the Thirties* (1964) and *Poetry of the Forties* (1968), included nine of his works, while Edward Lucie-Smith found space for two in his anthology *British Poetry since 1945* (1970), its editor praising Spencer in a head-note for 'precision of imagery' and 'truth to feeling'. Three years later, in *A Poetry Chronicle*, Ian Hamilton aptly noted that his poetry of the 1930s and 1940s resisted the dehumanizing effects of war and foreshadowed the modes of Movement writing. Yet the simplified notion that Spencer is a mere precursor of 1950s poetry needs strenuously combating. During the 1990s, Roger Bowen's *'Many Histories Deep': The Personal Landscape Poets in Egypt, 1940-45* (1995) and Jonathan Bolton's *Personal Landscapes: British Poets in Egypt during the Second World War* (1997) both included chapters concentrating on the understated and self-effacing virtues of Bernard Spencer, a writer whose poems, as Durrell wrote at the time of his death, recall those of Edward Thomas, adding that 'his best poems will certainly live as long as the best of Thomas.'

Uncollected Early Poems

Above, the fingers of the tree …

Above, the fingers of the tree
high above, the arched sky
stood immense, grave with cloud:
her eyes, turned to me
by her aliveness were made quick.
Between deliberate sky and slow river
for a glance, amazed, I held as tenant
more than was owed to them and their summer,
where their live world
ends, beyond this, alive.

Oxford Poetry (1930)

Departure

The hills begin their march again; Pauline
admired, untouched, is drowned out by their waves;
the old lady, whose sick bed, never seen
unearthed soon-silenced voices from the graves
now treads the night-waiting stars: and Destiny
takes moods and manners from the breathing one
unbodied now in brain; from the dead lady
her dying, and with some small leaf upon
a hedge, seen carelessly, shuts them up all
for good into the cupboards of the mind.

At loss, the mind grows older in this school
holds harder to life, if that's what is designed.

Oxford Poetry (1930)

Those near and dead who think there is another ...

Those near and dead who think there is another
Death to pray against, claim their memory –
thoughts that I believed three nations' frontiers
and a sea stretched to hide.
Mountains now blue over earth's rim
wished for, be near, big gods,
outbulk our small thinking
for fear these thoughts and my loathing,
strong acid, burn away your shadows
while distance still promises, untrusted,
while they are strangers
on the skirt, there, of the sky
still, and the people crowd to the carriage windows.

Oxford Poetry (1930)

Two Poems

i

My pulling on of shoes
My opening of doors
Speaking – the hundred acts
That serve my hourly use

Are then not disparate
Are nationals of one blood;
Closer, the raiding eyes
The thoughts around each gate

Are surely dyed the same;
In these, too, lover is,
And I, since I have loved you,
In everything I change
On the world must write your name.

That for sense enough keen
Within a street I must
From the rest show different;
And though I walk still here
I breathe, from what I had been,
Your love's whole air distant.

ii

Her hands waking on her lap
Let out in me a prisoner,
Her hands' unclasping fired the train
That lit my mind with her:

I saw her limbs were a well full
From the same source that moved the day's
Swift over heart of slow; she was all
Desires walking their natural ways.

(Suddenly I saw this. Surprise
Was yet such sort as understood
How long this truth, she being near,
Had housed in bone, run in the blood.)

Also, though to no coward mind,
She was healing, and of Sleep's nature.
I saw that in her love I would find
Sharpness to cut the sun into
This sensual tent in which I am blind.

Oxford Outlook (February 1932)

Poem

Who sees the rain fall into the Spring land
And the sun's attack from hill to hill behind,
Who in the wind, from a new quarter blowing,
Smells the year turning, the new hungers preying;

Who feels at pulse the general advance
And each defence marched down by suns and rains,
Now on him too the hands strong above choice
Pressing to strange streets, promising no ease;

Young, may he have his wish, have from the start
A credit of pride to overtide first doubt;
Success on his first making or ordering
Shine down remembered failing, stammering.

From friends through various disguise may he tell
The close spies weaving against will
Urging to give place to an admired one,
Be blunted with kind names, or use caution.

Sometimes with lover feel that unique force
That makes the 'I' all things and every place,
For lover is new, lover is from outside,
Stronger than the tower where the man is tied.

Fused in these hours to all that has world's name
Into one circuit with them with no break,
— World run the rivers of its strength through him,
World that he nerved himself against, and was weak.

Oxford Outlook (May 1932)

For seeing whole I had been too near my friends ...

For seeing whole I had been too near my friends:
When we drank or drove I came near to one,
Near to another in speaking of a woman:
What could I hold back, using their blood, their brain?

In part only I saw them. Then in the train
I crossed fields that had never known their fire;
An evening country turning, hedges and trees
Not leaved with their words and laughter, as those were.

The brow of Summer matched against their quickness
Made them seem far and overshadowed them.
They must spill apart and change whom I thought firm;
I saw them draw like green things to their time.

Oxford Poetry (1932)

Such height of corn, so many miles ...

Such height of corn, so many miles
Of Summer's uncountable heads held up,
One standing mane, to the dusk lights
Lit on the hills —

Suddenly held all my mind. Earth
Smelled, and was the wealthiest table laid.
Earth, like a precious grain-ship, sailed
With its cargo's worth.

'There I must change,' 'there was denied,'
'There failed.' Dark as the cloud I saw ride
West above the fields, was the thought;
'Wanting what men do, from what plenty
I must go wide.'

Oxford Poetry (1932)

Uncollected Translations

Odysseus Elytis

The Mad Pomegranate-Tree

In these whitewashed courtyards where the South Wind blows
Whistling through arcaded rooms, O tell me
Is it the mad pomegranate-tree
That darts into the light scattering her fertile laughter
With whims and whispers of the wind
O tell me is it the mad pomegranate-tree
That shakes with newborn foliage at dawn
Opening all her colours high with shudders of triumph?

When the naked girls awake in the plains
Reaping the clovers with their fair hands
Tossing the depths of their slumber
O tell me is it this mad pomegranate-tree
That slips the lights in their fresh baskets
That overflows their names with songs
Is it the mad pomegranate-tree
That flights the shadows of the world?

The jealous day adorns herself with seven glowing wings
Surrounding the eternal sun with a million prisms
O tell me is it this mad pomegranate-tree
That grasps a horse's mane with a hundred lashes
In her runaway race
Sometimes sad and sometimes grumbling
O tell me is it the mad pomegranate-tree
Shouting the dawn of a new hope?

O tell me is it this mad pomegranate-tree
Rejoicing in the far-away
Shaking a handkerchief of leaves and fresh fire
A sea pregnant with a thousand ships
With waves that run and roll for ever
Towards untrodden shores, O tell me
Is it the mad pomegranate-tree
That creaks her rigging high in the lucid air?

In the grape-blue heights feasting and flaring
Defiant, dangerous, tell me
Is it the mad pomegranate-tree
Smashing with light clean in the middle of the world
The tempests of the demon
Spreading from end to end
The yellow mane of dawn
Embroidered with crops and songs
O tell me is it the mad pomegranate-tree
That swiftly unfastens the silk dress of the day?

In April's petticoats and the cicadas of August
O tell me, she who plays, she who works, she who drives us crazy
shaking from Menace all his bad black shadows
Pouring drunken birds into the sun
O tell me she that opens her wings in the breast of things
In the breast of our deep dreams
Is it the mad pomegranate-tree?

Translated by **Nanos Valaoritis** *and* **Bernard Spencer**

First published in *New Writing and Daylight 7 (1946)*

George Seferis

The Mourning Girl

You sat on the rock waiting
as the night came on
and the pupil of your eye showed
how much you suffered.

And your lips were drawn in a way
exposed and trembling
as if your soul were whirled like a spinning-wheel
and your tears were pleading.

And you had in your mind the thought
of yielding to tears
you were a body falling from its bloom
back to its seed.

But there was no cry from your heart's breaking:
that breaking became
the meaning, scattered upon the world
by the sky, all stars.

Translated by **Bernard Spencer**

Broadcast on The BBC Third Programme (1957)

Denial

Upon the hidden beach
white as a dove
we were thirsty in the mid-day heat
the water was bitter.

Across the yellow sand
we wrote her name.
Marvellously the breeze blew:
scattered our writing.

We were daring then, we were brilliant,
full of longing and passion:
we snatched our life. What fools!
Life has changed now.

Translated by **Bernard Spencer**

Broadcast on The BBC Third Programme (1957)

Bernard Spencer

University Of Madrid Lecture

The lecture exists as 11 numbered hand-written pages of manuscript, in blue biro on lined paper, to which is attached a cyclostyled handout entitled 'Poems by Bernard Spencer' containing nine works. It is held in the Bernard Spencer archive at Special Collections, the University of Reading, catalogue number BSP 2/4/1 [MS 5369]. The text has been lightly edited for consistency of accidentals and capitalizations, while the paragraphing and layout have been adjusted a little here and there for ease of reading. I have also indicated, when necessary, where the poems are to be read.

I feel I should explain why I am not offering you a lecture on some more important subject than my own poems. In fact this is not even a real lecture. It sounds a bit 'pushing,' as we say, to come here and talk about my own work. But the fact is that I had been away on sick leave and hadn't got anything else ready when I was asked to contribute to this English-American week. And I was told that a reading of my own poems with a bit of talk about them was something which you might accept instead of a regular lecture. In fact, I was persuaded into doing this by my great friend Dr Sophia Martin Gemero and Professor Pujals. Now Professor Pujals and I first met by letter. It was at a time when after spending six very happy years in Madrid at the British Institute I had been moved to a job in Athens. (Everyone wants a job in Madrid...) Anyhow, I was in Athens, in about 1956, when I received a letter from Dr Pujals saying things which I thought very flattering about some poems which I had recently published in *The London Magazine*. The poems he liked had Spanish subjects, or backgrounds. Now this was very gratifying, very pleasing to me, especially as coming from someone I didn't know, except that he was a distinguished member of the staff of the Instituto de España in London. And to take the trouble to write to me! When you publish a poem in a magazine you usually get no reaction at all. It is like a sailor shipwrecked on a desert island who throws a bottle into the sea with a message in it ... or like dropping a stone down a well ...

And then last year Dr Pujals very kindly wrote an article about my poems in the *Filologia Moderna*.[1] So by the combined forces Dr Sophia Martin Gemero and Dr Pujals, you can see how I was persuaded to give this talk to you today.

I think there is a certain interest in the biography of any artist.[2] I will give you the relevant facts of mine very briefly. I am told that at the age of two I came back

---

[1] Esteban Pujals, 'Poemas de Bernard Spencer', *Filologia Moderna* no. 3, Madrid, abril 1961, pp. 19-27. Spencer adds the marginal comment: 'I ought really to read that. So much better!'

[2] A marginal note beside this sentence reads: 'What kind of a poet / What is involved in writing poetry / What poets are trying to do.'

from a childrens' party reciting, although rather indistinctly, some verses from *The Lays of Ancient Rome*, written in the beginning of the nineteenth century, by Macaulay. Some strong visual images and an infectious, swinging metre. I had apparently heard some grown up repeat them. I suppose I had that much of the poet in me that I was already fond of words. Sometime before I was five, because I remember the house where I did it, I ate a whole newspaper. I remember the difficulty I had in finishing it. I suppose I was fond of print. I learned to read rather earlier than most children, mostly through boredom, and read anything I could find, indiscriminately and always enthusiastically. I suppose I was not meant to be a critic. My parents lived abroad and I was brought up by guardians in remote places in the English countryside. I had to find my own entertainment – and to amuse myself – most of the time; and I suppose a certain amount of loneliness and boredom nourishes the artistic imagination. What you haven't got you invent. When I was at school I used to tell imaginary adventure stories to the other boys[3] – though some of the others could do that also – and later on I used to make up funny poems to make people laugh. As I grew older, while still a schoolboy, I read lots of poetry of the nineteenth century – the Romantics, especially Keats, William Morris, Swinburne and Matthew Arnold; and in the twentieth century such Romantics of this period as Masefield and James Elroy Flecker, both of whom wrote poetry which was based on travel abroad. I was lucky enough to travel abroad myself, while still a schoolboy, for holidays to France, Switzerland, Italy and Belgium. I mention this because I used to pray that I should be a traveler abroad when I grew up, just as I used to pray that I should be a poet, and both prayers have been to some extent answered! I think my travels, which have been mostly around the Mediterranean, have had a good deal to do with my poetry, both because of the stimulus of seeing many varied places, and because I have been exposed to some extent to the literature of other countries.

Anyhow, to return to my later schooldays, under the influence of the Romantic poets I have mentioned I began to write poems which curiously enough sounded a bit like bad Keats and Shelley, and from one point of view were not so funny as my earlier ones. But I remember, with the money given me for a school prize, buying not only the earlier works of W. B. Yeats, the great Irish poet who died only a little before the last world war, but also a volume of George Herbert, the Seventeenth Century poet. And he has always remained one of my great admirations because of his deep feeling, his essential innocence, and his sparing and curious use of words. His sense of a tight pattern. This was a new sort of influence, no longer of the Romantic school, and you will see that it connected with what I was thinking about and reading later. At Oxford University I continued studying Latin and Greek, which was a healthy influence in the sense of making you careful about how many words you use – not to use too many. The advice that Latin and Greek literature give is: think hard while

[3] Marginal remark: 'Once told a story which went on for two years. Tolstoy put to shame.'

you feel warmly. There is a story on this topic about a poet who showed a poem of his to Ezra Pound, the American poet and important critic, whose views about poetry made a deep impression on such different poets as W. B. Yeats and T. S. Eliot. Ezra Pound read the poem through and said: 'You could have written the same poem with two syllables less.'

At Oxford I published poetry in the styles that were accepted then: one of the styles owed a good deal to T. S. Eliot, a style which was reserved, ironical and dry. To show you what our admirations in literature were then, I will quote to you a little rhyme written by a university student of that time – even though he was from Cambridge and not from Oxford. There is in English an old prayer which used to be recited by children when they went to bed. It is this, and it calls on the names of the disciples: 'Matthew, Mark, Luke and John / Bless the bed that I lie on.'[4] In order to show the literary influences of those times, the student wrote: 'Eliot, Rabelais, Dryden, Donne / Bless the bed that I lie on.' T. S. Eliot at that time was writing critical essays, which you no doubt have read, very much praising the poetry of the seventeenth century, and recommending our return to that tradition. So we might have continued writing this learned sort of poetry, full of references, if it had not been for the International Financial Crisis – the Slump – which prevailed from 1929 on until 1932 and beyond, and, following that, the steady growth of international tensions, the rise of the Nazi State in Germany, the Italian occupation of Abyssinia, the Civil War in Spain. Millions became unemployed in Europe. Many people in the 1930s were wondering whether they would lose their job in the following month, and they were also wondering how soon their country would be at war.

In this way there arose the so-called Social Poetry of the 1930s, in which the subject of poetry was often Man in his Social Situation, and also the impending war. Leading figures in this movement were W. H. Auden and Stephen Spender, both of whom had travelled and seen conditions in Europe, not only in England. They used to write for a magazine called *New Verse*, to which I also used to contribute. The general view among these poets, supported by poems and critical articles from the editor, Geoffrey Grigson, was that the poet should not be a withdrawn visionary, but one in the middle of the events of his time, with a view that extended beyond the frontiers of his country. (Colloquialism of language, less scholarly than Eliot).

One poem of mine, which dates from this time, is in the well-known anthology *Contemporary Verse*.[5] It is rather staccato, and awkward, in the manner of the time,

---

[4] Spencer cites the first couplet of a quatrain by John Davenport in *Cambridge Poetry* (London: Hogarth Press, 1929): 'Eliot, Rabelais, Dryden, Donne / Bless the bed that I lie on, / Blake and Rimbaud, Marvell, Voltaire, / Swift, Joyce, Proust and Baudelaire.'

[5] At this point Spencer has written 'BOOK', which may mean that he showed the audience a copy of *The Penguin Book of Contemporary Verse* ed. Kenneth Allott (1950), which contains 'Allotments: April' (1935) and 'On the Road' (1947). His subsequent remarks make it clear that he has the first of these poems in mind.

but I still think it does what it sets out to do, which is to show how man in a setting of Nature and Spring is at the same time man in a setting of Society, of Politics and Economics. In 1939, whether we wanted it or not, we in England had to face Man in his Social Setting; a pessimist might say Man in his Preferred Social Setting – the one where he likes to be: The World War had started.

The Social School of Poetry no longer existed in its earlier sense. And this brings me to the first poem I want to read to you today: 'Base Town'. At the outbreak of the war between Greece and Italy, the so-called Albanian War, I was in Salonika in Northern Greece, which was the nearest big town to the front where the fighting was taking place: the date was 1940. Salonica is a very Macedonian sea-town, rather primitive, smelling strongly of fish and fruit and the kind of resinous wood which is burnt everywhere as fuel. There are some splendid Byzantine churches. The town with its bay is set among wild, barren hills, and in winter, when this campaign was mostly fought, it is intensely cold, especially when a North East wind, the 'Varda', sweeps down from Russia. In this poem I am trying to give the impression of what it is like to be near to a war, yet not quite of it. In verse 3 I mention the air raids which in fact one night entirely gutted or destroyed the inside of the hotel where I was staying. I had spent that particular night in another part of town because I had been celebrating someone's birthday! The air raids happened at fairly regular times, so we used to arrange to have our meals specially early or specially late so that we didn't have to get up in the middle of them to go to the shelters. I have tried to give the weird, uneasy feeling of not actually *seeing* the enemy, except his aeroplanes, and yet knowing that anyone you spoke to might be an enemy agent or sympathizer. And indeed you yourself were suspicious in the eyes of other people. ['Base Town' – see page 255].

As I have said, I have spent a lot of my life in countries around the Mediterranean, and for me the olive tree is a sort of symbol of this part of the world, and also of the ancient civilizations, especially the Greek civilization, which flourished there. That is what I am speaking about in the third verse where I am thinking of how these trees which often look so ancient themselves, 'crones' in verse 1, must have been the background to the building of new towns and the destruction or falling to pieces of the same towns. They are like spectators at a play which is human history.

This poem came to me when I was on a long bus journey in Israel, going East from the coast near Haifa and up into the hills. I remember that the bus passed through miles and miles of olive groves as the road climbed. For most of the time I had not got a seat and had to stand; and I was peering out at the olive trees and going over in my mind all the things I had been thinking about olive trees for years – how old they look, and how I like the colour of them, and how I don't like eating 'aceitunas'[6] – how there was something rather grim

---

[6] Spanish for 'green olives'.

or dour about them, and yet something beautiful and attractive; in fact I was talking to myself, a little bit to pass the time on the long journey, and I found that what I was saying to myself was beginning to be a poem. And here it is: ['Olive Trees' – see page 256]. You may notice that the hard consonants in the first verse suggest the hard, forbidding quality of the trees; and the soft long sounds in the second verse correspond to the change of thought. And I want the sounds at the end of the fourth verse to give an impression of heaviness and stoniness.

In 1958, shortly before I returned to Spain, I went to Turkey to work at the University of Ankara for six months, and I was taken one holiday time for a journey by car through the plain of Anatolia, where you can drive for two hours without seeing a village or even a house, only sometimes a flock of sheep with their wild-looking shepherd. It was after this journey that I wrote the next poem, 'Feathery Grasses'[7] [See page 257]. After crossing the plain we drove over the mountains and went to look at the remains of some ancient Greek towns on the South coast of Turkey. These towns, although overgrown with grass and weeds, often have recognizable remains of temples and theatres standing, with their semi-circular tiers of stone seats. So much loneliness and emptiness and all those ruins put me in a state of melancholy excitement. I was half attracted by it and half afraid. And the impulse to write poetry is partly the impulse to *sort out and understand* confused, worrying feelings. So I wrote this poem. What is the trap? What was I afraid of? Later, at his request, I read the poem out to a fellow poet, John Betjeman, and he cried out 'Oh! Eternity!' That is as good an answer as any.

In 1956 I left Madrid for some years, and before I left I thought I would like to put down the feelings I had for this city. I had for some time been writing a prose journal[8] in order to have some record of what it was like to live here, and so in this poem, 'Notes by a Foreigner' [see page 258], I am as it were talking to myself, as one does in a journal, and when I say *YOU* it means *ME*. I love Madrid, but the way I see it is probably different from the way another person would. And a foreigner sees it differently from a person who belongs to the city. That is the first meaning of the poem, but all poems have different depths of meaning, and the poem is not just about Madrid but about any town, and eventually it is about the strangeness of being in the world at all, the feeling that you may have invented the whole thing. More precious because you have? In the sixth and seventh verses there is a phrase 'dust-doomed' about the famous vivid Madrid sunsets. It is not 'dust' – 'doomed sunsets' etc ... I find it hard to make

---

[7] This is the earlier title and opening line of the poem called 'Delicate Grasses' in *With Luck Lasting* (Hodder and Stoughton, 1963) and subsequent printings.

[8] Though believed to have been lost when Roger Bowen published his edition of Spencer's *Collected Poems* (Oxford University Press, 1981), the Madrid Journal written in a green covered exercise book has been found, returned to the estate, and is now in the archive at Reading, with the catalogue number: BSP 2/10/1-2 [MS 5369].

printers and typists use the hyphen and not the dash. I am not quite sure what 'dust-doomed' means, but it sounds good! It is something to do with the dust in the air accounting for the extreme brilliance of the sunset, and the sunset itself having the appearance of doom and flames.

The next two poems were both written in Madrid. The first one, 'From my Window' [see page 259], is about the essential separation of different groups of people in a large city. The students in the first lines have nothing to do with the rich. And the poet, although he can see the rich behind their windows, is not likely to meet them and he can't even hear their voices, but only see them waving their hands. And the poor children, who are playing a game of Try to Catch Me, have nothing to do with the other groups. And finally the dog has to find company in the fire until it hears another dog barking a long way off.

The second poem, 'Morning in Madrid' [see page 259], is trying to do one of the things which poetry sometimes can do – to get the inscape or essence of something. It also contains an onomatopoeic tribute to those creatures I admire so much, the Madrid donkeys. I think the poem, being so short, gets a certain lightness from its feminine endings: 'calling', 'falling' – 'drifted', 'lifted'.

The next poem, 'In Athens' [see page 260], has a mood of tenderness and frustration and a certain irony. I was walking one day in Athens near the main square, which is called the Syntagma or Constitution Square, when a girl of about seventeen passed me whom I at first thought I recognized, in fact knew well. Well, I didn't. It must have been that she was like someone whom I knew and loved years and years ago. Yes, but Who? This part of Athens is very near the part where the ancient city stood, near the Acropolis, and I thought of those discussions on love and the emotions in the Dialogues of Plato (Platon) where he speaks of the human soul as being drawn by horses that sometimes pull in different directions – the horses of Impulse and the horses of Reason – in fact how love can play the hell with people – and play silly tricks on them too, as is expressed in one of the same dialogues, I think by Aristophanes, who Plato makes tell the story of how the Gods, to punish humanity, cut everyone in half, just as you cut an apple, and since then everyone has gone around searching for his or her other half. And in the second part of the poem there is a feeling of wonder at how all these things, the girl, the thoughts, the place should have come together – the surprise Twist of Fate – the Twist in the Plotting[9] ... In this poem you will see that I have not used rhyme because the turning, drifting, exploring nature of the thought seemed not to be suitable for rhyme. Too heavy handed.

My poems are often in the technical sense dramatic. That is to say they often present a figure or several figures in a landscape, which may be a city, at a moment of action or strong feeling, and these moments I feel have a bearing on certain truths about life which I am rediscovering. But of course the

---

[9] Spencer adopted this phrase for the title of his limited edition of 25 poems published in 1960.

rediscovery can't happen in the way of being told something, A=B, but only as a total experience of an artistic kind. The last poem I read to you was like that, and so are the two which follow. First 'The Lottery Sellers' [see page 261]: a familiar sight not only in Madrid but in other cities where I have lived. One of the sellers is a man, one a woman, and the woman is blind. That is why her gaze is 'lifted over roof tops'. I find too, that blind people often have strange, remote voices. These then turn into the personifications of Luck and Wealth which they offer their clients.

The next poem ['The Rendezvous' – see page 262] presents a very contemporary scene. It is that of a city, and I was living in one like this, where political rioting is taking place, and the satisfactions of the mob, which the army has had to be called in to restrain, have for the moment taken first place. Profounder, more human values have been for the time forgotten. As you walk down the empty street at night you see the political slogans on the walls; you see the soldiers, and you reflect that this is the town where two people had a *rendezvous*.

March 1962

Poems By Bernard Spencer

Base Town

Winter's white guard continual on the hills;
The wind savaging from the stony valleys
And the unseen front. And always the soldiers going,
Soldiers and lorries beating the streets of cobbles,
Like blood to where a wound is flowing.

War took friends, lights and names away. Clapped down
Shutters on windows' welcome. Brought those letters
Which wished to say so much they dared not say.
The proud and feminine ships in the harbour roads
Turned to a North-East grey.

Curious the intimacy we felt with Them;
We moved our meals to fit Their raids; we read
Their very hand across each bomb-slashed wall.
Their charred plane fallen in the cratered square
Held twisted in it all

Their work, Their hate, Their failure. Prisoners
Bearded and filthy, had bones, eyes and hair
Like other men in need. But dead like snow,
Cold like those racing winds or sirens' grief,
Was the hate which struck no blow:

The fear of speaking was a kind of tic
Pulling at the eyes. If stranger drank with stranger
It seemed thief drank with thief. Was it only every
Night, the fall of the early and lampless dark?
I remember it so often. And the lie,
The twist of reason,
The clever rumour planted in the nerves,
The dossier infecting like a coccus;
all these became for us the town, the season.

These, and the knowledge that to die,
Some stony miles north of our wintering
Was a more ordinary thing.

Olive Trees

The dour thing in olive trees
is that their trunks are stooped like never dying crones,
and they camp where roads climb, and drink with dust and stones.

The pleasant thing is how in the heat
their plumage brushes the sight with a bird's wing feeling:
and perhaps the gold of their oil is mild with dreams of healing.

The cold thing is how they were
there at the start of us; and one grey look surveyed
the builder imagining the city, the historian with his spade.

The warm thing is how they are
first promise of the South to waking travellers:
of the peacock sea, and the islands and their boulder-lumbered spurs.

Feathery Grasses

Feathery grasses blowing in the wind,
grass out of cracks among tiered seats of stone
where a Greek theatre swarmed with audience,
till Time's door shut upon
the stir, the eloquence.

A hawk waiting above the enormous plain,
lying upon the nothing of the air,
a hawk who turns at some sky-wave or lull
this way, and after there
as dial needles prowl.

Cool water jetting from a drinking fountain
in crag-lands, miles from any peopled spot,
year upon year with its indifferent flow;
sound that is and is not;
the wet stone trodden low.

There is no name for such strong liberation;
I drift their way; I need what their world lends;
then, chilled by one thought further still than those,
I swerve towards life and friends
before the trap-fangs close.

Notes by a Foreigner

Their opaque, restless eyes,
the last place you will find a clue to this town;
eyes that face yours or hunger past you,
darknesses cut from a woman's evening gown.

Encounters with frequent phantoms,
women whose beauty lays a hand on your gut:
the sound of the impetuous language,
blurred as if the tongue still savoured fruit.

Your wish to build them all
into one vision, with traffic bells, the fine
knives of the whistles, and the blind,
tapping to the world like caught souls down a mine.

The shuffle of evening crowds
past cinema lights; each sixteenth-century square
where the bronze kings and heroes rein
their grave war-stallions back: and everywhere

Blocks without hope going up,
windowless brick down two gaunt sides, that back
on wastes of sand and dazing lion-light
through which walk women in their mourning black.

Illusion, your old failure
to see except as a foreigner. There is just
a sense in which your town never
was true, for all its trams and banks and dust

-doomed sunsets like the hell
over a town bombarded, and for all
that light that stays a half hour more
as though mad cocks had given the dawn a call,

The echo-light no town
(of this at least you are sure), can parallel;
when things mean more yet fade, like places
you half remember, a now-not-beating bell.

From My Window

Now when the University students have abandoned
their game of bowls in the garden, with their cries of 'Two' or 'Six'
and the evening sky goes soured milk,

There are left the brightening windows of the rich owners of flats;
their meaningless finny gestures, dumb departures and entries;
a deaf man's theatre twenty times.

And quite indifferent towards the students or the rich
there are left the children of the poor, playing tag on a sandy waste,
and miles off southward ring the trams.

Alone on a building site a watchdog stalks by the fire,
wooed and repulsed by the jump-away flames, or raised its head
at a barking that chips a hole in the distance.

Morning in Madrid

Skirmish of wheels and bells and someone calling:
a donkey's bronchial greeting, groan and whistle,
the weeping factory sirens rising, falling.

Yelping of engines from the railyard drifted:
then, prelude to the gold-of-wine of morning,
the thunderstorm of iron shutters lifted.

In Athens

Her hank and swing of hair
then – the whole face in a glance – the rounding line
of cheek, the childlike
mouth that is learning yet to be composed,
the chin, the joy of the neck; you know each feature
about this stranger
like things you have learned by finger-tips or drawing.

The knock inside your chest:
someone you loved was like her; there is given
neither name nor time, except it was long ago:
the scene, half caught, then blurred:
a village on the left perhaps, fields steeply rising.

A perturbation of pulse,
and a word your body is trying to make you hear
on a city corner. It is so much like
the twist in the plotting of things she should pass here
so near where they talked well on love
two civilizations ago, and found
splendid and jeering images: horses plunging,
that apply cut, the Hidden One.

A wryness,
and a name your body is trying to make you hear ...

The Lottery Sellers

Beneath a gun grey sky
– with a wind savage out of Tartar places
– he barks four words to hurrying, lowered faces
and shakes his tickets with their potent numbers;
fluttering fortunes.

Gaze lifted over roof tops,
she calls four words in out-of-nowhere tones,
nailed as though cold could no more search her bones,
and droops her tickets lucky past all longings
or strength of stars.

Perhaps it will snow tonight:
two voices still keep with you as you go:
Luck never saw the sky hang charged with snow;
Wealth trembles, hugs his rag suit to his chest,
on a cold hell's corner.

The Rendezvous

I take the twist-about, empty street
– balconies and drapes of shadow
– and glimpse chalk slogans on each wall,
(now governments have done their work)
that the fanatic or the duped,
even children are taught to scrawl:
the patriotic, 'Tyrants', 'Vengeance',
'Death to', etc.

Hooped
the barbed wire lies to left and right
since glass crashing, cars on fire,
since the mob howled loose that night,
gawky, rusty, useful wire
with little dirty fangs each way,
(what craftsman makes this fright?).
Black on the chemist's lighted window
steel helmets, rifle tops. I sense
the full moon wild upon my back
and count the weeks. Not long from this
the time we named comes round.

And true
to loves love never thought of, here
with bayonet and with tearing fence,
with cry of crowds and doors slammed to,
waits the once known and dear, once chosen
city of our rendezvous.

Patricia McCarthy and Johnny Marsh

Lost Footsteps

A few fragments from a collaboration between writer and artist, consisting of poems in various voices, images and installations based around the life of Camille Claudel, Rodin's mistress whom Rodin believed was more gifted, even, than himself. Partly due to his rejection of her as his long-term mistress or wife, she was locked up in a lunatic asylum, for the last thirty years of her life and died in the Asile de Montverdergues in the Luberon in October 1943, aged 79. She was the sister of Paul Claudel, poet, playright and diplomat.

Patricia McCarthy

La Salle des Pas Perdus

Camille speaks

In the corner of the room, beneath the recitative
of cackles from the female inmates in third class,
the pianola rescued from scrap creaks out its tunes.

Its felt-covered fingers have no agility, no talent
for rubato, dynamics or pedalling, as they push up
through perforated holes in rolls of cardboard sheets.

I sit in another corner, listening to the rip and tear
of minds like thick sheets, the *salle des pas perdus* a hole
where the segregated, clad in folds of emaciated skin,

Clotho-like, leap sideways. Their clumsy arabesques –
unrelated to art nouveau, to the intricacies of Islam –
mock Debussy's *Arabesque No 1* with its cascades

of triplets that, despite the heavy mechanics, waterfall
through me. No one knows I was his lover, my right hand
in my left as if it were in his; how I re-shape the women

into the fluent curves of showgirls in the Folies Bergère
until they grace his music, lips reddened by cherry-juice,
cheeks rouged by cochineal stolen from bottles

reserved for dyeing the icing on cakes of the first class.
Yet when their empty charcoaled eyes and open legs lift up
for soldiers who come to steal, from the walled gardens,

vegetables we have home-grown, they trip over
their hanging skins, flailing back through my sight, through
the notes missed or misplayed, mad for the feel of any man.

Over and over the *Arabesque* repeats, and into it I inject
the expression recorded in my heart he called too hard for his.
What the tone-deaf women register I relegate to the backs

of monkeys on hurdy-gurdy barrels once drawn
by horses to the fairground of my young life, before
its slow burial in the sound-box of *la salle des pas perdus.*

Notes:

La Salle des Pas Perdus, literally meaning 'the hall of lost footsteps,' was the name of the communal living room in the asylum of Montdevergues. It is also the name given to waiting rooms on railway stations in France.

Debussy had an affair with an unknown woman who broke off abruptly with him. This woman was presumed to be Camille Claudel.

The *Folies Bergère* in Paris opened in 1869 and had its heyday in the 1920s and 30s.

Early pianolas were not capable of expression in the rolls of music they automatically played.

Fourteen visits in thirty years

Fourteen visits in thirty years
from chateau to asylum, from around
the world, he found her waiting still,

shrunken, dessicated, her expression
wiped clean of all anger, hostility.
She welcomed him from the iron frame

of her bed as if he appeared daily
with his similar proclivities.
Mon p'tit Paul, mon p'tit Paul.

As in childhood she muttered
his name like a song. Awed
by her body's ruined cathedral,

he tried, over the thin sheet, to smooth
the flagstones torn up in its aisles,
to restore the plaster in naves, filling

with his guilt and sorrow the hollows
from chapels desecrated between each rib.
Too late to straighten her life-force

like a dishonoured pillar broken in two;
to reply to *Mon p'tit Paul* – as if
they were still the pair racing woods

that ran with them, parting ears of corn.
Each time her eyes flickered open,
then shut, intense as ever, like his,

he saw what he had tried to ignore:
the stations of the cross shouldered
by her in isolation from her kind.

While the nurses gathered around,
blessing her new benignity,
her compliant starched simplicity,

he put his head in her hands,
shock-cold. He would nail himself
to her cross, and hang there instead of her,

splintered by her pain.
Fourteen visits in thirty years.
Mon p'tit Paul, p'tit Paul, p'tit Paul.

Masses said

The money that could have helped her out
he left to the Church for masses to be said
for her after she had gone. Epistles, gospels,

offertories fell against the dilapidated walls
of the chapel, the stones quarried from her heart.
Dominus vobiscum, the priest muttered to the wind

which, standing in for the faithful, chanted
a ghostly response: *Et cum spiritu tuo* –
blowing through statues too pious to be hers,

dimpling water like absent fingers in the font.
Sanctus...the bell tinkled thrice of its own accord
into the hiatus, raw, damp, lined with the bones

of leaves she had counted falling, one by one,
in slow motion, with the bits of her life.
He should have been there, her brother,

supplicant in a pew, her name with the Virgin Mary's
on his lips, chasing away the feral cats that slinked
up the aisle, rubbing against memories of her

more recent than his, their purr prolonging
the last note of the organ now defunct.
The money that could have helped her out

rattled in the collection box, worthless as tin
without his care for her body shunted from
carré number 10 in the graveyard in Montfavet

off sacred ground to the communal ditch for the insane.
Ite missa est. The cleric's dismissal brought
no thanks to God for the way she had been flung,

anonymous, sacrificial as the bread and wine
in the mass, sealed in the earth by a line
that stretched into a tight, sadistic, spade-etched grin.

Note: the words in Latin are part of the liturgy of the Tridentine Mass.

Johhny Marsh: Camille's Stations

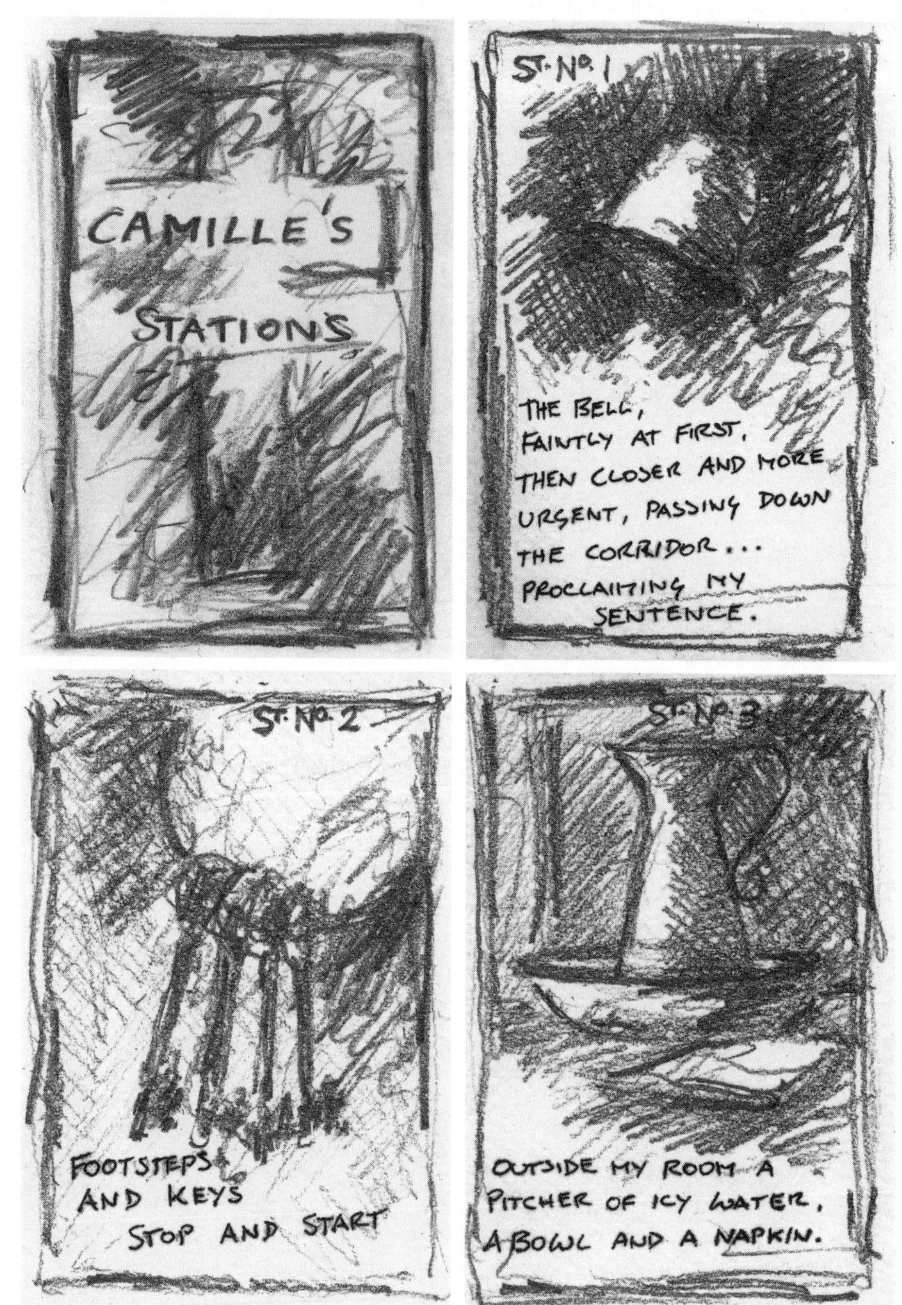

ST. No. 4
WHICH
OF MY
TWO DRESSES
TO WEAR
DRAGGING
A BROKEN
COMB
THROUGH
MY HAIR

ST. No. 5
WHO WILL
CARRY MY
BOWL, MY BREAD

ST. No. 6
TO BE,
TO THINK,
TO STARE,
AT.
NOTHING.

ST. No. 7
THE IMAGE OF MY
FACE UPON THE CLOTH
I BEAT.

ST. NO. 8
THE WOMEN
FIND SOME
HOPE
IN THE SOIL.

ST. NO. 9
I SHALL STAY, LAID
BEFORE ME, MYSELF,
A PILE OF PAPERS.

ST. NO. 10
STRIPPED OF
MYSELF...
I WRITE.

ST. NO. 11
B.
C.
NEVER
NEVER
TO LEAVE
TO ARRIVE
AN ETERNAL NOW.

ST. No. 12
I ATTEND TO MYSELF,
A PERFORMANCE, STILL,
HIS HANDS ABOVE THE
KEYS.

ST. No. 13
A PAUSE
BETWEEN
THE HANDS.

ST. No. 14
THROUGH THE
FILIGREE OF MY
WINDOW I CAN FLY
TO SET SOULS AFLAME
AND SCORCH THE MARBLE
TO LIME.

MONTDEVERGUES
ASYLUM
1914 - 1943